Setting Sights

Histories and Reflections on Community Armed Self-Defense

Edited by scott crow

Setting Sights: Histories and Reflections on Community Armed Self-Defense
Edited by scott crow

Essays by scott crow—"Liberatory Community Armed Self-Defense: Approaches toward a Theory," "On Violence, Disasters, Defense and Transformation: Setting Sights for the Future," "Sometimes Stories Reveal Themselves," "Introduction: As Rare as Flowers Rising through Concrete: Why Liberatory Community Armed Self-Defense?"—are licensed under a Creative Commons Attribution-ShareAlike 3.0 Unported License 2017

PM Press
PO Box 23912
Oakland, CA 94623
www.pmpress.org

Cover design by John Yates / www.stealworks.com
Cover photo by Leon Alesi / www.leonalesi.com
Interior design by briandesign

ISBN: 978–1–62963–444–9
Library of Congress Control Number: 2017942918

10 9 8 7 6 5 4 3 2 1
Printed in the USA by the Employee Owners of Thomson-Shore in Dexter, Michigan.
www.thomsonshore.com

*This book is dedicated to those who have
exercised power for collective liberation on
their terms by any means necessary.*

Dream the future
Know your history
Organize your people
Fight to win

Contents

● ● ● ●

ANALYSIS AND THEORY

● ● ● ●

HISTORIES OF THE TWENTIETH AND TWENTY-FIRST CENTURIES

Sometimes Stories Reveal Themselves

scott crow

> In . . . war, things get confused out there—power, ideals, the old morality, practical military necessity.
> —General Corman, in the film *Apocalypse Now*

This book grew organically out of conversations between people in Lawrence, Kansas, and Austin, Texas, which evolved into a collaborative pamphlet called *Desire Armed: An Introduction to Armed Resistance and Revolution*, released in 2006. (The people in Lawrence did the heavy lifting on the project, for which I am grateful.) The subjects varied from self-reflection and theory, to the history and basics of gun use. As a text, it was limited, but powerful.

When that pamphlet was written there were at most a handful of leftist, radical, or anarchist groups talking about the use of firearms at all, except in historical settings or some far-off revolutionary future. I was part of an anti-fascist defense caucus that trained on firearms use, safety, and tactical considerations together as part of our organizing within the Anti-Racist Action network. In Lawrence their organizing was largely around Kansas Mutual Aid and the John Brown Gun Club, which both focused on working with rural and low-income whites as part of food, housing, and other organizing programs.

Once released, the pamphlet took on a life of its own and now appears worldwide in many DIY and small press editions. I knew there was much more to be written, more histories to uncover, analyses and theories that needed to be heard and discussed by more people.

That's when the idea to expand the zine into this book, *Setting Sights: Histories and Reflections on Community Armed Self-Defense*, germinated. Over the next several years I researched materials, interviewed people, and collected new or undiscovered essays and articles from around the world on the subject of community armed self-defense. Almost twelve years later, this book is the culmination of that work. I hope you find it engaging and thought-provoking.

> Dream the Future
> Know Your History
> Organize Your People
> Fight to Win

scott crow
From the concrete jungle in the Gulf Coast Basin
2017

Gun Control Means Being Able to Hit Your Target

Ward Churchill

> The struggle of man against power is the struggle of memory
> against forgetting.
>> —Milan Kundera, *The Book of Laughter and Forgetting*

Once upon a time, believe it or not, the right inhering in all communities to defend themselves by force of arms against the violence of external assault was so well understood that it was not thought worthy of serious discussion.

Notwithstanding the contentions of Michael Bellesiles's *Arming America*, guns were as common as axes on the North American frontier during the period leading up to the thirteen colonies' armed struggle for independence, and far more essential to survival. Hence, the Second Amendment to the U.S. Constitution acknowledged the right of citizens to keep and bear arms and placed it quite solidly on a military footing having nothing whatsoever to do with a desire to preserve certain "sporting" indulgences for posterity. The character of this provision is readily apparent in the framers' explicit reference to the necessity of "a well regulated Militia" in defending the U.S. "free State" against armed aggression by foreign powers. Indeed, as John Grenier ably demonstrates in *The First Way of War*, the country's

military capacity remained almost *entirely* contingent upon the existence of local militias well into the nineteenth century. No less clarify-
ing are the numerous observations of Jefferson and others among the
"founding fathers" to the effect that an armed populace embodies the
most effective barrier to the domestic state itself evolving toward a
"tyranny."

On both counts it's obvious that the types of arms envisioned
were not of the variety used for hunting rabbits, squirrels, and deer,
but those employed by modern armies. In contemporary terms, this
would equate to *real* military-issue assault rifles, not the semiautomatic "civilian" models commercially available to the public. It would
also be well to remember that it was not especially unusual for local
militias, to say nothing of corporate entities like the American Fur
Company, to equip themselves with their own artillery, and that the
central government did little, if anything, to question—and less still
to curtail—their right to do so until the 1860s.

It can be argued, and rightly so, that since the society on whose
behalf these principles were set forth was composed all but exclusively of white settlers—this is to say, invaders—it was by definition
everywhere and always the aggressor, and consequently had no basis
upon which claim a right to self-defense, armed or otherwise. Put
another way, no matter how often or "savagely" indigenous peoples
might attack, they can *only* be seen as defending their own communities against the genocidal onslaught they were suffering. It follows
that, irrespective of the white supremacist hypocrisy imbuing the
outlook of those who enshrined it in written form, the principle holds.
American Indians had every right to fight back with every weapon
available to them, and one can only wish that these had included
rocket launchers and machine guns.

To be sure, the same applies with regard to the black chattel slaves
imported from Africa and later commercially "bred" in the U.S. by
white settlers who purportedly "owned" them and formally classified
them as a subhuman species. Plainly, the indigenous West African
communities from whence the slaves were forcibly taken had a natural
right to defend themselves by all possible means against this genocidal "enterprise," while those engaged in it had no corresponding
right at all. By the same token, there can be no valid claim to the "right
to self-defense" against slave revolts in the U.S., either by the slave

owners and traders themselves or by the broader white supremacist society that condoned, enforced, and accrued economic benefits from chattel slavery. Conversely, the slaves were inherently and undeniably vested with a right to slit not only the collective throat of their "masters" but also the throats of those of *whatever* complexion who'd comported themselves as either enablers or tacit beneficiaries of "the peculiar institution."

The principle holds as well for the black and red/black communities emerging in the aftermath of the structural adjustment of the U.S. economy passed off as "emancipation." The residents of Opelousas (Louisiana; 1868), Colfax (Louisiana; 1873), Wilmington (North Carolina; 1898), Atlanta (Georgia; 1906), Slocum (Texas; 1910), East St. Louis (Illinois; 1917), Tulsa (Oklahoma; 1919), Knoxville (Tennessee; 1919), Elaine (Arkansas; 1919), and Rosewood (Florida; 1923) were imbued with an unequivocal right to engage in armed self-defense against the officially sanctioned white paramilitaries—by no means consisting of only the Klan—who massacred them in a protracted campaign to restore African Americans to their "place" of racial subjugation and de facto enslavement. So too, those who organized to defend themselves and their communities with arms against the systematic reign of white terror inflicted for the same purpose but in a more generalized way—not just in "the South," but in every one of the forty-eight contiguous states (as far north as Duluth, Minnesota)—by the lynchings of well over four thousand black people between 1877 and 1950.

Any recitation of this sort can of course be extended at considerable length, including as it does those of Mexican heritage throughout the Southwest, hundreds of whom were lynched for the same reasons and during the same period while hundreds—or, more likely, thousands—of others were summarily executed along the border by Texas Rangers between 1910 and 1920. As well, there are the imported Chinese laborers who were not only expended like so much used toilet paper in the building of railroads and the depths of deep shaft mines in the western states, but at least two hundred of whom were massacred in places like Los Angeles (California; 1871) and Rock Springs (Wyoming; 1885). The labor movement must also be mentioned—certainly, it has suffered extraordinary levels of repressive violence at the hands of the corporate state—although with the qualification that its record of conscious adherence to the codes of white supremacy renders its station far more ambiguous than those of the communities already mentioned. Nonetheless, it too had—and retains—the elemental right to defend itself "by any means necessary."

As recently as the mid-1970s, this premise went without saying among those seriously committed to the struggle for liberation in the U.S. Here, merely pointing to Malcolm X, SNCC, RAM, the Panthers, the Lords, AIM, and other such obvious examples would be inexcusably glib. More revealing by far is the fact that Robert F. Williams's "rogue NAACP chapter" in Monroe, North Carolina, was in no sense alone—or deviant—in assuming a posture of armed self-defense in the face of Klan terrorism in 1957. The Regional Council of Black Leadership, a kind of "homegrown NAACP" led by Medgar Evers and T.R.M. Howard, had done so in Mississippi as early as 1951 (albeit with much less fanfare). Even the veritable icon of the "nonviolent freedom movement" of the '60s, Martin Luther King Jr., was quietly attended by armed security personnel from the 1955 Montgomery bus boycott onward, and he openly accepted such services from the Deacons for Defense and Justice on behalf of *all* participants in the 1966 "March Against Fear."

Despite the mythologies it fostered at the time, the very survival of the nonviolent movement would have been impossible absent the deterrent effect of a credible armed component, and such successes as it ultimately attained depended upon the backdrop of incipient guerrilla warfare and urban insurrections. Such, in variation, has been the case with all movements that have managed to improve the circumstances of their communities. To paraphrase Frederick Douglass, the capacity to deliver either words or blows is necessary, as both are invariably required.

Should there be any question as to which should be deemed the more essential, the answer has all along been provided by the U.S. elites themselves. Witness the urgency with which they sought to prevent native peoples from acquiring anything resembling a parity of firepower with the settlers, criminalizing the sale of arms and munitions to Indians and doing everything in their power—including the repeated use of military force—to prevent trade between foreign powers and the indigenous nations located within territorial boundaries claimed by the U.S. That firearms were forbidden to slaves is a given, but much the same pertained to black freemen in the antebellum South, and thereafter, as much as possible, they were denied and taken from persons of African descent, including—or especially—former Union soldiers, through various contrivances under the Jim Crow system of apartheid.

The same pattern prevailed vis-à-vis every community discussed above, the point in each instance being that so long as arms are in use by any particular element of a sociopolitical equation, to be disarmed is to be disempowered, and thus effectively subjugated, no matter *how* loudly or eloquently the situation might be decried. Those In Charge, always fully aware of this concrete reality, have been all the more acutely so since the wave of domestic insurgencies marking the "Long Sixties," circa 1958–1975. This accounts for the incredible and steadily accelerating militarization of the burgeoning U.S. police establishment since 1980, the even greater and more rapid expansion of an interacting "private security" apparatus, integration of the military itself into the sphere of domestic policing, as well as adoption of counterinsurgency doctrine and training in methods of applying it by every major police department in the country.

Concomitantly, there has been a staggering increase in the rates of incarceration—especially for young black men and American Indians of both sexes—with the number of people consigned to federal prisons alone having swollen by nearly 800 percent since 1980, quintupling in the overall penal system. Since the dawn of the new millennium, a little over two million people have been in lockup each year, 37 percent of them black, with a further 4.5 million on probation or parole. The upshot is that in the U.S. roughly a third of all black men under age sixty have done or are doing time, and the proportion of indigenous people is similar. While the impact on the targeted communities including familial disruption, lost income (both real and potential), and wholesale disenfranchisement has been the focus of much commentary, far less remarked upon is the fact that to have been "duly convicted" of a felony is to be permanently divested of the right to lawfully possess a firearm or, perhaps more instructively still, purely defensive body armor.

In substance, the disarmed and correspondingly disempowered condition in which African American and other communities of color were maintained under Jim Crow has simply been (re)imposed by other means. Actually, in light of the massive build-up of police personnel and armaments over the past forty years, the degree of disempowerment involved is objectively greater today than at any point since the end of Reconstruction. The glaring racial bias displayed in implementation of such sweeping policies as "stop and frisk" has in itself been sufficient to demonstrate the violation of even the most rudimentary level of human dignity. That the police have themselves assumed the role once fulfilled mainly by such "unofficial" entities as the Klan and White Citizens' Councils, randomly but regularly engaging in the exemplary murders—which is to say lynchings—of "uppity" young men and sometimes women of color, most often black or American Indian, serves to greatly amplify the desired message.

As to the latter, it remains no different from that conveyed in 1917, or a century earlier still: "Know your place, and stay in it. The price of forgetting or attempting to alter it, whether individually or collectively, will be far too high." As it's been continuously asserted over the past couple of generations that, whatever the country's "lingering imperfections," things have been gradually "getting better" in the U.S. since the "bad old days" of Jim Crow—most spectacularly in the surge of liberal drivel about how Barack Obama's election supposedly heralded the emergence of a "postracial America"—the question arises as to the material nature of the "place" assigned the communities most directly subjected to the onslaught of "law enforcement."

It should be noted in this regard that there *was* in fact a noticeable improvement in the conditions prevailing in African American communities toward the end of what James Forman termed "the high tide of black resistance" and on American Indian reservations following AIM's armed struggle in the same period. In both cases, however, such gains had been largely rolled back by the mid-1980s. Since then, things have gone steeply downhill. As of 2010, the median accumulated wealth of black families in the U.S. was less than $5,000, while that of white families was nearly twenty times as large—a disparity *greater* than in 1960—and for American Indians the gap was even more pronounced. This in itself reveals the falsity of the apologia that it simply "takes time" to overcome the inequities of America's "racist past." At the post-2010 rate of "improvement" in their circumstances, it would take the average black family *228 years* to reach an economic position equal to that now occupied by its white counterpart, and an indigenous family half again as long.

Plainly "things" have *not* "gotten better" for African Americans or American Indians—or for appreciable sectors of the Latino, Asian American, and Pacific Islander communities—since the days of Jim Crow. Overall, apart from voting rights and other such accouterments of formal democracy conceded as a result of the much-celebrated struggle for civil rights during the '60s, the material situation in communities of color in the U.S. is demonstrably *worse* now than it was then. Moreover, even the transparently co-optive concessions granted during that storied era of liberal "successes" are now being systematically repealed as white supremacy reasserts itself ever more brazenly. Witness, if you will, the composition of the newly installed Trump regime and the base that propelled its ascent to power.

It of course remains possible to counter the worst conditions structurally imposed by the existing order through a process of consciously detaching from it. This devolves upon the (re)building of subjugated communities through the organization of grassroots initiatives to maximize their capacity to approach or attain self-sufficiency on the basis of local resources, human and otherwise. Food production—community gardening even in "hard core" urban areas, as is being done in Baltimore, for example—to improve nutrition and reduce living expenses in inner city "food deserts" has been successfully taken on as an organizing focus in a number of locales. So too has the refurbishing of unlivable dwellings and dilapidated or abandoned public use facilities, establishing community-based health care services and educational programs ranging from mentoring and tutoring to whole schools, building or acquiring alternative energy sources such as solar panels and wind generators, revitalizing local parks and establishing recreational centers, providing both childcare and eldercare, as well as neighborhood transport and security services.

Much of this effort has been undertaken and often expanded through the organization of co-ops both within and between communities pursuing similar agendas, facilitating trade in a variety of locally produced foodstuffs and other commodities as well as the pooling and sharing of technical skills, experience, and labor. The co-op model has also been used in (re)establishing small shop manufacturing and corresponding job opportunities within largely disemployed communities, thereby reducing the burden of necessarily participating in the broader cash economy. It is worth bearing in mind that since the mid-nineteenth century, co-ops have been organized in numerous contexts, for a range of purposes, often on a large scale, and have tended to be successful whenever they've not been squelched by Those In Charge.

While there is much more to be said in these connections, none of it is especially mysterious. Liberals have been paying lip service to the concept of community building for the past half century, all the while purporting to seek its realization through electoral politics and passage of legislation underwriting assorted federal programs (thus nullifying the prospect of community control). Self-styled progressives have taken essentially the same approach, albeit with a greater reliance on private funders and a more leftward cant to their rhetoric. In contrast, anarchists have from time to time actualized something akin to genuine community self-sufficiency in various places, although such efforts have largely been both situational and transient. On the whole, only the Black Panther Party in its prime provided a model that was effective, replicable, and potentially sustainable. While the Party itself foundered, largely as the result of official repression but also due to a complex range of factors that needn't be addressed here, its concept remains no less viable today.

The crux of what distinguished the Panthers' approach was its appreciation of the link between community self-sufficiency and the capacity to reject the impositions of external forces such as the police, thereby achieving community control of key institutions. Any community succeeding in such an endeavor would present what Noam Chomsky has described as "the threat of a good example" and necessarily be targeted for destruction by Those In Charge as a means of deterring imitation and consequent erosion of the existing order. This was precisely the dynamic at work in the earlier-cited massacres in Colfax, Tulsa, Elaine, and elsewhere. Consequently, as the Panthers saw it, community building would be pointless absent the readiness to physically defend what had been built against those bent on destroying it.

This view, to be sure, flies squarely in the face of what has passed— or been passed off—as an oppositional politics in the U.S. since 1975. It may or may not have been simply a "failure of nerve," as many analysts—myself included—have argued, but somehow, just as the liberation struggles of the preceding years were bearing tangible fruit and the Vietnamese people's war was exposing still deeper cracks in the empire, the notion that armed struggle of *any* sort was "counterproductive"—and (in the words of feminist Robin Morgan) "inherently sexist"—became the conventional wisdom of the white Left. Shortly thereafter came the "retreat into theory": on the one hand, French postmodernist esoterica was avidly embraced in an abstract struggle to supplant the "Sartrean paradigm" of existentialist collectivity with its individuated Heideggerian antithesis, and on the other, Homi Bhabha emerged as a luminary of "postcolonial theory" on the strength of his discovery that the only truly revolutionary activity is to be found in the reading of lots and lots of books and scribbling indecipherable tracts about the experience.

That the CIA had been covertly subsidizing, publishing, and promoting such gibberish since the late 1940s for the express purpose of undermining the Left's ability to actually *do* anything has been thoroughly documented by Frances Stonor Saunders, Gabrielle Rockwell, and others. As it turned out, the operation would appear to have exceeded its goal, as the bulk of the so-called New Left dissolved by the late 1980s. Of what remained, apart from a handful of tiny sectarian groups like the RCP, the term "radical" had been jettisoned in favor of "progressive," and what has been called the "hegemony" or, less politely, the "tyranny of nonviolence" had been firmly established, along with a strict compliance with the parameters of dissent permitted by the state.

Apart from the weeklong 1992 insurrection in South Central Los Angeles, following the acquittal of four cops charged in the videotaped beating of a black motorist, the confrontational mass actions marking the late '60s and early '70s had by that point completely disappeared. Indeed, "protest demonstrations" had largely become a carefully scripted matter of marching like self-herding sheep along assigned routes leading into fenced off "free speech zones," and more than a few progressives sought to require the signing of a "pledge of nonviolence" before allowing anyone to participate even in *that* sort of travesty.

Beginning with the 1999 WTO meeting in Seattle, a few groups, most prominently the black blocs, (re)introduced a much more diverse and productive range of ideas and tactics to the protest scene, with the result that participants in such actions were publicly condemned by progressives of the "Gene Sharp school" with a venom conspicuously lacking in their criticisms of the WTO itself (and neoliberalism more generally). By and large, the pattern has prevailed into the present, as evidenced by dynamics on display in the highly publicized and self-aggrandizing Occupy movement of 2011–2013, which may account for the rapidity with which it fizzled even without being subjected to substantial repression. Whether the still more recent Movement for Black Lives will do better remains to be seen, although the signs have become increasingly mixed.

In any case, since the early '80s a prime signifier of bona fide progressive credentials—along with banning smoking, the building of speed bumps, and better bike paths in affluent white neighborhoods—has been the advocacy of gun control. To be clear, "gun control" in this parlance means to severely restrict—or, better yet, prevent—possession of a broad range of firearms, not only by "convicted felons" and persons diagnosed as suffering psychological disorders but by the entire "civilian population." Weapons to be proscribed include "assault rifles," certain types of shotguns, and handguns, as well as large capacity magazines and several varieties of ammunition. No emphasis whatsoever is placed on a concomitant disarming of the police and other components of the enforcement apparatus, or even constraining the array of weaponry and equipage they've long since become accustomed to wielding.

Undeniably, there's a lot left to be unpacked here, and, for anyone genuinely setting out to pursue fundamental rather than cosmetic changes to the sociopolitical/economic order of the U.S., perhaps even more to rethink. Much has been forgotten about how to effectively engage in grassroots community organizing over the past forty years and must be relearned if any sort of liberatory momentum is to be attained. Most saliently, the centrality of the right of armed self-defense must be restored to the consciousness of those seeking radical change. Fortunately, there remain an aging few who were active in the struggle "back in the day." Some of them are still at it and have never recanted what they then knew to be true. They have much knowledge to impart. As well, lines of continuity joining then and now *have* occasionally been reflected during the interim in the armed defense of communities by younger activists, most often in collaboration with movement elders. In these examples too there are important lessons to be gleaned.

The present book offers a very solid selection of what might be described as windows into the actualities as well as the potentials attending self-defense both during the Long Sixties and more recently, thereby making a substantial contribution to the process by which the necessary relearning can and must occur. It is thus a tool of immense utility not only in the struggle to reempower oppressed communities of color, but others as well, not least those once known as "hidden communities," LGBT, targets of rape (both female and male), victims of domestic violence, the physically/mentally other-abled among them. Each is equally and innately endowed with the right to defend oneself "by any means necessary."

Exercising that particular right, however, requires proficiency in employing the "means." It follows that those presently lacking such basic skills are in need of acquiring them, and that providing the requisite instruction—as is even now being done in a number of localities—should be seen as a high priority by those undertaking the task of organizing for community self-sufficiency and empowerment. After all, what "gun control" *really* means is being able to hit your target, and with *that* understanding, we must *all* embrace it. While that in itself will not accomplish the raft of changes to which we mutually aspire, none of them will ultimately be possible without it.

As Rare as Flowers Rising through Concrete: Why Liberatory Community Armed Self-Defense?

scott crow

The world has been in tumult for decades, with more crises still ahead of us—from ecological (climate change, destruction of the natural world) and economic (neoliberalism, the 1%) to political (oppression, corruption, authoritarianism) and wars (both small- and large-scale). The sky is not falling, but these slow disasters will demand new approaches and open new possibilities. I think it's time for all of us within civil society to think about how we want to respond, autonomously and collectively, without waiting to be saved by the same reactionary governments and corporations that have produced the crises in the first place.

This anthology, *Setting Sights: Histories and Reflections on Community Armed Self-Defense*, is part of an emerging and growing body of thought that is both assessing and reassessing the role that community armed self-defense has played worldwide within struggles for justice. This body of work seeks to articulate an ethical framework that is deeply rooted in power-sharing and collective liberation.

In the following pages we will see that guns aren't *the* answer to creating just, sustainable, or liberatory societies, but that they can and do have an important role that is worth exploring. We will discuss the ways they have been used in extraordinary circumstances

1

for vulnerable communities to defend themselves without relying on the state. And we will see how collective arms offer possibilities for self-determination through community self-reliance.

Setting Sights covers people and communities who have resorted to armed self-defense as part of their struggles for liberation, justice, or basic human rights. Most of these stories are about those who engaged in social or political struggles for autonomy or self-determination—the agency to determine their own futures within their neighborhoods and communities.

The pieces gathered in this book include personal essays, journalistic accounts, interviews, communiqués, and original source documents representing a spectrum of international voices from revolutionaries, activists, scholars, and journalists in the twentieth and twenty-first centuries. Together, they focus on two major and sometimes overlapping themes: "Histories" and "Analysis and Theory."

Histories: Here are collected stories of individuals or communities from around the world; some are celebrated parts of political movement history, while others are mostly unknown. We draw from many underrepresented stories of those who out of necessity took up arms as part of other larger political projects to protect themselves and those around them from brutal attacks at the hands of mobs, racist hate groups, drug cartels, or even governments. Many of these narratives reveal more than just the armed actions or heroic struggles; we get to learn about the process and the feelings and the tensions that arise when communities try to exercise their power through resistance.

Analysis and Theory: These chapters explore some of the broader considerations about gun rights, liberatory theory, and armed struggle, as well as reflecting on the spectrum of violence, gun control and gun policy, and the ideas of community and self-defense in both narrow and broad terms.

This book examines and explores the ideas of a liberatory collective defense, as we find it in our histories and as we develop it further moving toward unknown futures.

If we are truly going to transcend Power and structural violence that is involved in maintaining it, or if we want to truly support oppressed communities' defense against modern-day fascists, then we will at some point engage in the use of force, whether or not we want to or like it.

Even if the armed components are a comparatively miniscule portion of the political activity we all engage in, they remain the most dangerous. It is a serious undertaking that needs to be considered, thought out beforehand, strategized for, and practiced. We want to hit the target we're aiming for, tactically and politically. This book is one step in that process.

ANALYSIS AND THEORY

Liberatory Community Armed Self-Defense: Approaches toward a Theory

scott crow

Notions of Defense

> I wanted you to see what real courage is, instead of getting the idea that courage is a man with a gun in his hand. It's when you know you're licked before you begin but you begin anyway and you see it through no matter what. You rarely win, but sometimes you do.
>
> —Harper Lee, *To Kill a Mockingbird*

In this essay, I will try to sketch a set of potential practices, praxis, and thinking centered on the narrow use of what I name as *liberatory community armed self-defense*. This distinct concept draws upon the histories of community self-defense, as practiced by various groups of people worldwide, and from the liberatory principles derived from anarchist and anti-authoritarian traditions.

The concept of *community armed self-defense* is a distinct development from grassroots social and political organizing models and notions of *community defense*, which at their core assert the right of oppressed peoples to protect their interests "by any means necessary." That would include signing petitions and voting on one end of the spectrum to extralegal means of direct action, insurrection, or

7

rebellions on the other. The Black Panther Party, for example, engaged in community defense not only through their armed patrols but also through their *survival programs*, which opened health clinics and free schools in poor black neighborhoods otherwise lacking these kinds of services. This essay is an attempt at a critical reassessment of *liberatory community armed self-defense*: to reenvision the histories and analysis, to examine the praxis and bring these lessons forward to future engagements, and to broaden and strengthen our tactics and responses to crisis.

In the first part I attempt a brief working definition and explain how this range of actions differs from those of standing militaries, guerrillas, or other types of armed forces and combat engagements. The section that follows develops some emerging principles or ethics rooted in the anarchist values of egalitarianism and power-sharing.

A Working Definition

Liberatory community armed self-defense is the collective group practice of temporarily taking up arms for defensive purposes, as part of larger engagements of self-determination in keeping with a liberatory ethics.

I am proposing liberatory community armed self-defense as a distinct idea born of a reassessment, spanning decades, of the historical experience of armed struggle and broader theories of the *right of self-defense*.

Self-defense usually describes countermeasures employed by an individual to protect their immediate personal safety, and sometimes their property. Within the U.S., self-defense is discussed almost exclusively in legal terms relating to "rights" recognized by governments or constitutions, and only occasionally as human rights. By limiting the discussion to the rights attached to individuals, this framing fails to consider community interests, structural violence and oppression, and collective actions. The discourse thus completely neglects the defense of communities *as such*, and especially leaves out the political demands of people of color, women, immigrants, queers, and poor people.

Community self-defense in any form is not defined by laws but by ethics based in need (to protect) and the principles of anarchy (whether people call it that or not) by which groups of people collectively exercise their power in deciding their futures and determining how to respond to threats without relying on governments.

As a concept, *liberatory community armed self-defense* attempts to take into account unrecognized types of violence and the limits marginalized groups face in their ability to determine their own futures or collectively protect themselves. For example, in 1973, when the American Indian Movement took up arms to defend "their people" in the occupation at Wounded Knee, they did so to bring attention to the horrible living conditions on the reservations and the violence their communities faced both from a lack of basic services and from armed vigilante squads. The town of Wounded Knee was not itself under attack, but it represented what First Nations were facing everywhere. AIM's stand was a clear example of community armed self-defense, but it doesn't fit neatly into existing typologies of self-defense.

Some Important Distinctions
Liberatory community armed self-defense is different from other forms of armed action for two major reasons. The first is that it is temporary but organized. People can train in firearms tactics and safety individually or together but would be called on more like a volunteer fire department—only when needed and in response to specific circumstances. Second, and possibly more importantly, power-sharing and egalitarian principles are incorporated into the group ethics and culture long before conflict is ever engaged. These two overarching ideas separate it from most armed conflicts.

For instance, right-wing militias—like the anti-immigrant patrols of the Minutemen Militia along the U.S./Mexico border, or the racist Algiers Point Militia operating in the aftermath of Hurricane Katrina— have *nothing* to do with the type of community armed self-defense rooted in collective liberatory principles. These militias are built on abstract fears and racist beliefs, conspiracy theories, and a macho culture where the strongest or loudest is the leader. They are typically organized in military-type hierarchies with no real accountability to the people in civil society and the communities they operate within. These types of militias are far too similar to the types of the groups the people profiled in this book have had to defend themselves *against*.

That said, the adoption of armed tactics in any conflict or threat situation always has the potential to morph temporary defensive measures into permanent military hierarchies unless conscious efforts to counter that tendency and share power are maintained. A liberatory approach is necessary to minimize, or at least mitigate, that danger.

Below are quick summaries of more common armed conflict group configurations. They are listed here to provide a very rudimentary understanding and to draw both distinctions and parallels between them.

Armed Forces/Law Enforcement
Organized mechanisms of Power that use state-sanctioned "legitimized" violence to maintain the status quo of unequal power distribution. They tend to be highly organized and hierarchical. Examples include police departments, private security firms, and national militaries.

Guerrilla Armies
Small groups using hit-and-run military tactics in a form of asymmetrical warfare. Examples include Fidel Castro's communist 26th of July Movement during the 1960s Cuban Revolution or the anarchists operating within the Kurdish region under the banner of International Revolutionary People's Guerrilla Forces (IRPGF) during the Rojava revolution.

Paramilitary or Militia Organizations
Volunteer citizen military formations composed of nonprofessional fighters who train together for potential combat. In the U.S., these groups typically oppose the federal government but inhabit a subculture and organizational structure derivative of the professional military. Examples include the Oath Keepers, Three Percenters, and the Ku Klux Klan.

Terrorists
Historically, the use of intentionally indiscriminate and horrific violence against civilians to create fear in furtherance of a political, religious, or ideological aim by nonstate actors. Examples are the Army of God in the U.S., al-Qaeda, and ISIS. The term is sometimes cynically used by politicians and media to describe any opposition, such as the Earth Liberation Front and Greenpeace.

Armed Propaganda/Propaganda by the Deed
Violent actions meant to inspire others and spark insurrections or revolutions. Tactics include, but are not limited to, bombings, armed takeovers of buildings, armed expropriations from banks, and assassinations. These actions are usually followed by communiqués sent to media stating the political reasons for the actions. Groups like the Angry Brigade in England and the Red Army Faction in Germany were examples of this.

Armed Insurrection
Also known as rebellions, these events are characterized by open resistance of masses of people against Power/authority. Usually precipitated by a spontaneous triggering event, and not organized beforehand. The "spark" for the uprising has usually been preceded by longer-term unaddressed grievances.

Proposed Principles

The armed component should never become the center; otherwise we risk becoming standing militaries. To avoid that, and to equalize power as best we are able to, a liberatory analysis is necessary to nurture those who are learning to exercise their power, and for those who need to be accountable to their groups or communities. The liberatory framework is built on anarchist principles of mutual aid (cooperation), direct action (taking action without waiting on the approval of the authorities), solidarity (recognizing that the well-being of disparate groups is tied together) and collective autonomy (community self-determination).

Defensive arms should be used only for the goals of collective liberation and not to seize permanent power, even if their use could potentially, and possibly necessarily, escalate conflicts. In any case, arms are not the first line of defense and are only taken up after other forms of conflict resolution have been exhausted.

The use of arms is only effective for the long term if it is part of a *dual power* framework. Dual power means resisting exploitation and oppression, while also developing other initiatives toward autonomy and liberation as part of other efforts in self-sufficiency and self-determination.

Those engaged with guns should hold the same power as others involved in other forms of community defense or self-sufficiency.

Carrying arms should be seen as a privileged task, with the same importance as childcare, growing food, or taking out the garbage—and not more. To maintain a balance of power, rotate all armed tasks and training among all those willing to participate. All firearms training needs to include dynamic and evolving liberatory ethics and practices in addition to how-to and safety. Within any training or operation, there should be an emphasis on challenging internalized assumptions about class, gender, and race to interrupt typical gun culture.

Reflections and Questions toward a Theory

These notes are only a beginning. Many questions remain, including those concerning organization, tactical considerations, the coercive power inherent in firearms, accountability to the community being defended and to the broader social movement, and ultimately, one hopes, the process of demilitarization. For example: Do defensive engagements have to remain geographically isolated? Are small affinity groups the best formations for power-sharing and broad mobilization? How do we create cultures of support for those who engage in defensive armed conflict, especially with respect to historically oppressed people's right to defend themselves? What do those engagements of support look like? Additionally there are many tactical considerations and questions to be discussed and debated to avoid replicating the dominant gun culture. How do we keep arms or arms training from becoming the central focus, whether from habit, culture, or romanticization?

The ideas in this essay come from two decades of dissecting and reassessing my own life, as well as many long conversations over the years with others who took up arms in varying contexts. One of the collective thoughts that emerge from all of those experiences is that none of this should be taken lightly. Careful thought and practice will be necessary to avoid many unintended consequences.

There *can* be an end to the senseless violence for domination or resources. But if we want to transcend violence in the long term, we may need use it in the short term. We thus need to ask ourselves some tough questions about our approaches and our methods. When is armed engagement appropriate? How would we want it to look? How do we create cultures of tacit or direct support and include people who would never themselves engage in armed defense? How will we keep from centralizing power? When do the consequences outweigh the benefits? There are no blueprints; we have to create this together step by step. We need to challenge ourselves and overcome our self-imposed limitations and shed our preconceptions of what resistance and liberation are like. When we do, we will gain confidence in potentially using deadly tools with a liberatory consciousness. That means we have to understand that the values of power-sharing and openness are every bit as important as the power of carrying loaded weapons.

For me, collective liberation is not about fetishizing arms as the only true means toward freedom but about exploring the options in a realistic and thoughtful manner. Arms will never offer the only answer to exercising or equalizing power. Only we can do that, but they can be a deterrent against real threats, and can greatly expand our tools of liberation!

Politicians Love Gun Control: Reframing the Debate around Gun Ownership

Neal Shirley/North Carolina Piece Corps

> Never in history has violence been initiated by the oppressed.
> How could they be the initiators, if they themselves are the result
> of violence? ... There would be no oppressed had there been no
> prior situation of violence to establish their subjugation.... It is
> not the unloved who initiate disaffection, but those who cannot
> love because they love only themselves.
>
> —Paolo Freire, *Pedagogy of the Oppressed*

Culture Wars

In the United States, I am often told, the "culture war" is in full effect. Heated debates around controversial issues like abortion, same-sex marriage, and religion in public institutions abound. In many of these cases there is undoubtedly some level of grassroots support for the various entrenched sides of the debate; the elite Human Rights Campaign, for example, does manage to successfully pull away millions of dollars from queer folks every year. But on the level of policy decisions, the actual positions adopted in these "cultural wars" are usually decided by elite members of such groups, manipulated into thirty-second sound bites, easily simplified into emotional appeals, and transformed from an issue of freedom or liberation—the ability to love and relate to anyone of any gender one chooses, for example—to an issue of institutional and legislative policy—the ability to experience all the institutional privileges of marriage, which will continue to be denied to those who choose to not have their relations sanctified by a government.

Perhaps the most surprising thing about those supposed culture wars is how similar the major actors are to each other. Both sides are represented by well-dressed, well-funded, usually white individuals, whose organizations are large, bureaucratic, extremely hierarchical, single-issue, and not electoral in focus. We are reminded more of governments competing for territory or corporations aggressively trying to buy out each other's production facilities, with all the passive inhabitants or workers held in the balance, rather than an authentic, grassroots social movement directed at casting off society's repressive mores.

Somewhere in the midst of these cultural wars, and fitting into this pattern quite nicely, lies the issue of gun control. Though as a public controversy it may have been surpassed in recent years by other "cultural" topics, gun control remains an extremely divisive subject. Because this debate cuts to the heart of the meaning of government itself and thereby is directly related to the success or failure of liberation movements throughout the world, and because pro– and anti–gun control stances in this country are both usually characterized by racist, capitalist, and progovernment discourse, I am hoping to contribute to a complete reframing of this debate.

Primarily this reframing depends upon two things: one, a look at historic and contemporary social movements where access to firearms has been a decisive factor and, two, the perspective that government is best fundamentally characterized as the "monopoly of force" in a society. This means simply that a government is the only institution or group of people in a society which can "legitimately" use violent coercion against others. For example, if a family is evicted from their home at gunpoint by a police officer, that cop's violence is not punished but is in fact financially rewarded by our society. If that same family physically refuses to leave, however, they will end up behind bars. Whatever one's opinion about government may be, it is clear that the legitimacy of this state violence is not innate but constructed in our society by this same group of governing people in their very power position. I am defining government as the *monopoly of force*, because I think this is the simplest, most common, and least controversial definition available, and because it reflects back on the decisive nature of any debate on whether or not civilians should have access to weapons. I am defining government in this way because it helps us to orient ourselves in the direction of creating a more peaceful, secure society that is not founded upon violence, which is something I believe nearly everyone (except perhaps politicians and weapons industry bosses) on both "sides" of the gun control debate desires.

The Major Players

In one corner of the gun control debate are folks who remain firm believers in one's right to bear arms, and who are (unfortunately) represented institutionally by the National Rifle Association (NRA), a very large organization that is funded by a massive U.S. arms industry. These folks are a mixed bunch indeed: some want guns for hunting purposes, some want guns to protect them from communists, or from terrorists, or from chaos and ecological collapse, or from tyranny and fascism, or they are racists and fascists and want to "protect themselves" from people of color, or perhaps they want to better serve tyranny in its use of systemic violence against those same people of color, as was done by white supremacist vigilante groups cooperating with police in the aftermath of Hurricane Katrina in New Orleans. This camp draws a great deal of support from white poor rural and working-class folks, though they are "represented" by a multi-billion-dollar arms industry and its lobbyist, the NRA. People opposed to gun control in the U.S. tend to be right-wing, progovernment folks in their practical attitudes toward domestic and international military and police repression, yet somehow they see themselves as fighting against government control.

If nothing else, then, right-wing anti–gun control tendencies in the U.S. are a mass of contradictions. Probably the best example of this is the NRA's newest propaganda, "Freedom in Peril," a large pamphlet detailing in full color the abuses heaped upon gun owners by crazed liberal politicians. Using language like "It's inevitable that terrorists will infest America for generations to come" while arguing that it is antiterrorism legislation that will result in "the final disarmament of law-abiding Americans," this pamphlet jumps from one paranoid fear to another, regardless of consistency. On one page we see an image of an old woman on the ground, disarmed and surrounded by violent riot police, but on the next page we see a poor policeman being gagged, unable to arrest "illegal aliens." Rather than have a coherent position on the relationship between government and gun ownership, the NRA will in one sentence discuss how chaos and fear provide an excuse for government tyranny, while at the same time promote that same fear through millenarian talk of terrorism, impending ecological disaster, animal rights "terrorists," and racist images of gangs. The NRA is in a difficult position that naturally gives rise to contradictions: it is an explicitly procapitalist institution embedded in the political elite of our country, yet it must appeal to the "average Joe's" resentment of the authority and wealth of these same elite. The result is confusing at best.

It should be pointed out, however, that unlike pro–gun control institutions like the Coalition to Stop Gun Violence, the NRA does offer its rank-and-file constituency real practical support. For example, if a member's gun is stolen, the NRA will replace that gun at no charge whatsoever, which can add up to hundreds if not thousands of dollars of support for individual members. This benefit alone is enough for many people who completely disagree with the NRA's politics to join up.

The historical roots of the anti–gun control position are complicated and somewhat unique to the United States, so they deserve mention as well. In colonial times, one of the British strategies for controlling an increasingly rebellious and independent colonial population was prohibiting the possession of firearms, especially in the context of local militias. In this sense, for many people, the "right to bear arms" was fundamentally connected to the "freedoms" guaranteed by the new United States. Paradoxically, in its fight against the British and its simultaneous attempt to centralize power in the new nation, George Washington's Continental Army also attempted to disband local armed militias, creating a sense of resentment as well as loyalty to the new national government.

This resentment fueled the fire of later rebellions by poor white farmers, such as Shays' Rebellion, to which the national government responded first with a Riot Act that put farmers in jail without trial and restricted weapons ownership, then with brutal violence and hangings, and then by drawing up a new constitution in 1781 that ultimately centralized power into an even more powerful national elite. One farmer involved in this rebellion, Plough Jogger, said at an illegal assembly:

> I have been greatly abused, have been obliged to do more than my part in the war; been loaded with class rates, town rates, province rates, Continental rates and all rates...been pulled and hauled by sheriffs, constables, and collectors, and had my cattle sold for less than they were worth....The great men are going to get all we have and I think it is time for us to rise and put a stop to it, and have no more courts, nor sheriffs, nor collectors nor lawyers.[1]

Though they certainly contradict the right-wing political positions of the NRA and its politicians, Jogger's words do lie at the foundation of much anti–gun control sentiment in this country. It should be pointed out that in the midst of Shays' Rebellion a far more brutal system of violence was being used to repress African slaves and their moves for freedom, a repression which also depended upon denying access to weapons. This pattern of denying weapons to oppressed classes and ethnicities is a globally consistent trend, reflected in right-wing Nazi Germany, left-wing Communist Russia, and everywhere in between.

In the other corner are advocates of increased gun control, which quite simply means increased government control over our ability to access, train with, and use weapons, including for self-defense. Institutions like Handgun Control, Inc. and the Brady Campaign to Prevent Gun Violence lobby for gun control legislation and give money to federal candidates, especially in regards to assault weapons and handguns. These institutions have contributed a total of only $1.7 million dollars to gun control advocates since 1989, while the NRA has given ten times that amount to lobby for greater access to guns. They did, however, succeed in passing an assault weapons ban called the Brady Bill in 1994, which has since expired. This bill in fact did little to curb assault weapons ownership because of large loopholes and a grandfather clause that made it legal to own assault weapons manufactured prior to 1994. The Brady Bill was passed largely on misconceptions and ignorance: many people thought they were pushing for a ban on automatic weapons, when in fact it was already illegal to own those without a separate license, and the bill instead had an overly vague focus on semiautomatics.

The ideological roots of the pro–gun control position in the U.S. are also based around a number of differing cultural perspectives and sentiments. There are folks who have concerns about the number of handgun-related homicides in inner-city areas; white people whose already racist impulses have been fueled by racist media portrayals of dangerous, young Black and Brown men; anti-war activists who believe that gun control must go hand in hand with opposing war; people concerned about domestic violence against women and children via handguns; and politicians courting a pro–gun control population. The basic logic of much gun control advocacy is that violence is bad, and guns are often used in violence, therefore guns are bad, therefore it would be better if the government was the only entity able to use them (presumably against everyone else?). Gun control advocates tend to be more liberal, middle- and upper-class white people, who have far less experience with institutional violence than others in this country and are more likely to be able to depend on police for protection. It is also important to point out that in no way do gun control advocates, as such, push for the government to have less access to firearms or for fewer circumstances where the government is allowed to use those weapons.

Part of the pro–gun control position is related to the power which corporate media has in reporting crime. As Michael Moore points out in *Bowling for Columbine*,[2] crime rates have been generally dropping on a national level since the early '90s, yet media representations of criminal acts, crime shows, and the people they portray as a criminal class (predominately young Black men) have all increased dramatically. This creates a public perception that gun-related crime is increasing when it actually is not, thereby creating an environment of fear ripe for increased government control of weapons ownership. Interestingly, racist media portrayals of "dangerous young Black men" are also at the heart of much anti–gun control sentiment, in the sense of white folks wanting to protect themselves from this "threat." In either case, predominately wealthy, white institutions are lobbying a predominately white government to control communities of color, which have been constructed as a threat by white corporate media.

Rather than identifying the causes of domestic violence and property crime (such as male-dominated family structures and living in a very class- and race-stratified society) or targeting governments themselves as the major purveyors of violence throughout the world, gun control advocates focus on civilian ownership of "the tools of violence." In avoiding the root causes of violence, thereby avoiding the physical struggle it would require to fix these systemic problems, and in actively supporting a violent U.S. government's monopoly of force by helping them to monopolize that force, pro–gun control folks also stand on a bed of contradictions.

Gun control advocates will often find themselves being "against" the government when it comes to war, police brutality, corporate welfare, and free trade rulings but actively support the government's monopoly of force via gun control. In this sense many advocates of gun control consider themselves involved in other "movements" but believe that social movements are most effective when they are not able to use physical force or even the threat of physical force. Gun control advocates thus hope to limit social movements' methods of changing government and corporations' behavior to proper "democratic" channels, channels which these same "progressives" themselves will admit are corrupt. It is this belief about social movements, their reliance upon the moral benevolence and democratic channels of our country's ruling elite, and the role of weapons access that I hope to elaborate on in the next section.

Social Movements and Access to Weapons

The project of laying out all the social movements where access to weapons was a decisive factor in success or failure is daunting and can in fact never be complete. It does seem pertinent, however, to mention just a few instances where the use of weapons, or at least their availability, has played a major role in the United States. For this section I am basically defining a social movement as a gathering of people throughout a society who are, with increasing momentum, trying to change some fundamentally oppressive, inegalitarian, or hierarchical aspect of that society. The abolitionist movement in pre–Civil War times is an example, as are the labor movement of the early twentieth century, the U.S. civil rights movement and consequent Black Power movement, the gay liberation movement of the late '60s and '70s, the women's liberation movement of that same era, the "anti-globaliza-tion" movement—as it was dubbed by the corporate media—of recent times, and the animal rights/liberation movement as it continues to have successes today.

A social movement might challenge just one aspect of a society's structure or it could have a broader revolutionary vision. In either case, one fundamental trait of every social movement is that it challenges some aspect of a government's "monopoly of force." This may be in the forefront of that movement's language and perspective, such as in the anti–Vietnam War movement, which focused more directly on economic issues but clearly stood in physical and often violent oppo-sition to the power of police and Pinkerton thugs as strikebreakers. The primary point for this discussion is that any movement which is successfully attempting to take some fraction of power away from a society's ruling elite will face violence from that same group of people, who have up to that point solidly maintained their monopoly of force and are therefore "allowed" to use violence.

They are allowed to use that force not because of a divine or moral right or democratic "legitimacy" but because they are the ones with the financial and political connections to be able to summon the mili-tary, the police, or paramilitary and/or white supremacist groups like the Ku Klux Klan and Pinkerton thugs. This will be true and has been true whether the government and economic elite in question are capi-talists or communists, Democrats or Republicans, dictators or "freely" elected professional politicians. It is not a question of the ideology those in power claim but one of power itself. For this reason, self-defense is always a vital issue for any successful movement.

As was already stated, one of the many methods of control used during chattel slavery by white owners was not allowing slaves to handle weapons of any kind. During slave uprisings like Nat Turner's rebellion these rules were obviously ignored, and the northern aboli-tionist movement managed to at least sometimes use armed force as well, such as in John Brown's raid on Harpers Ferry. White and Black members of the Underground Railroad, who managed to free thou-sands of slaves via their clandestine networks, were also armed, as was Harriet Tubman, their most famous freedom fighter. Ultimately, over five hundred thousand men would be killed in a civil war waged by the U.S. government to maintain its territory and power, but which was in its later years portrayed as a war against slavery. In the words of historian Howard Zinn:

> It would take either a full-scale slave rebellion or a full-scale war to end such a deeply entrenched system [of slavery]. If a rebellion, it might get out of hand, and turn its ferocity beyond slavery to the most successful system of capitalist enrichment in the world. If a war, those who made the war would organize its consequences. Hence, it was Abraham Lincoln who freed the slaves, not John Brown. In 1859, John Brown was hanged, with federal complicity, for attempting to do by small-scale violence what Lincoln would do by large-scale violence several years later—end slavery.[3]

Spontaneous uprisings like Nat Turner's rebellion and John Brown's raid on Harpers Ferry, as well as the more continuous struggle of clandestine networks, all had a tremendous impact on the ultimate sustainability of chattel slavery in the U.S.

Movements by poor farmers in this country have almost always required the use of arms, at least as a threat if not in their active use. This is true of North Carolina's Regulators movement against taxation, the Anti-Renter movement of the Hudson Valley, Shays' Rebellion, the populist movement of the late nineteenth century, and numerous others. It was true as well of the early labor movement, before the more revolutionary ambitions of the Knights of Labor and the Industrial Workers of the World (IWW) were sold out for the bureaucratic, conservative, management-friendly style of the AFL-CIO, which is now in drastic decline. Members of the IWW repeatedly had to defend themselves with rifles and pistols, sometimes against government Gatling guns, at picket lines, marches, and other labor conflicts. The United Mine Workers were only able to unionize parts of West Virginia after the bloody battle of Blair Mountain of 1921, in which ten thousand armed miners were fired upon by twenty-five thousand U.S. Army troops.[4]

If we move on to the late 1960s, a time when the "peace" movement was at its peak, we can hardly find peace anywhere. The civil rights movement had been repeatedly targeted with brutal violence by white people in and out of government uniform. It was clear to increasing numbers of civil rights activists that even the more modest goals of peaceful integration and equal opportunity were not going to be achieved by a nonviolent movement. Even the earlier "nonviolent" protests to integrate handfuls of Black students in the South required the violent presence of thousands of armed federal troops. It was also blatantly apparent that the police were targeting both northern and southern Black communities, not protecting them, and that if anyone were to protect those communities from violence, it would be the residents themselves. It was in this environment that the Deacons for Self-Defense, the Black Panther Party for Self-Defense, the Young Lords Party, and other revolutionary organizations formed.

These went on to be some of the most effective revolutionary organizations this country has ever seen, completely changing the face of Black and Brown politics forever. Despite predominantly white liberal calls for nonviolence, which spoke of class and race privilege more than wisdom, these organizations fed the hungry, educated their communities, formed free health clinics, successfully used armed cop-watch patrols to lessen police brutality,[5] and created a new kind of politics around mutual aid and self-determination. The Black Panthers themselves were armed, and their social programs were made possible partly with the additional revenue of the Black Liberation Army, a clandestine organizations that freed prisoners and robbed banks to fund programs in poor communities of color. Ironically, it was right-wing governor of California Ronald Reagan who introduced some of the country's first gun control legislation, explicitly as an attack on the Black Panthers.

To move on to a more contemporary social movement, the "anti-globalization" movement was known for bringing a new era of street fighting and militancy to the stale, reformist, and ineffective activism of an earlier decade. Beginning in the U.S. after the effective shutdown of World Trade Organization talks in Seattle in 1999, this movement never actually reached a point of armed resistance before being abruptly cut short by 9/11. Nevertheless, the international roots of this anti-globalization, which would more accurately be labeled a movement against neoliberal capitalism, lie in the successful armed insurrection of poor indigenous folks from southern Mexico called the Zapatistas. The more recent U.S. movement against the war in Iraq has had almost none of this militancy or direct action, and given current troop increases of twenty thousand to that land now ravaged by four years of occupation, has been remarkably unsuccessful in changing the U.S. government's behavior.

A final example of the presence of weapons in U.S. social movements can be seen in the Common Ground Collective, a large and still-growing radical relief effort which began in the days after Hurricane Katrina devastated New Orleans. Cofounded by an ex–Black Panther named Malik Rahim, Sharon Johnson, and an anarchist from Texas, scott crow, and organized by hundreds of in- and out-of-town anarchists, Earth First!ers, Food Not Bombs volunteers, Ninth Ward residents, radical street medics, previous civil rights and Black Power activists, and others, Common Ground was the first group to open a free walk-in health clinic in the lower Ninth Ward after the storm. Since then they have opened several free health clinics, distributed tens of thousands of dollars worth of food and supplies, gutted hundreds of houses, helped tenants fight evictions, raised awareness and opposition to the massive gentrification being attempted by the City in Katrina's aftermath, and generally brought a practical approach to the anger that New Orleans residents have toward bureaucrats in the Red Cross, National Guard, NOPD, and FEMA. Relevant to our discussion is the origins of Common Ground, whose core group of cofounders began as an armed response to white supremacist vigilante groups who were, with permission and cooperation from New Orleans police, out on patrol "looking for looters." Malik, crow, and others contacted friends in the city and asked them to bring not food and supplies, but guns. Their initial standoff with the white vigilantes successfully pushed the racists out of their neighborhood and cleared the way for the organizing work Common Ground would soon begin.[6] One can only imagine how many lives might have been saved and how New Orleans might have changed for the better had more resources been freed up from the financially inefficient, bureaucratic strangleholds of the Red Cross and National Guard and instead been used to promote the kind of radical, grassroots relief efforts of Common Ground Collective.

This is an extremely brief overview of a wide range of diverse, complicated movements, but it points to a fairly obvious reality: firearms are a fact of life when it comes to social movements in the U.S. They may not always or even often be visibly present, but access to them has been a necessary component of most large social movements this country has experienced, especially when we factor in international resistance to U.S. foreign policies and economic interests. The role of firearms in struggles for dignity, autonomy, justice, civil rights, security from police brutality, economic equality, and freedom does not require a justification, simply an observation. There is no identifiable social movement in this country, including the ones whose results we hold most dear in our daily lives, that has not needed to use some kind of violence or threat of violence to challenge the U.S. government and economic elite's "monopoly of force." It is hypocritical to appreciate the elimination of chattel slavery, or the eight-hour workday, or even government programs like Head Start, which began as a pale imitation of Black Panther free breakfast programs, while simultaneously attempting to limit or eliminate civilian access to the tools that had helped to achieve these changes. This goes without mentioning the deeper, broader, more fundamental changes which will be required if we want to get their "monopoly of force" off our backs for good.

A New Stake in the Culture War

Observing that guns have been instrumental in U.S. social movements and declaring that they will inevitably play some kind of role in any movement that attempts to challenge the "monopoly of force" held by the economic and political elite is not equivalent to saying that firearms are a good thing. It is not a moral apology for an arms industry that has helped create a world were death is more welcomed than life, where the killing of animals is more often considered a "sport" than a necessary but respectful and sustainable human activity, where war and genocide are always right around the corner. Firearms undoubtedly represent to many people patriarchy and machismo and will continue to do so no matter how many "revolutionaries" own them.

In short, guns are not a morally or politically neutral tool, any more than electricity derived from fossil fuels or cellular phones that use coltan.[7] But for some reason, while few claim that future social movements will succeed without the at least temporary use of electricity and cell phones, quite a number of these movements' more conservative actors claim that guns have no place in our midst. Their strange follow-up to this is that the government, previously assumed to be an enemy of freedom, equality, and integrity, ought to be the only institution able to use these tools.

Nevertheless, it has to be constantly reemphasized that guns are by themselves nothing more than wood and steel and plastic, that they are not "the revolution," nor are they even a primary force in it. That force is people. Inspiring people to change the world requires practical steps toward that end, and this means acknowledging the reality that we are living in. Weapons and the necessity of self-defense are a part of that reality. Whether we have to confront this reality now or in twenty years, clearly it will be easier to confront if we have access to the right tools.

To return to a criticism of the traditional anti–gun control attitudes as well as pro–gun control advocates, probably the fundamental factor on both sides of this debate is white supremacy. Traditional right-wing gun nuts in this country are notoriously racist, and the propaganda put out by the NRA reflects this. Behind this is a paranoid fear of people of color, ultimately the desire to become an unpaid police officer in some fictitious race war to come. The white supremacy of the liberal gun control position is more subtle, but its results are perhaps even more heinous because they are enacted through the U.S. government. Whether out of an equally racist fear of armed people of color, or out of a more "benevolent" desire to "help" communities where gun violence is common, predominately white liberals use gun control to legislate the freedoms of communities of color to which they have no accountability, no legitimacy, and no connection. The fundamental effect of this kind of legislation is predictable: rather than reducing violence in communities of color, such laws give racist cops one more thing with which to harass, detain, arrest, and brutalize people of color.

For those who are (justifiably) concerned about gun violence but are not a part of these communities themselves, there are many more effective options at hand for approaching peace. The most obvious of these is supporting voluntary armistices themselves. One example might be the "Multi-Peace Treaty," a voluntary treaty organized and officially put into effect by multiple gangs from Los Angeles on April 28, 1992. When 250 Bloods and Crips marched on the Los Angeles City Council to announce this peace treaty and to ask for financial support in creating an economic infrastructure that would make this peace last, the city council was completely ambivalent. One council member suggested they apply for a $500 grant. Even after gang homicide tallies plunged, police still responded with skepticism. Cops began to break up peaceful meetings of members from different gangs, and then arrested a key architect of the treaty, Dewayne Holmes, who was in turn sentenced to seven years in prison for a ten-dollar robbery. Gang member Kershaun Scott wrote in the *Los Angeles Times*, "Now that we're chilling they want to attack us. Isn't that ironic?"

For those interested in supporting gang peace efforts in L.A., there were many options, including vocal support of the treaty and opposition to police efforts to undermine it, support for Dewayne Holmes's legal defense, as well as raising funds to support community members' creation of self-managed infrastructure that would render gangs less necessary. White people effectively did none of these. The least sensible of any of these options would be imposing more white control over communities of color through the enactment of legislation that allows white police to forcefully disarm community residents, but this option seems to get the most airtime and in fact is the most common.

At this point is it clear that both sides of the gun control debate in the U.S. are completely inadequate and, in fact, rooted in some form of white, institutional control and racist attitudes. This should come as no surprise considering who the major institutional players are and that they are both fundamentally supportive of the U.S. government. It also seems that much of what determines where someone stands in this debate is determined not by a realistic, open-minded assessment of our political options but by cultural considerations like whether or not one is "comfortable" or "grew up" around weapons. This is not an adequate basis for any kind of politics. No matter what our personal comfort level may be with violence or weapons, our heads cannot be in the sand when it comes to the recognized historical necessity of self-defense. This is especially true when it comes to anti-racist, anti-capitalist, anti-government movements like the ones this country so desperately needs.

Gun control advocates affirm that only the government ought to be able to use firearms, and therefore by definition they support that elite's "monopoly of force," even as they claim to abhor the results of that force. In their white supremacy, support for police and military forces, and institutionalization at the hands of the NRA, most anti–gun control folks also support this same "monopoly of force." To choose between these two positions, then, is to have no choice at all. A reframing of this debate is obviously necessary, and I hope that this piece is a useful step in that direction. We do not have to choose between racist institutions and their arms industry backers, on the one hand, and legislation-happy white liberals, on the other. We can support efforts toward peace and freedom in communities plagued by gun violence, challenge the roots of domestic violence, and fight against war abroad, all without giving police one more excuse for repression and thereby strengthening their "monopoly of force."

Part of this is simply a matter of admitting (or for many of us, proudly declaring!) that middle-class white liberals do not always or even often know best. It also means recognizing that the ways in which "cultural" debates are institutionalized in our country reflect the way our society is structured, so that either side of the debate is imbued with the racist, homophobic, sexist, capitalist, and hierarchical logic that characterize "our" institutions. We need to rework these debates so that our beliefs can be enacted directly in our lives and our communities, without being mediated by lobbyists and professional politicians. Instead of being oriented toward the compromised electoral positions of the right and left, our stake in the "culture wars" should be oriented toward the practical needs of our communities and our own ethical principles of freedom, equality, decentralization, and dignity.

Notes

An earlier version of this essay appeared in a limited zine circa 2008 under the authorship of North Carolina Piece Corps.

1   Howard Zinn, *A People's History of the United States* (New York: Harper and Row, 1980), 92.
2   Though Moore's politics contain all the normal contradictions and basic conservative impulses of other U.S. liberals, this documentary does at times do a good job of pushing the gun control debate beyond issues of "safety" and into discussions around race, corporate media, and our culture of fear.
3   Zinn, *A People's History of the United States*, 171.
4   This battle was also the first and only time that airplanes have bombed U.S. civilians on continental U.S. soil, and it was done by our "own" government.
5   Especially in Oakland, California, statistics on police killings of African Americans from before and after the emergence of the Panthers' armed patrols show the positive effect of those patrols. This was made possible because it was legal to carry firearms as long as they weren't concealed.
6   Ed. note: These armed actions and the birth of the Common Ground Collective are recounted in detail in scott crow's book *Black Flags and Windmills: Hope, Anarchy, and the Common Ground Collective* (Oakland: PM Press, 2014 [2nd edition]).

7   Production of cell phones currently requires tantalum powder, derived from the rare mineral coltan, found mainly in the Democratic Republic of Congo. It is estimated that nearly three million people have died in a four-year resource war over this mineral, not to mention the ecological destruction of the mining process itself.

Gun Rights Are Civil Rights

Kristian Williams and Peter Little

> One of the quickest ways for an Afro-American to lose some of
> his white friends is to advocate self-defense against white racist
> savages.... Our belief in this principle has cost us some of our
> phoney white friends, however, we have also gained some true
> ones.
>
> —Robert F. Williams, writing in *The Crusader*, 1960

Conventional wisdom identifies gun control as a "liberal" agenda and
gun rights as "conservative." In practice, history demonstrates a telling
unity between the two "opposing" camps on gun control policy. The
current debates reflect historic and contemporary struggles over race,
class, and the politics of violence and power in society as a whole.

The Second Amendment reads: "A well regulated Militia, being
necessary to the security of a free state, the right of the people to
keep and bear Arms shall not be infringed." The focal debate over gun
control hinges on a couple of questions about what this sentence really
means. It appears to secure the states' right to organize their own
militia, but does it also establish the individual's right to keep a gun?
And if it does, does that right depend on his (real or potential) participation in the militia system? Is the individual gun owner protected

against interference by the state, or from other private citizens, or only from the federal government? The Amendment contains a deep ambiguity about the relationships between individual gun owners, the militia, the state, and the federal government.

The rest of the Constitution does nothing to clarify matters. Article I, Section 8 grants Congress the power to create "Militia to execute the Laws of the Union, suppress Insurrections and repel Invasions"; Congress was also made responsible for "organizing, arming, and disciplining, the militia." James Madison asked, rhetorically, "For whose benefit is the militia organized, armed and disciplined? for the benefit of the United States." Yet he also argued in *The Federalist Papers* that armed citizens, organized into a state militia, provided a safeguard against the power of the national government. Was the militia, then, a check on government authority or its instrument?

Amid the questions and confusions, two things are clear: the Second Amendment is not about hunting, and it was never the intention of the framers to arm blacks.

There has always been gun control in America. Starting in the colonial period and continuing after the revolution, the law was careful to identify whole categories of people who were barred from carrying guns—slaves, free blacks, Indians, poor whites, non-Protestants, and even some heterodox Protestant sects. The militia—which never performed particularly well in military engagements—was chiefly responsible for putting down insurrections, and in the South, for organizing slave patrols to police the black population.

After the Civil War, Southern states sought to preserve this tradition with "Black Codes" that barred blacks from owning guns, serving as jurors, and otherwise participating in society as full citizens; at the same time, terrorist organizations like the Ku Klux Klan simply continued the work of the slave patrols, using violence to restrict blacks' travel, suppress their political activity, and disarm them.

Blacks resisted, of course, sometimes with their own armed militias—and, for the brief flowering of democracy referred to as Reconstruction, they did so with the backing of the federal government. In 1867, Congress dissolved the entire Southern militia system because it excluded blacks, and some states barred ex-Confederates from carrying guns. In 1871 the federal government sent ten thousand obsolete muskets to South Carolina for use by the black militia. The state government invested another $90,000 to convert the guns to breechloaders, and bought a thousand additional rifles as well. It was less than a year, though, before Governor Robert Scott caved in to white pressure and disarmed South Carolina's black militia.

The balance swung fatally back in the favor of whites following the Colfax Massacre of 1873. It is only the scale of the violence that marks Colfax as unusual for the period of reaction. A contested election, a battle between black and white militia, and the massacre of black prisoners ended with more than a hundred dead black men and three dead whites. The local authorities declined to proffer murder charges, but the federal government charged ninety-eight people with violating the 1870 Enforcement Act, which made violations of the Fourteenth Amendment a federal crime.

Part of the government's case centered on the right of blacks to bear arms. Prosecutors argued that because the whites attacked in part to disarm the black militia, they were guilty of violating their Second Amendment rights. But in the decision *United States v. Cruikshank*, the Supreme Court determined: "bearing arms for a lawful purpose is not a right granted by the Constitution.... This is one of those amendments that has no other effect than to restrict the power of the national government." The Court further decreed that the Fourteenth Amendment "prohibits a State from depriving any person of life, liberty, or property, without due process of law; but this adds nothing to the rights of one citizen as against another."

In principle the Court denied both the individual right to bear arms and the national government's ability to protect civil rights. In practice, the Court sided with the organized and armed white population against the black, and determined that the constitution did nothing to establish or protect the rights of the latter against the former. In practice, *Cruikshank* marked the end of Reconstruction.

Over the course of the next hundred years the Court slowly came to recognize that the Bill of Rights limited state, as well as federal, action, and civil rights legislation made individual violations actionable. Somehow the right to bear arms was left behind.

At both the state and national levels, gun regulations continued to be drafted, passed, and enforced in ways that selectively disarmed the poor and minorities. In the 1941 case *Watson v. Stone*, the Florida Supreme Court overturned the gun conviction of a white man; Justice

Buford wrote in his concurring opinion that "The Act was passed for the purpose of disarming negro laborers. . . . [It] was never intended to be applied to the white population and in practice has never been so applied." A quarter century later, Robert Sherrill, a gun control supporter, said that the 1968 federal Gun Control Act was "passed not to control guns but to control blacks." Even less subtle was California's "Panther Law," passed in 1967 for the specific purpose of ending the Black Panther Party's armed patrols against police brutality.

As white supremacy has refined its presentation, judges and politicians have learned subtlety. Since the Civil Rights period the language of white supremacy has shifted, hiding behind the veneer of judiciality and racialized notions of criminality. Beyond this, the changing relationship of old form white supremacists to a globalized, multicultural state has shifted the politics of Klan and militia groups from a proxy to a potentially insurgent role. This has resulted in a federal government less sanguine about white paramilitaries (the warm reception of the Minutemen in some border areas notwithstanding).

Many gun regulations continue to disproportionately affect people of color—bans on guns in housing projects, "Saturday Night Special" laws that take the cheapest pistols off the market, and laws that prevent felons or probationers (even those accused of nonviolent crimes) from owning firearms. Although the NRA sometimes argues that gun laws discriminate against the poor and minorities, the organization has repeatedly demonstrated a telling unity with gun control advocates in its support for mandatory sentences, federalized prosecutions, increased policing, and other "tough on crime" policies that also disproportionately affect these same groups. The race-coded rhetoric stresses keeping guns out of the hands of "criminals" while respecting the rights of "law-abiding, responsible hunters, sport shooters, and collectors."

Significantly, the *Heller* decision, while establishing the individual right to bear arms, also leaves in place the prohibition against felons owning guns.

There's a common-sense appeal to denying guns to criminals, if it is assumed that "criminals" constitute a static and readily identifiable class of people. In practice, such policies are a handy way of institutionalizing racism: the police pay disproportionate attention to people of color, so those people are more likely to have records—which can be used, with circular logic, to justify more scrutiny. With more scrutiny and less leeway, people who have already been to prison are more likely to return, usually on some technicality like a parole violation. Thus the criminal justice system serves as not just a means of punishing crime but also a legal mechanism for stripping minorities of their basic rights. It probably shouldn't be surprising that it works that way to deny them guns, given that most states also use it to deny them the vote.

In this context, the dispute between "liberal" gun control proponents and "conservative" gun rights advocates is a sustained disagreement about the relationship between armed whites and the government. Liberals trust the state to respect the rights of individuals and to protect them against crime and disorder; they see no role for gun ownership under the rule of law. Conservatives retain some suspicion of government regulation and don't believe the state capable of protecting decent law-abiding people; they see gun ownership both as an emblem of citizenship and as a protection against those they see as criminals—historically, blacks, and at present, immigrants as well. The disagreement is over who should have guns; the point of agreement is over who *shouldn't*. As currently construed, both the gun control and the gun rights arguments—that is, both the liberal and the conservative positions—represent the defense of white supremacy.

Notes

This essay originally ran in a shorter form as "Talking about Guns, Fighting about Race," in the September 2008 issue of *In These Times*, responding to the Supreme Court's *Heller* decision. The full version then ran under this title on July 1, 2010, at BringTheRuckus.org, on the occasion of the *McDonald* decision extending the Fourteenth Amendment's protections to include the right to bear arms

Notes for a Critical Theory of Community Self-Defense

Chad Kautzer

> You should all go out with your sticks. What is the use of demon-
> strating for freedom and going unarmed? Don't come to meet-
> ings without sticks in the future, men and women alike.... It is
> no use pretending. We have got to fight.[1]
>
> —Sylvia Pankhurst, suffragist,
> quoted in the *New York Times*, 1913

In his speech "Communication and Reality" (1964), Malcolm X famously said: "I am not against using violence in self-defense. I don't call it violence when it's self-defense, I call it intelligence."[2] He made a similar point in his Harlem speech introducing the newly founded Organization of Afro-American Unity: "It's hard for anyone intelligent to be nonviolent."[3] To portray self-defensive violence as natural, in no need of justification, or as so commonsensical that it could barely be called violence, has a depoliticizing effect. Since the goal of Malcolm X's speech was to undermine critiques of armed black resistance, this effect was intentional. For good reasons, he was attempting to normal-ize black people defending themselves against the violence of white rule. When Malcolm X did speak of self-defense as a form of violence, he emphasized that it was lawful and an individual right. In his most famous speech, "The Ballot or the Bullet" (1964), he explicitly states: "We don't do anything illegal."[4] This was also, of course, how the Black Panther Party for Self-Defense justified their armed shadowing of the police in Oakland, California, in the late 1960s: it was their Second Amendment right to bear arms and, more specifically, their right under California law to openly carry them.[5]

To develop a critical theory of community defense, however, we need to move beyond the rhetoric of rights or the idea that all self-defensive violence is quasi-natural or nonpolitical. The self-defense discussed here is *political* because the *self* being defended is political, and as such it requires both normative and strategic considerations. This is a different kind of project than the one we find in the words and deeds of Malcolm X and the Black Panthers. It seeks to articulate the dynamics of power at work in self-defense and the constitution of the self through its social relations and conflicts. Because communities of color defend themselves as much against a culture of white supremacy as they do against bodily harm, their self-defense also undermines existing social hierarchies, ideologies, and identities. If we were to limit ourselves to the language of individual rights, these interconnections, which are found throughout our everyday social relations, would remain concealed. Violence against women (but not only women), for example, has a gendering function, enforcing norms of feminine subordination and vulnerability. Resistance to such violence not only defends the body but also undermines gender and sexual norms, subverting hetero-masculine dominance and the notions of femininity or queerness it perpetuates. Since the social structures and identities of race, gender, class, and ability intersect in our lives, practices of self-defense can and often must challenge structures of oppression on multiple fronts simultaneously.

In the following, I do not focus on the question of whether self-defensive violence is justifiable, but rather on why it is political; how it can transform self-understandings and community relations; in what contexts it can be insurrectionary; and why it must be understood against a background of structural violence. It is necessary to clarify these dimensions of self-defense for two reasons in particular. First, arguments advocating armed community defense too often discuss the use of violence and the preparations for it as somehow *external* to political subjectivity, as if taking up arms, training, or exercising self-defensive violence do not transform subjects and their social relations. The influence of Frantz Fanon's *The Wretched of the Earth* (1961) on the early Black Panthers, Steve Biko, and others derives precisely from Fanon's understanding of the transformative effects of resistance in the decolonizing of consciousness.[6] "At the individual level," Fanon writes, "violence is a cleansing force. It rids the colonized of their inferiority complex, of their passive and despairing attitude."[7]

The second reason for clarification is to distinguish the strategies, ways of theorizing, and forms of social relations within liberatory movements from those within reactionary movements. There is an increasingly influential understanding of self-defense today that reinforces a particular notion of the self—a "sovereign subject"—that is corrosive to horizontal social relations and can only be sustained vis-à-vis state power. This notion of the self runs counter to the goals of nonstatist movements and self-reliant communities. To be aware of these possibilities and pitfalls allows us to avoid them, a goal to which the following sketch of a critical theory of community self-defense seeks to contribute.

Resistance and Structural Violence

At the National Negro Convention in 1843, Reverend Henry Highland Garnet issued a rare public call for large-scale resistance to slavery: "Let your motto be resistance! *resistance!* RESISTANCE! No oppressed people have ever secured their liberty without resistance. What kind of resistance you had better make, you must decide by the circumstances that surround you, and according to the suggestion of expediency."[8] I describe resistance as opposition to the existing social order from within. As Rev. Garnet suggests, it can take different forms, such as self-defense, insurrection, or revolution. We can think of an *insurrection* as a limited armed revolt or rebellion against an authority, such as a state government, occupying power, or even slave owner. It is a form of *illegal* resistance, often with localized objectives, as in Shays' Rebellion (1786), Nat Turner's Rebellion (1831), the insurrections on the *Amistad* (1839) and *Creole* (1841), the coal miner Battle of Blair Mountain (1921), Watts (1965), Stonewall (1969), and Attica (1971).

Distinguishing between defensive and insurrectionary violence is complicated, since our location within relations of domination informs our subjectivity and assessments of such violence. In the

Amistad case, for example, white officials initially described it as a rebellion and thus a violation of the law, but later redescribed it as self-defense when the original enslavement was found to be unlawful. In a rare reversal, the U.S. Supreme Court recognized the captives on the *Amistad* as having selves worthy of defense. That was not in question among those rebelling, of course, but it does indicate the political nature of the self and our assessments of resistance. "Since the Other was reluctant to recognize me," writes Fanon, "there was only one answer: to make myself known."[9] On the *Amistad*, rebellion was the only way to make known the selves of the enslaved, meaning that their actions were simultaneously a defense of their lives and a political claim to recognition. A sustained insurrection can become *revolutionary* when it threatens to fundamentally transform or destroy the dominant political, social, or economic institutions, as with the rise of the Zapatista Army of National Liberation in Mexico in 1994 and the recent wave of Arab uprisings in the Middle East and North Africa, including most significantly Rojava (Western Kurdistan).

The armed rebellion led by John Brown in 1859, which seized the United States arsenal at Harpers Ferry, was intended to instigate a revolution against the institution of slavery. Although the insurrection was quickly put down, it inspired abolitionists around the country and contributed to the onset of the U.S. Civil War. Brown's rebellion was not a slave revolt (and thus not an act of self-defense), but it does highlight the nature of structural violence. Henry David Thoreau, the inspiration for Gandhi's nonviolent civil disobedience and, in turn, that of Martin Luther King Jr., wrote the most insightful analysis of this violence at the time. In his essay "A Plea for Captain John Brown," Thoreau defends Brown's armed resistance and identifies the daily state violence of white rule against which the insurrection took place:

> We preserve the so-called peace of our community by deeds of petty violence every day. Look at the policeman's billy and handcuffs! Look at the jail! Look at the gallows! Look at the chaplain of the regiment! We are hoping only to live safely on the outskirts of *this* provisional army. So we defend ourselves and our henroosts, and maintain slavery.... I think that for once the Sharps rifles and the revolvers were employed in a righteous cause [i.e., Brown's insurrection].[10]

Clearly revealed in this passage is how the so-called security of one community was achieved by oppressing another and making it insecure. To truly understand the insurrection, Thoreau argues, it must be viewed as a response to illegitimate structural violence. He enumerates the commonplace mechanisms of this rule, which, for the white community, fades into the background of their everyday lives: law and order upheld by a neutral police force, enforced by an objective legal system and carceral institutions, and defended by an army supported by the Constitution and blessed by religious authorities. The violence of white supremacy becomes naturalized and its beneficiaries see no need for its justification, for they see their interests reflected back to them in their objective institutions, making those interests and the violence that supports them appear normal. This violence goes almost unnoticed by those it sustains but not, of course, by those it oppresses. "The existence of violence is at the very heart of a racist system," writes Robert Williams in *Negroes with Guns* (1962). "The Afro-American militant is a 'militant' because he defends himself, his family, his home and his dignity. He does not introduce violence into a racist social system—the violence is already there and has always been there. It is precisely this unchallenged violence that allows a racist social system to perpetuate itself."[11]

We all exist within hierarchical social structures and the meaning and function of violence, self-defensive or otherwise, will be determined by our position vis-à-vis others in these structures. FBI Director J. Edgar Hoover, for example, described the self-defensive practices of the Black Panther Party as "the greatest threat to the internal security of the country" and thus insurrectionary, if not revolutionary.[12] Surely his assessment had more to do with the threat self-reliant black communities posed to white domination in the country than with the security of government institutions. "When people say that they are opposed to Negroes 'resorting to violence,'" writes Williams, "what they really mean is that they are opposed to Negroes defending themselves and challenging the exclusive monopoly of violence practiced by white racists."[13] These structures of domination and monopolies of violence are forms of rule that operate in the family, the city, and the colony, and resistance to their violence, both dramatic and mundane, "makes known" the selves of the subjugated.

A satisfactory notion of *self-defense* is not obvious when we view self-defensive acts within the context of structural violence and understand the *self* as both embodied and social. Akinyele Omowale Umoja, for example, defines self-defense as "the protection of life, persons, and property from aggressive assault through the application of force necessary to thwart or neutralize attack."[14] While this is appropriate in many contexts, the primary association of self-defense with *protection* does not capture how it can also reproduce or undermine existing social norms and relations, depending on the social location of the self being defended. Describing the effects of his defense against a slaveholder, Frederick Douglass, for example, wrote that he "was a changed being after that fight," for "repelling the unjust and cruel aggressions of a tyrant" had an emancipatory effect "on my spirit."[15] This act of self-defense, he asserts, "was the end of the brutification to which slavery had subjected me."[16] Our understanding of self-defense must, therefore, account for the *transformative* power of self-defense for oppressed groups as well as the *stabilizing* effect of self-defense for oppressor groups.

Social Hierarchies and Subject Formation

To see how self-defense can have several effects and why a critical theory of self-defense must, therefore, always account for relations of domination, we need to understand in what way the self is both *embodied* and *social*. By *embodied* I mean that it is through the body that we experience and come to know the world and ourselves, rather than through an abstract or disembodied mind. The body orients our perspective, and is socially visible, vulnerable, and limited. Much of our knowledge about the social and physical world is exercised by the body. Our bodies are sexed, raced, and gendered, not only "externally" by how others view us or how institutions order us—as, for example, feminine, masculine, queer, disabled, white, and black—but also "internally" by how we self-identify and perform these social identities in our conscious behavior and bodily habits.[17] By the time we are able to challenge our identities, we have already been habituated within social hierarchies, so resistance involves unlearning our habits in thought and practice as well as transforming social institutions. As David Graeber writes, "Forms of social domination come to be experienced in the most intimate possible ways—in physical habits, instincts of desire or revulsion—that often seem essential to our very sense of being in the world."[18]

40

Since our location within social hierarchies in part determines our social identities, the self that develops is social and political from the start. This does not mean that we are "stuck" or doomed to a certain social identity or location, nor that we can simply decide to identify ourselves elsewhere within social hierarchies or somehow just exit them. To be sure, we have great leeway in terms of self-identification, but self-identification does not itself change institutional relations or degrees of agency, respect, risk, opportunity, or access to resources. These kinds of changes can only be achieved through social and political struggles. Our embodied identities are sites of conflict, formed and reformed through our practical routines and relations as well as through social struggle. Since the actions and perceptions of others are integral to the development of our own, including our self-understanding, we say that the self is *mediated*, or is formed *through* our relations with others in systems of production, consumption, education, law, and so forth.

W.E.B. Du Bois theorized black life in a white supremacist society as experiencing one's self as split in two, a kind of internalization of a social division that produced what he called "double-consciousness," or "this sense of always looking at one's self through the eyes of others, of measuring one's soul by the tape of a world that looks on in amused contempt and pity." The disconnect between one's self-understanding and the perception of others, cleaves one's self-consciousness in two: "an American, a Negro; two souls, two thoughts, two unreconciled strivings; two warring ideals in one dark body, whose dogged strength alone keeps it from being torn asunder."[19] Although one may view oneself as capable, beautiful, intelligent, and worthy of respect, the social institutions one inhabits can express the opposite view, namely, the "amused contempt and pity" for one as inferior. Part of the experience of oppression is to live this *othering* form of categorization in everyday social life. Even when one consciously strives to resist denigration and to hold fast to a positive self-relation, the social hierarchy insinuates itself into one's self-understanding. In the most intimate moments of introspection, a unified self-consciousness escapes us because our self-understanding can never completely break from the social relations and ideologies that engender it. Social conflict is internalized, and it takes great strength just to hold oneself together; to live as a *subject* when others view and treat you as little more than an *object*, and when you are denied the freedoms, security, and resources enjoyed by others. Ultimately, only by undermining the social conditions of oppression through collective resistance can the "double-consciousness" Du Bois describes become one.

Racism produces race and not the other way around. Racial categories emerge from practical relations of domination, unlike ethnic groups, which are cultural forms of collective life that do not need to define themselves in opposition to others. Racial categories are neither abstract nor biological, but are social constructions initially imposed from without but soon after reconfigured from within through social struggles. As with all relations of domination, the original shared meanings attributed to one group are contrary to the shared meanings attributed to other groups and, thus, often exist as general dichotomies. This oppositional relation in meaning mirrors the hierarchical opposition of the groups in practical life—a fact that is neither natural nor contingent. Masculinity and femininity, for example, are not natural categories: they are social roles within a social order and thus have a history just as racial groups do. Yet, like those of race, the social and symbolic relations of gender are not contingent. Indeed, masculinity and femininity exhibit a certain kind of logic that we find in every institutionalized form of social domination. Because gender is a way of hierarchically ordering human relations, the characteristics associated with the dominant group function to justify their domination. Group members are said to be, for example, stronger, more intelligent, and more moral and rational. Nearly every aspect of social life will reflect this, from the division of labor to the forms of entertainment. In reality, the dominant group does not dominate because it is more virtuous or rational—indeed, the depth of its viciousness is limitless—but due to its dominance it can propagate the idea that it is more virtuous, rational, or civilized. "The colonial 'civilizing mission,'" writes María Lugones, "was the euphemistic mask of brutal access to people's bodies through unimaginable exploitation, violent sexual violation, control of reproduction, and systematic terror."[20]

It is often said that history is written by the victors, but that is only half the truth; they also create social norms, mythologies, and scientific discourses to justify their rule. They seek to turn the existence of oppression into an expression of nature that would be irrational to resist. This is what is meant by the idea that "racism produces race."

The existence of social domination—in, for example, white supremacy, colonial capitalism, or heteronormative patriarchy—contributes to the social construction of group identities that reflect and in turn justify that domination. "Cultural ideals of manhood and womanhood," writes Martha McCaughey, "include a cultural, political, aesthetic, and legal acceptance of men's aggression and a deep skepticism, fear, and prohibition of women's."[21] The subordinate groups are characterized as *essentially* weaker, less intelligent, overly emotional, and morally degenerate; each of which logically call for the dominant group's leadership, discipline, and protection. The daily interpersonal and state-sponsored violence that supports domination becomes a necessary mechanism to enforce this supposedly natural order. Law, violence, intimidation, institutional and scientific discourses, and informal social practices all reinforce the inferior characteristics attributed to the subordinate groups, thus denying or limiting group self-determination and access to social, cultural, and economic resources. These denials and limitations disable people from developing and self-determining, and are in turn used as evidence of their inferiority.

George Yancy writes that the "Black body has been historically marked, disciplined, and scripted and materially, psychologically, and morally invested in to ensure both white supremacy and the illusory construction of the white subject as a self-contained substance whose existence does not depend upon the construction of the Black qua inferior."[22] This *racial formation* is both a material and ideological process fueled by white supremacy.[23] Yancy rightly notes how whiteness is invested with an attribute that obscures the dependencies that constitute it, namely, *independence*. The fundamental dependency of the oppressor on the oppressed is concealed in all ideologies of social domination. Although the very existence of the colonist, capitalist, white supremacist, and patriarch relies on the continuous exploitation of others, they propagate the idea of an inverted world in which they are a "self-contained substance," free from all dependencies. This is the camera obscura of ideology that Marx discusses in *The German Ideology*. The supposedly natural lack of autonomy of the subordinated groups is, we are told, the reason for social hierarchy. Workers depend on capitalists to employ and pay them, women need men to support and protect them, people of color require whites to control and decide for them, and so forth.

Resistance to domination reveals the deception of this inverted world, destabilizing the practical operations of hierarchy and undermining its myths—for example, of masculine sovereignty, white superiority, compulsory heterosexuality, and capital's self-creation of value. "The reification of gender as natural, particularly men's invulnerability and women's helplessness—in popular media, in traditional rape and self-defense laws, and even in crime prevention advice for women and college rape prevention programs—is a central tenet of rape culture," writes Martha McCaughey.[24] Violence and various forms of coercion support these myths, but such violence would be ineffective if some groups were not socially, politically, and legally structured to be vulnerable to it.

Social relations unequally distribute levels of risk and vulnerability to different groups and the dichotomous pairings of social identities described above can also be calculated by the level of vulnerability each group has. This vulnerability to violence, exploitation, discrimination, disrespect, and toxic environments that limit life chances and undermine the social and material conditions of autonomy is not the choice of the individual. Ruth Wilson Gilmore defines racism as "the state-sanctioned or extralegal production and exploitation of group-differentiated vulnerability to premature death."[25] Changing the equation on group-differentiated vulnerability strikes a blow to social domination and undermines group identities structured by it. This is not to say that vulnerability can be completely overcome. The social nature of our projects and selves guarantees that the conditions that enable or disable us can never be completely under our control, and those very same conditions render us vulnerable to both symbolic and physical harm. Self-defensive practices cannot therefore eliminate vulnerability, but they can reduce it for particular groups and undermine it at a structuring principle of oppression. Training in self-defense, writes McCaughey, "makes possible the identification of not only some of the mechanisms that create and sustain gender inequality but also a means to subvert them."[26]

The Politics of Self-Defense

If we accept a social, historical, and materialist account of group and subject formation, and understand that groups are reproduced with the help of violence, both mundane and spectacular, then we can see why self-defense functions as more than protection from bodily harm. It is not merely an empirical question, or somehow external to the formation of our political subjectivity. If we acknowledge that we are hierarchically organized in groups—by race, gender, and class, for example—which makes some groups the beneficiaries of structural violence and others disabled, harmed, or killed by it, we see how self-defense can either stabilize or undermine domination and exploitation. Self-defense as resistance from below is a fundamental violation of the most prevalent social norms and bodily habits. As McCaughey writes: "The feminine demeanor that comes so 'naturally' to women, a collection of specific habits that otherwise may not seem problematic, is precisely what makes us terrible fighters. Suddenly we see how these habits that make us vulnerable and that aestheticize that vulnerability are encouraged in us by a sexist culture."[27] Organized examples of resistance to this structured vulnerability include the Gulabi or Pink Sari Gang in Uttar Pradesh, India, the suffragists of "The Bodyguard," trained in jiujitsu, as well as numerous queer and feminist street patrol groups.[28] McCaughey calls these self-defensive practices "feminism in the flesh," because they are simultaneously resisting the violence of patriarchy, while reconfiguring and empowering one's body and self-understanding.[29] We could similarly think of the self-defensive practices of the Black Panthers, Young Lords, Deacons of Defense and Justice, Brown Berets, and the American Indian Movement as *anti-racism* and *decolonialism in the flesh*.

Although self-defense is not sufficient to transform institutionalized relations of domination, unequal distributions of resources and risk, or the experience of double-consciousness, it is a form of decolonization and necessary for other kinds of mobilizations. The praxis of resistance is also an important form of self-education about the nature of power, the operations of oppression, and the practice of autonomy.[30] When conditions are so oppressive that one's self is not recognized at all, self-defense is de facto insurrection, a necessary *making oneself known* through resistance. While the most common form of self-defense is individual and uncoordinated, this does not make it any less political or any less important to the struggle, and this is true regardless of the mind-set or intentions of those exercising resistance.[31]

We must, however, also be attentive to how resistance, and even preparations for it, can instrumentalize and reinforce problematic gender and race norms, political strategies, or sovereign politics. A critical theory of community self-defense should reveal these potentially problematic effects and identify how to counter them. There is, for example, an influential pamphlet, *The Catechism of the Revolutionist* (1869), written by Sergey Genadievich Nechayev and republished by the Black Panthers, which describes the revolutionist as having "no personal interests, no business affairs, no emotions, no attachments, no property, and no name." This nameless, yet masculine, figure "has broken all the bonds which tie him to the social." But who provides for the revolutionist and who labors to reproduce the material conditions of his revolutionary life? Upon whom, in short, does the supposed independence of the revolutionist depend?

Although the machismo and narcissism here is extreme to the point of being mythical—George Jackson said it was "too cold, very much like fascist psychology"—it does speak to a twofold danger in practices of resistance.[32] The first danger is that self-defensive practices are part of a division of labor that falls along the traditional fault lines of social hierarchies *within* groups. Men have, for instance, too often taken up the task of community defense in all contexts of resistance, which has the effect of reproducing traditional gender hierarchies and myths of masculine sovereignty. Considerations of self-defense must therefore be intersectionalist and aware of the transformative power and embodied nature of resistance, as discussed above. The group *INCITE!*, for example, seeks to defend women, gender nonconforming, and trans people of color from "violence *directed at* communities (e.g., police brutality, racism, economic exploitation, colonialism, and so on)" as well as from "violence *within* communities (e.g., sexual/domestic violence)."[33]

The second danger is a commitment to the notion of a sovereign subject, which is the centerpiece of authoritarian political ideologies and motivates so many reactionary movements. The growing number of white militias, the sovereign citizen movement, as well as major shifts in interpretations of the Second Amendment and natural rights, are contributing to an increasingly influential politics of self-defense with a sovereign subject at its core. For this sovereign subject—whose freedom can only be actualized through domination—the absolute identification with abstract individual rights always reflects an implicit dependency on state violence, much the way the revolutionist of the

Catechism implicitly relies on a community it refuses to acknowledge.[34] The sovereign subject's disavowal of the social conditions of its own possibility produces an authoritarian concept of the self, whose so-called independence always has the effect of undermining the conditions of freedom for others.

Although one objective of self-defense is protection from bodily harm, the social and political nature of the self being defended makes such resistance political as well. Self-defense can help dismantle oppressive identities, lessen group vulnerability, and destabilize social hierarchies supported by structural violence. The notion of a sovereign subject conceals these empowering dimensions of self-defense and inhibits the creation of self-reliant communities in which the autonomy of each is enabled by nonhierarchical (and nonsovereign) social relations being afforded to all.

Notes

1 "Jiu-Jitsu for Militants: Sylvia Pankhurst Also Wants Them Drilled and to Carry Sticks," *New York Times*, August 20, 1913, 4.

2 Malcolm X, "Communication and Reality," Speech to Domestic Peace Corps, December 12, 1964, in *Malcolm X: The Man and His Times* (New York: Macmillan, 1970), 313.

3 Malcolm X, Organization of Afro-American Unity (OAAU) Founding Rally in Harlem, June 28, 1964.

4 Malcolm X, "The Ballot or the Bullet," in *Let Nobody Turn Us Around: An African American Anthology*, ed. Manning Marable and Leith Mullings (Lanham, MD: Rowman & Littlefield, 2009 [2nd edition]), 404–13.

5 See Joshua Bloom and Waldo E. Martin Jr., *Black against Empire: The History and Politics of the Black Panther Party* (Berkeley: University of California Press, 2013), 45–62.

6 See Bobby Seale, *Seize the Time: The Story of the Black Panther Party and Huey P. Newton* (New York: Random House, 1970), 25–26.

7 Frantz Fanon, *The Wretched of the Earth*, trans. Richard Philcox (New York: Grove Press, 2004), 51.

8 Henry Highland Garnet, "Let Your Motto Be Resistance!," in *Let Nobody Turn Us Around*, 62.

9 Frantz Fanon, *Black Skin, White Masks*, trans. Richard Philcox (New York: Grove Press, 2008 [1952]), 95.

10 Henry David Thoreau, "A Plea for Captain John Brown," in *Essays: A Fully Annotated Edition*, ed. Jeffrey S. Cramer (New Haven, CT: Yale University Press, 2013), 211.

11 Robert F. Williams, *Negroes with Guns* (New York: Marzani & Munsell, 1962), 76. In the final pages of his book, Williams quotes at length from Thoreau's text on John Brown, which he says he always keeps with him.

12 Cited in Bloom and Martin, *Black against Empire*, 3.

13 Williams, *Negroes with Guns*, 76.

14 Akinyele Omowale Umoja, *We Will Shoot Back: Armed Resistance in the Mississippi Freedom Movement* (New York: New York University Press, 2013), 7.

15 Frederick Douglass, *The Life and Times of Frederick Douglass*, in Frederick Douglass, *Autobiographies* (New York: Library of America, 1994), 591.

16 Ibid.

17 See Judith Butler, *Gender Trouble: Feminism and the Subversion of Identity* (New York: Routledge, 1990) and Iris Marion Young, "Throwing like a Girl," in Iris Marion Young, *On Female Body Experience* (New York: Oxford University Press, 2001), 27–45.

18 David Graeber, *Possibilities: Essays on Hierarchy, Rebellion, and Desire* (Oakland: AK Press, 2007), 16.

19 W.E.B. Du Bois, *The Souls of Black Folk*, in *Writings* (New York: Literary Classics of the United States, 1986), 364–65.

20 María Lugones, "Toward a Decolonial Feminism," *Hypatia* 25, no. 4 (Fall 2010): 744.

21 Martha McCaughey, *Real Knockouts: The Physical Feminism of Women's Self-Defense* (New York: New York University Press, 1997), 3.

22 George Yancy, *Black Bodies, White Gazes: The Continuing Significance of Race* (Lanham, MD: Rowman & Littlefield, 2008), 1.

23 See Michael Omi and Howard Winant, *Racial Formation in the United States* (New York: Routledge, 2014).

24 McCaughey, *Real Knockouts*, 7.

25 Ruth Wilson Gilmore, *The Golden Gulag: Prisons, Surplus, Crisis, and Opposition in Globalizing California* (Berkeley: University of California Press, 2007), 28.

26 McCaughey, *Real Knockouts*, 89.

27 Ibid., 90.

28 See Che Gossett, Reina Gossett, and A.J. Lewis, "Reclaiming Our Lineage: Organized Queer, Gender-Nonconforming, and Transgender Resistance to Police Violence," *Scholar & Feminist Online* 10, nos. 1–2 (Fall 2011–Spring 2012), http://sfonline.barnard.edu/a-new-queer-agenda/reclaiming-our-lineage-organized-queer-gender-nonconforming-and-transgender-resistance-to-police-violence/.

29 McCaughey, *Real Knockouts*, 90. See also Ann J. Cahill, *Rethinking Rape* (Ithaca: Cornell University Press, 2001).

30 As Fanon writes: "The colonized subject discovers reality and transforms it through his praxis, his deployment of violence and his agenda for liberation." Fanon, *Wretched of the Earth*, 21.

31 See Christopher B. Strain, *Pure Fire: Self-Defense as Activism in the Civil Rights Era* (Athens, GA: University of Georgia Press, 2005).

32 George L. Jackson, *Blood in My Eye* (New York: Random House, 1972), 3.

33 INCITE! Women of Color Against Violence, *Color of Violence: The INCITE! Anthology* (Cambridge, MA: South End Press, 2006), 1–2.

34 As Errico Malatesta writes: "Freedom is not an abstract right but the possibility of acting: this is true among ourselves as well as in society as a whole. And it is by cooperation with his fellows that man finds the means to express his activity and his power of initiative." Errico Malatesta, *Life and Ideas: The Anarchist Writings of Errico Malatesta*, ed. Vernon Richards (Oakland: PM Press, 2015), 80.

Three-Way Fight: Revolutionary Anti-Fascism and Armed Self-Defense

J. Clark

> We are not simply in a conflict with the state in its present incarnation, but in a three-way fight against it and its authoritarian opponents.
>
> —CrimethInc.[1]

Prologue: A Specter Haunting Rural America

Protesters blockade a highway in opposition to government land management policies. Law enforcement officers use Tasers, dogs, tear gas, and "First Amendment zones" to control protesters. Armed protesters face down federal agents over issues of sovereignty.

These scenes could easily describe an Earth First! forest defense campaign, a mass protest against the Republican National Convention, or an American Indian Movement occupation from the 1970s, respectively. Instead, they all played out in southern Nevada in April 2014, during the "Battle of Bunkerville," when right-wing militias answered the call to arms of a wealthy, white settler rancher named Cliven Bundy.[2]

After a protracted dispute over cattle grazing rights on Bureau of Land Management (BLM) land, federal agents began confiscating Bundy's cattle to recoup unpaid grazing fees. Bundy declared a "range war" and called for support. Organized militias and unaffiliated individuals from across the country responded, providing armed security details, setting up armed checkpoints, and confronting federal agents.

The BLM quickly ceased their operation and released Bundy's cattle. Bundy, however, continued to call on supporters and local sheriffs to disarm all federal agents, remove entrance stations to federal parks, and block interstate highways. In speeches, he declared, "We're about ready to take the country over with force!" and invoked a long history of populist right-wing "patriot" movements,[3] rejecting the authority and legitimacy of the federal government and proclaiming his sacred right to the land on which his cattle graze. Perhaps the only thing more remarkable than how quickly the Far Right was able to mobilize a mass-based armed response to confront the feds was how quickly the feds surrendered.

Nonetheless, even before Bundy opined about whether Black people were better off picking cotton as slaves, and before he blamed abortion and welfare for ruining America, the movement coalescing around him represented the germinating seeds of an insurgent, right-wing populism eerily reminiscent of fascism.

What Is Fascism Anyway?

Fascism is a reactionary mass political movement that is hostile to both revolutionary socialism(s) and liberal, bourgeois democracy. Fascist movements are rooted in perceptions of community/national decline and obsessive myths of community/national rebirth and greatness. They therefore seek, through redemptive violence, to purge or "cleanse" the community/nation of "corrupting" or "alien" elements, replace the current ruling elite with their own idealized class, and impose their new brand of "order" on the rest of the populace.[4]

Fascism "is never a mere puppet of the ruling class, but an autonomous movement with its own social base."[5] Historically, fascism has often functioned to defend capitalism against instability, crisis, and the revolutionary Left. At times, the state and its security apparatus have cooperated and colluded with fascists to undermine or attack the Left, lending credence to narratives that fascism is simply a tool of the ruling class or the most extreme manifestation of the state and capital.

However, fascist movements have also pursued agendas that clash with capitalist and ruling-class interests in significant ways, sometimes taking positions that seem in line with the Left while maintaining authoritarian and reactionary underpinnings. For example, right-wing and fascist elements have long opposed neoliberal globalization on the grounds that it is an attack on national sovereignty and the privileged position of white men in Western society. In the mid to late 2000s, after the anti-war Left had mostly withered into irrelevance, various right-wing elements vocally criticized the wars in Iraq and Afghanistan for compromising the state's capacity to police the U.S.-Mexico border and other internal "threats." A subset of the right-wing anti-war tendency is also hostile toward Israeli colonialism and the U.S.'s complicity, presuming both to be manifestations of various anti-Semitic conspiracy theories. Whether it's environmentalism, opposition to law enforcement, or distrust of bankers, the Far Right's oppositional politics are always grounded in authoritarian values.

It is sometimes said that fascism is revolutionary, in that it seeks to overthrow or seize state power. But I prefer to only use the term "revolutionary" to refer to movements that seek a more fundamental and liberatory transformation of existing social relations. I instead refer to fascism's "insurgent" nature, as insurgencies can come from a variety of political positions.

Twenty-first-century fascism, in particular, does not always look like the traditional forms of fascism that we are used to seeing. Some contemporary fascists have "shifted away from traditional fascism's highly centralized approach to political power and toward plans to fragment and subdivide political authority."[6]

These different forms of fascism are still built on authoritarian ideologies and belief systems but may use certain anti-authoritarian language, strategies, and tactics to achieve their goals. For example, prominent fascist groups over the previous decades have opposed all government authority above the county level, advocated strategies of "leaderless resistance," or sought to establish the racist, right-wing equivalent of temporary autonomous zones. One of the patriot militia groups that mobilized support for Cliven Bundy calls itself Operation Mutual Aid,[7] appropriating a central tenet of anarchism in its defense of "private property, lives, and liberty to exercise God-given rights ... codified in the Declaration of Independence and Bill of Rights."[8]

So-called Third Position fascism often espouses an explicitly anti-capitalist politics. "National Anarchism," for example, blends anti-statism, anti-capitalism, and decentralization/hyperlocalism (along with many anarchist symbols) with its own special brand of anti-Semitism, racial determinism and separatism, homophobia, and anti-feminism.[9]

Similarly, Keith Preston's "anarcho-pluralism" seeks to replace centralized nation-states with small-scale political entities through a "pan-secessionist" coalition among a wide range of oppositional movements from "white nationalists, Patriot/militia groups, Christian rightists, and National-Anarchists, [to] left wing anarchists, liberal bioregionalists/environmentalists, and nationalist people of color groups."[10] His end goal, though, is to empower "a handful of superior individuals [to] rise above the bestial mass of humanity," a starkly anti-liberatory and authoritarian vision masquerading as revolution.[11]

This appropriation of the symbols, language, and tactics of the anti-authoritarian Left does more than just muddy the waters; it also reflects "an ideological split in fascist circles as the younger generation attempts to update its organizational models for the 21st century."[12] Early 20th-century, industrial-era totalitarianism relied on the central power of the nation-state to impose its vision. Today, "in the era of outsourcing, deregulation, and global mobility," the decentralist currents in fascism express "a new social totalitarianism" that "look[s] to local authorities, private bodies (such as churches), and direct mass activism to enforce repressive control."[13]

Celebrating decentralized resistance without an analysis of the political aims and content of that resistance ignores the role of "illegal violence on the part of fascists, paramilitaries, gangs, drug cartels, mafias, and authoritarian revolutionary movements [in forming] an essential aspect of domination."[14] If the last century taught the revolutionary Left "the consequences of using hierarchical means to pursue supposedly non-hierarchical ends," this century may teach us "how supposedly non-hierarchical means can [still] produce hierarchical ends."[15]

Political Tectonics in the Age of Crisis

Recent history has demonstrated that, like anti-authoritarian and anti-capitalist ideas, fascism also finds increasing support from the downtrodden and dispossessed people subjugated and alienated by neoliberal globalization, cycles of economic crisis and austerity-driven "recovery," climate change, and the expansion and reconfiguration of modern empires.

The Left often assumes that the discontent spawned from these crises and contradictions of contemporary capitalism will always translate into support for the Left.[16] But anarchist philosopher John Clark (no relation to this author) observes that these crises and contradictions do not exist in a vacuum. When analyzed concretely, "in the context of the totality of social relations, they can be expected to lead in a direction determined largely by the prevailing institutional structure and the dominant political culture"—that is, in the United States, one of white supremacist settler-colonialism, class exploitation, and hetero-patriarchy.[17] "The disquieting but inescapable conclusion is that [capitalism's contemporary] transformative contradictions might very well transform in a rightist, authoritarian, or even fascistic direction."[18]

In Greece, protracted economic crisis and suffocating austerity measures imposed under intense pressure from the European Commission, European Central Bank, and International Monetary Fund led to an intense period of social upheaval and a dramatic rise in the visibility of radical and anarchist organizing. But it also brought about a sharp increase in scapegoating immigrants and support for the fascist Golden Dawn party. In the 2012 parliamentary elections, Golden Dawn won nearly 7 percent of the vote, up from 0.5 percent just three years earlier, to capture its first seats in parliament. Emboldened by their electoral victory, members and supporters of Golden Dawn escalated and increased their violent—and sometimes deadly—attacks on immigrants, queers, and leftist political opponents.

The Euromaidan uprising in Ukraine in the spring of 2014 was particularly disorienting for North American radicals, because at first glance it was easy to identify with the street fighting and rioting. But in the midst of Ukraine's multifaceted power struggle, fascists constituted "a powerful minority in the anti-Yanukovych campaign."[19] "The neo-fascists from Svoboda [Freedom party] and Pravy Sektor [Right Sector] [were] probably the vanguard of the movement, the ones who pushed it harder than anyone."[20] Genuine anti-authoritarian/anti-capitalist elements were nearly invisible, while fascists reportedly appropriated anarchist symbols and even the image and legacy of anarchist Nestor Makhno. The "accepted and leading role" of

Euromaidan's fascist organizations was "a breakthrough and set a new benchmark for fascists across Europe."[21]

In France, the previously marginal far-right National Front party won municipal elections in fourteen cities in March 2014, and then captured a quarter of the national vote in the 2014 European Parliament elections. Right-wing insurgencies and coups in Venezuela[22] and Thailand, respectively, and electoral victories for hardline nationalists in India[23] and parts of Europe fill in the picture of a global reactionary shift in the current moment of overlapping crisis. It is not yet clear whether the Far Right in these countries will simply get absorbed into the current ruling class and act as the new right hand of capital, or whether their parliamentary gains will act as a foothold from which to further build their mass base and advance insurgent aims.

The United States has not been an exception to this trend. The Far Right in the U.S. is perhaps more inclined than elsewhere to adopt decentralized forms and anti-authoritarian language, due in part to the cultural and political mythology of individualism and federalism in U.S. The Far Right has also "worked diligently for decades at the [local] grassroots level in many areas"—through churches, civic organizations, and local political structures, for example—"to create the cultural preconditions for reactionary grassroots [politics]."[24] This allows the right to wage their reactionary battles state by state, city by city, and school board by school board.

Yet the Far Right also faces barriers to their power that contributes to growing radicalism and militancy in their ranks. Despite some electoral gains for the Tea Party,

> they will never be able to muster the strength to defeat finance capital and the political mainstream on parliamentary grounds. Assuming no unforeseen economic amelioration, the conditions that are developing and radicalizing the far-right ... will only deepen. Yet with a decided inability to advance any further through parliament, the possibility of a right-wing break with the ballot box as the [primary] terrain of political struggle will begin to loom ever larger on the horizon. The popular base and the historical conditions for a new form of Fascism or proto-Fascism, called by a much different name, will continue to grow unless relentlessly combated by a genuine, militant U.S. Left.[25]

A possible turn toward extralegal, militant, collective action by a growing right-wing mass movement is evidenced by Minutemen-style border militias, Tea Party disruptions of Democratic town hall meetings, the growing tendency of right-wing groups to openly display firearms at any protest they attend, and the mobilization of armed patriot militias to confront the federal government in defense of oppositional twenty-first-century settler ranchers. If this movement is effectively mobilizing for war with the feds over a bunch of cattle and the specter of a centrist president that they think is too socialist, "what will happen if [anarchists and the radical Left] are the next ones who piss these guys off?"[26]

Greensboro Was a Massacre

On November 3, 1979, the multiracial Communist Workers Party held a "Death to the Klan" march in Greensboro, North Carolina. At CWP rallies in the area over the previous months, they had openly carried firearms for self-defense, due to death threats and acts of violence against them. But for this particular event, local law enforcement had required that the CWP remain unarmed to receive a permit.

During the march, a caravan of Klansmen and members of the American Nazi Party drove up to the CWP march and stopped. The fascists emerged from their vehicles, pulled firearms from the trunks, and opened fire, killing five core CWP members and wounding eleven other organizers and bystanders. Unlike previous similar events in Greensboro, local police were not present during the march, evidence of the police collusion with the fascists in the attack. Nonetheless, the CWP's unarmed presence at this march, despite known threats, provided a ripe opportunity for an open fascist attack. One unarmed CWP member got to his car to retrieve his handgun and returned fire, albeit ineffectively.

Had the CWP maintained an effective armed presence at the march as they had at others, it is extremely unlikely that the attack would have occurred. The history of Klan action in the South during the civil rights movement shows that their power and gall were greatly diminished when met with organized armed opposition.[27] The Greensboro massacre greatly deflated the power and capacity of the CWP, which transitioned from revolutionary communism to social democratic activism before fully dissolving a few years later.

The Greensboro massacre was also "a pivotal event for the U.S. far right" in part because "it broke the suspicion and animosity" that had previously "kept Klansmen and Nazis at odds with each other."[28] The subsequent "collaboration, cross-over, and interchange between the two branches of the far right" shifted the "movement's ideological center of gravity" from "segregationism to fascism—away from restoring the old racial order, to new dreams of creating a new whites-only homeland or overthrowing the U.S. government entirely."[29]

As a chilling reminder that that the past doesn't pass, one of the neo-Nazi participants in the Greensboro massacre, Frazier Glenn Miller, made national headlines in 2014 when he fatally shot three people outside a Jewish community center in Kansas City, after decades of fascist organizing.

Bashing the Fash: Anti-fascism Everywhere

In the struggle against the state and capital, we run the risk of being outflanked by fascism and the insurgent right. Don Hamerquist states, "The real danger presented by the emerging fascist movements and organizations is that they might gain a mass following among potentially insurgent workers and declassed strata through an historic default of the Left. This default is more than a possibility, it is a probability, and if it happens it will cause massive damage to the potential for a liberatory anti-capitalist insurgency."[30] CrimethInc.'s commentary on the events in Ukraine similarly foreshadows "a future of rival fascisms, in which the possibility of a struggle for real liberation becomes completely invisible."[31]

To guard against this trend we cultivate a movement that is both revolutionary and explicitly anti-fascist.[32] "Anti-fascism without revolution…guarantees capitalism's continuing misery and devastation… [while] revolution without anti-fascism … all but ensures that the insurgent right will ace out the insurgent left."[33]

On the one hand, we must oppose, disrupt, and undermine the fascist/insurgent right and their organizing, as well as help build support for the targets of right-wing violence and scapegoating.[34] On the other, we must organize to fight the conditions from which fascism grows, such as capitalism and its current austerity programs, which intensify the impact of economic crisis on marginalized communities.

We must also recognize and address the potentially reactionary positions within our own movements. For example, many environmental/anti–climate change movements propagate narratives of catastrophe and apocalypse that can inadvertently fuel reactionary ends.[35] Similarly, Occupy's myth about the 99% flattened out a lot of differences of race, class, and ideology, reinforcing many of the nationalist myths about the U.S. and allowing right-wing elements (like the "End the Fed" crowd) to feed off Occupy's popular appeal.

Also, recent anti-fascist movements in the U.S. have encountered several major pitfalls, including hypermacho behavior and related patriarchal tendencies and getting stuck in a mostly reactive posture. Emphasizing armed self-defense here admittedly runs the risk of compounding both of these problems—simply one more example of anti-fascists preferring supposed militancy over the less dramatic work of building a broad anti-fascist culture and politics in revolutionary movements; one more instance of anti-fascists jumping at some emergent fascist threat but never proactively building a positive anti-fascist strategy.[36] Confronting these challenges is imperative to building effective revolutionary, anti-fascist movements.

Reciprocally, our organizing should engage the communities that tend to form the mass base for the insurgent Right, pushing on the internal tensions and inconsistencies in their politics, to divide the misguided from the true believers. For example, in Arizona, anarchists openly carried firearms during their campaign against the neo-Nazi National Socialist Movement (NSM) as part of a larger strategy to engage and split the local libertarian movement over their contradictions around immigration and white supremacy. One participant wrote:

> We carried firearms openly against the NSM, not just for self-defense, or so that the NSM would know we were armed, but also informed by the memory of having seen pacifist anti-war liberals denounce armed anti-war libertarians at protests during the early days of that movement in Arizona. We wanted to differentiate ourselves from the liberals in the eyes of both groups. We knew the significance that would have. And the right wing libertarians responded. Quite a lot of them came out to the [anti-Nazi] action.[37]

The goal was "to divide [the local libertarian movement], neutralize it and, hopefully, to cause a shaking out of its more truly libertarian elements toward advancing the attack on Capitalism and State ... [and breaking] with the overall fascist tendency, the reactionary free market ideology and the infantile patriotism."[38]

One area anarchist reflected on the personal impact of the actions: "This is the first time I have physically seen anarchists at demonstrations carry firearms with them—and I have to say that the experience was very empowering to see."[39] While emphasizing that "the way forward is collective action" and organizing by oppressed communities, they also declare, "if we are going to go up against people like the NSM, we should be prepared to defend ourselves."[40]

In Kansas and Colorado, anarchists used their involvement with gun culture to distribute political literature—primarily focused on class struggle and critiquing white supremacy—to mostly white working-class communities at local gun shows.[41] From Texas to North Carolina to Oregon, anarchists and radical anti-fascists have quietly prepared to defend their homes and organizing spaces. This preparedness can make all the difference.

The struggle against fascism and the insurgent Right is largely political. Accessible political education and collective organizing against the ideology and practice of private property, white supremacy, and patriarchy, for example, can do more to curb the power and legitimacy of insurgent right-wing populism in a country where private property and white, male privilege are widely seen as synonymous with liberty.

This struggle is often physical as well as political, however, and building a capacity for armed self-defense is paramount. Armed self-defense is sometimes necessary to provide physical protection—autonomous of the state—from fascist terror, and to create and maintain the space in which to wage our political struggles.

Hurricane Katrina and the Showdown in Algiers

In the power vacuum in New Orleans immediately following Hurricane Katrina, a group of radicals used armed self-defense to create the space from which to launch broader grassroots organizing and relief efforts.[42] White militias had formed in several neighborhoods throughout New Orleans, including the Algiers Point neighborhood on the West Bank of the Mississippi River.[43] Algiers Point is a small, wealthy, white neighborhood that is surrounded by the much larger Algiers and West Bank neighborhoods, which are predominantly poor and Black.

The militias were composed of white men from various socioeconomic backgrounds, ostensibly to protect their private property and secure "law and order" locally in the absence of the state. But much like the police, their actions mostly amounted to intimidation and harassment of Black people on the street in any number smaller than the patrolling militia.

The militias self-organized to enforce the racial hierarchy in an area where the state's violence was no longer actively present.[44] They threatened many desperate unarmed people of color, even killing some, which they later bragged about to Danish media.[45] The actions of these militias and the paternalistic, white supremacist attitudes of many rescuers escalated tensions between all who were desperate and left to their own devices in the storm's aftermath.

In the wake of the storm, some Texas anarchists responded to a call for support from Malik Rahim, an organizer and former Black Panther who lived in Algiers and was witnessing and experiencing the militia's racial policing. They snuck into the city under martial law to get to Rahim's house, armed and ready to support the defense of the community and their friends from the racist attacks and harassment of the militias.

Together with residents of the neighborhood, they sat on Rahim's porch and went out on informal armed patrols to keep the white militias at bay. When a truck with some of the Algiers Point militia pulled up in front of Rahim's house, as it had several times before to shout threats at Rahim, an armed stand-off ensued. But this time, faced with an armed and organized opposition, the militia abruptly left.

Without the presence of an organized, armed opposition to the Algiers Point militia, violence against poor people of color in Algiers would likely have been much worse than it was. The presence of whites and Blacks working together to defend a community against the racist militias was often cited by local residents as having eased tensions in a racially and economically divided area that was devastated in many ways before Katrina ever came ashore.

Moreover, armed self-defense helped create the space for broader grassroots organizing and relief efforts to take place. The militia's power had been clearly diminished after facing armed opposition, and it continued to wither as aid and food distribution sites, free medical clinics, and independent media centers were developed into full operations.

The aftermath of Hurricane Katrina and particularly the struggles and organizing in Algiers offer a tiny and intensified example of both what is at stake and what is possible in the world today. John Clark explains that the hurricane "offers abundant evidence of how crisis creates ideal opportunities for intensified economic exploitation, what has since then come to be called 'disaster capitalism,' and also for increased repression, brutality, and ethnic cleansing, which might be called 'disaster fascism.'" But "it also creates the conditions for an extraordinary flourishing of mutual aid, solidarity, and communal cooperation, something we might call 'disaster anarchism.'"[46]

Open Carry, Ferguson, and the Three-Way Fight

More recent struggles against white supremacy and police brutality paint a messy picture of the different political forces mobilizing around race, property, state violence, and individual rights to own and carry firearms. Much of the recent open-carry movement has been driven by the largely white male libertarian right, a reaction to a perceived decline of their collective power and an assertion of the right to overtly threaten their historic violence in public. Whether promising to march through historic Black neighborhoods in Houston or organizing meet-ups at local fast-food joints across suburban Middle America, much of open carry has blatantly smacked of white male entitlement and explicitly sought to normalize their armed presence in public spaces.

When John Crawford, a Black man, was shot dead by police for carrying a toy rifle at a Walmart in Ohio, a state that allows open carry, much of the national open-carry movement was remarkably silent on the matter. The white male core of the movement was too overcome by their racist stereotypes about Black criminality and violence to see the obvious implications: white people get to open carry and Black people get a fusillade of bullets for trying to exercise a comparable right. And this was but one episode in a long history of communities of color in the U.S. being legally and extralegally denied the right to self-defense.[47]

One Ohio open-carry group, however, partially recognized some of the dynamics underlying Crawford's murder. They mobilized several dozen activists to a protest at the Walmart where Crawford was murdered by police, openly carrying firearms along with their signs decrying the racist double standard in how police and citizens view people carrying firearms, and the police violence that results.[48] In Texas, a group of Black activists from various political tendencies formed the Huey Newton Gun Club to flip the script on open carry, marching in Houston and Dallas while carrying firearms.[49] Both instances point to possibilities for creative engagement with the contradictions in the populist libertarian right.

The events surrounding the 2014 uprising in Ferguson, Missouri, provide another model of community defense and the challenges it presents. After the murder of Michael Brown, and again after the county prosecutor and the grand jury refused to indict the officer, outraged community members smashed, burned, and looted area businesses and police vehicles, making good on the maxim of "no justice, no peace." During the unrest, a local Klan chapter began distributing fliers threatening lethal force against protesters and warning that the protests had woken a "sleeping giant."[50] In the midst of these riots in November, a local Black church that had been critical of the local police and prosecutor and was where Michael Brown's stepfather had recently been baptized, was burned down, despite being several miles from any of the protests. Many suspect Klan involvement.[51]

After the first night of post–grand jury protests in November, the right-wing "patriot" group the Oath Keepers began mobilizing in Ferguson.[52] Founded by a former Ron Paul staffer, the Oath Keepers are a national network of retired and active law enforcement and military personnel who vow to disobey any orders that they deem to be unconstitutional.[53] It is part of the right-wing patriot movement and had a large presence at the "Battle of Bunkerville" with Cliven Bundy.

A cursory reading of their stated mission might lead one to think that the Oath Keepers mobilized in Ferguson against the police murder of an unarmed Black youth or the extreme police violence against protesters. In reality though, they saw the government's real transgression as the failure to prevent property destruction by an angry and historically oppressed community.[54]

The Oath Keepers spent only a few days posting up on the rooftops of commercial buildings with rifles and binoculars before area law enforcement told them to leave and threatened legal action for operating a security service without a license. Incensed, the Oath Keepers promised to instead join the protesters but were back on patrol a few days later. Like much of white America and the political establishment, the Oath Keepers were much more committed to the protection of private property than the struggle against white supremacy or police violence. Yet their relationship with the state, even though they were composed largely of agents of the state and fulfilling some of its primary functions, seemed to oscillate between guarded suspicion and open hostility.

Conclusions?

In moments of crisis and upheaval, political lines and alliances can shift quickly. Right-wing elements that in one moment act largely in concert with the state can pivot to a much more system-oppositional but still reactionary posture as the state reacts to threats to its legitimacy from several directions. But whether these elements are acting in direct concert with the state (as in Greensboro), against the state (as in Nevada), or in a relative absence of state control (as in Ferguson and New Orleans), they still pose a threat to our revolutionary movements against white supremacy, patriarchy, capitalism, and the state.

The shape the future takes may hinge on our movements' ability to respond dynamically and appropriately to rapidly shifting conditions, to build communities and networks of revolutionary solidarity and mutual aid, and to defend those communities and networks. Armed self-defense is an area that the radical Left in the U.S. has neglected, but which may be necessary for the survival and relevance of our future organizing in the face of a growing insurgent fascism.

¡No pasaran! ¡Siempre anti-fascista!

Notes

This piece is derived from an essay that I pseudonymously wrote with scott crow in 2006. Many thanks to Lena M., Julie R., scott crow, and Alexander Reid Ross for thoughts, feedback, and edits.—J. Clark

1 "The Ukrainian Revolution & the Future of Social Movements," *CrimethInc.*, March 17, 2014, http://crimethinc.com/texts/ux/ukraine.html, accessed June 25, 2017.

2 Grace Wyler, "An Armed Standoff in Nevada Is Only the Beginning for America's Right-Wing Militias," *Vice*, April 16, 2014, http://www.vice.com/read/

an-armed-standoff-in-nevada-is-only-the-beginning-for-americas-right-wing-militias, accessed June 25, 2017.

3   The patriot movement is a loose collection of groups and people who believe that strict (and some might argue selective) adherence to the U.S. Constitution is necessary to rein in a tyrannical (and sometimes "socialist") federal government and its "New World Order." Various strands run the gamut from militias, conspiracists, white nationalists, and Christian fundamentalists.

4   For deeper explorations, see Don Hamerquist, et al., *Confronting Fascism: Discussion Documents for a Militant Movement* (Montreal: Kersplebedeb, 2002); Matthew Lyons, "Two Ways of Looking at Fascism," *Journal of the Research Group on Socialism and Democracy Online*, March 8, 2011, http://sdonline.org/47/two-ways-of-looking-at-fascism/, accessed June 25, 2017; Matthew Lyons, "What Is Fascism?" *Political Research Associates*, December 12, 2000, http://www.politicalresearch.org/what-is-fascism; Kevin Passmore, *Fascism: A Very Short Introduction* (Oxford: Oxford University Press, 2002); Robert O. Paxton, "The Five Stages of Fascism," *Journal of Modern History* 70, no. 1, March 1998, http://w3.salemstate.edu/~cmauriello/pdfEuropean/Paxton_Five%20Stages%20of%20Fascism.pdf, accessed June 25, 2017.

5   Lyons, "What Is Fascism?"

6   "Third Position," *Political Research Associates Archive*, http://www.publiceye.org/fascist/third_position.html, accessed June 25, 2017 (quoting Chip Berlet and Matthew N. Lyons, *Right-Wing Populism in America: Too Close for Comfort* (New York: Guilford Press, 2000), 267.

7   Cheryl K. Chumley, "Militias Head to Nevada Rancher's Standoff with Feds: We're Not 'Afraid to Shoot,'" *Washington Times*, April 11, 2014, http://www.washingtontimes.com/news/2014/apr/11/militias-head-nevada-ranchers-standoff-feds-were-n/, accessed June 25, 2017.

8   Operation Mutual Aid (2014) http://operationmutualaid1.webs.com/, accessed April 18, 2014; inactive July 4, 2017; see also "Operation Mutual Aid Militia," *Terrorism Research & Analysis Consortium* (2014), http://www.trackingterrorism.org/group/operation-mutual-aid-militia, accessed June 25, 2017; see also https://www.facebook.com/OperationMutualAid/.

9   Spencer Sunshine, "Rebranding Fascism: National-Anarchists," *Public Eye Magazine* 23, no. 4 (Winter 2008), http://www.publiceye.org/magazine/v23n4/rebranding_fascism.html, accessed June 25, 2017.

10 Matthew N. Lyons, "Rising Above the Herd: Keith Preston's Authoritarian Anti-statism," *New Politics*, April 29, 2011, http://newpol.org/content/rising-above-herd-keith-prestons-authoritarian-anti-statism, accessed June 25, 2017.

11 Ibid.

12 "Fighting in the New Terrain: What's Changed Since the 20th Century," *CrimethInc.*, August 23, 2010, http://www.crimethinc.com/texts/recentfeatures/terrain.php, accessed June 25, 2017.

13 "Third Position," *Political Research Associates Archive* (quoting Berlet and Lyons, *Right-Wing Populism in America*, 267).

14 CrimethInc., "Say You Want an Insurrection," *Rolling Thunder*, no. 8 (Fall 2009): 8, available at http://crimethinc.com/texts/recentfeatures/insurrection.php, accessed June 25, 2017.

15 "Fighting in the New Terrain."

16 Sasha Lilley, "Great Chaos Under Heaven: Catastrophism and the Left," in Sasha Lilley et al., *Catastrophism: The Apocalyptic Politics of Collapse and Rebirth* (Oakland: PM Press, 2012), 54.

17 John P. Clark, *The Impossible Community: Realizing Communitarian Anarchism* (New York: Bloomsbury Publishing, 2013), 30–31.

18 Ibid., 31.

19 Mark Ames, "Everything You Know about Ukraine Is Wrong," *Pando Daily*, February 24, 2014) http://pando.com/2014/02/24/everything-you-know-about-ukraine-is-wrong/, accessed June 25, 2017.

20 Ibid.

21 Tash Shifrin, "Ukraine: No Tears for Yanukovych, No Cheers for New Regime or Fascists in Its Midst," *Dream Deferred*, February 25, 2014, http://www.dreamdeferred.org.uk/2014/02/no-tears-for-yanukovych-no-cheers-for-the-new-regime-or-the-fascists-in-its-midst/, accessed June 25, 2017.

22 George Ciccariello-Maher, "#LaSalida? Venezuela at a Crossroads," *The Nation*, February 22, 2014, http://www.thenation.com/article/178496/lasalida-venezuela-crossroads, accessed June 25, 2017.

23 Matthew N. Lyons, "Reading 'The Solstice'—Kasama on Right-Wing Mass Movements," *Threewayfight*, June 15, 2014, http://threewayfight.blogspot.com/2014/06/reading-solstice-kasama-on-right-wing.html, accessed June 25, 2017.

24 Clark, *The Impossible Community*, 266.

25 "On Shutdowns and Party Politics," *Dirt Road Revolutionary*, October 7, 2013, https://dirtroadrevolutionary.wordpress.com/2013/10/07/on-shutdowns-and-party-politics/, accessed June 25, 2017.

26 "Psycho Hicks," *RednBlackSalamander*, April 25, 2014, http://rednblacksalamander.deviantart.com/art/Psycho-Hicks-450072949, accessed June 25, 2017.

27 The history of armed self-defense in the South during the civil rights and Black freedom movement is very instructive in this regard. See Charles E. Cobb, *This Nonviolent Stuff'll Get You Killed: How Guns Made the Civil Rights Movement Possible* (New York: Basic Books, 2014); Lance Hill, *The Deacons for Defense: Armed Resistance and the Civil Rights Movement* (Chapel Hill: University of North Carolina Press, 2004); Timothy Tyson, *Radio Free Dixie: Robert F. Williams and the Roots of Black Power* (Chapel Hill: University of North Carolina Press, 1999); Akinyele Umoja, *We Will Shoot Back: Armed Resistance in the Mississippi Freedom Movement* (New York: New York University Press, 2014).

28 Matthew N. Lyons, "Frazier Glenn Miller, Nazi Violence, and the State," *Threewayfight*, May 8, 2014, http://threewayfight.blogspot.com/2014/05/frazier-glenn-miller-nazi-violence-and.html, accessed June 25, 2017.

29 Ibid.

30 Don Hamerquist, "Fascism & Anti-fascism," in Don Hamerquist et al., *Confronting Fascism*, 16 http://kersplebedeb.com/mystuff/books/fascism/fashantifash.php, accessed June 25, 2017.

31 "The Ukrainian Revolution & the Future of Social Movements."

32 "Anti-repression, Anti-fascist Strategizing Suggestions," *Black Orchid Collective*, October 16, 2012, https://blackorchidcollective.wordpress.com/2012/10/16/anti-repression-anti-fascist-strategizing-suggestions/, accessed June 25, 2017.

33 Michael Staudenmaier, "Anti-Semitism, Islamophobia, and the Three Way Fight," *Upping the Anti*, no. 5 (2007), http://uppingtheanti.org/journal/article/05-the-three-way-fight-debate, accessed June 25, 2017.

34 For ideas and accounts of anti-fascist strategies and tactics, see CrimethInc. Workers' Collective, *Recipes for Disaster: An Anarchist Cookbook* (Olympia: CrimethInc., 2004), specifically the chapters "Anti-Fascist Action" and "Infiltration," https://archive.org/details/RecipesForDisasterAnAnarchistCook book, accessed June 25, 2017; K. Bullstreet, *Bash the Fash: Anti-fascist recollections 1984–1993* (London: Kate Sharpley Library, 2001), https://libcom.org/library/bash-the-fash-anti-fascist-recollections-1984–1993, accessed June 25, 2017.

35 Eddie Yuen, "The Politics of Failure Have Failed: The Environmental Movement and Catastrophism," in Sasha Lilley et al., *Catastrophism: The Apocalyptic Politics of Collapse and Rebirth* (Oakland: PM Press, 2012), 15.

36 Some of these critiques were raised in response to the first version of this piece back in 2006. See "The Three-Way Fight and Militant Antifascism: A Short Review," *Threewayfight*, November 16, 2006, http://threewayfight.blogspot.com/2006/11/three-way-fight-and-militant.html, accessed June 25, 2017.

37 "JT Ready Is Dead: Fascism and the Anarchist Response in Arizona, 2005–2012," *Fires Never Extinguished: A Journal of the Phoenix Class War Council*, June 1, 2012, http://firesneverextinguished.blogspot.com/2012/06/jt-ready-is-dead-fascism-and-anarchist.html, accessed June 25, 2017.

38 "High Noon Is Too Late for Tea: Seeking Ways to Engage and Oppose the Tea Party Movement," *Fires Never Extinguished: A Journal of the Phoenix Class War Council*, April 7, 2010, http://firesneverextinguished.blogspot.com/2010/04/high-noon-is-too-late-for-tea-seeking.html, accessed June 25, 2017.

39 "Phoenix: Where Anarchists Pack Heat and Send Nazis Packing," *Fires Never Extinguished: A Journal of the Phoenix Class War Council*, November 9, 2009, http://firesneverextinguished.blogspot.com/2009/11/phoenix-where-anarchists-pack-heat-and.html, accessed June 25, 2017.

40 Ibid.

41 "Rednecks with Guns and Other Anti-racist Stories and Strategies," *Defenestrator*, no. 51 (2011): 14–15, http://multi.lectical.net/content/rednecks_guns_and_other_anti_racist_stories_and_strategies, accessed June 25, 2017.

42 The original version of this section was coauthored with scott crow, and is recounted in greater detail in his book *Black Flags and Windmills: Hope, Anarchy, and the Common Ground Collective* (Oakland: PM Press, 2014 [2nd edition]), 46–70.

43 For in-depth reporting on the racist militias in post-Katrina New Orleans, see A.C. Thompson, "Katrina's Hidden Race War," *The Nation*, December 17, 2008, http://www.thenation.com/article/katrinas-hidden-race-war, accessed June 25, 2017.

44 "This 'autonomous attempt to impose hierarchies in miniature,' when allowed to develop in a zone temporarily abandoned by the State, takes the form of

warlordism. Rule by local mafia, by religious cultists, by the toughest guys on the block … [And] fascism is the ideology [that] warlordism tends towards. With its wild warrior ethos and its scorn for 'feminine' bourgeois civility, warlordism has always been the social myth that traditional fascism has dangled before its men." Karl Kersplebedeb, "Thinking about Warlordism," *Sketchy Thoughts*, August, 29, 2010, http://sketchythoughts.blogspot.com/2010/08/thinking-about-warlordism. html, accessed June 25, 2017.

45 Rasmus Holm, dir., *Welcome to New Orleans* (Fridthjof Film, 2006), https://www. youtube.com/watch?v=V__lSdR1KZg, accessed June 25, 2017.

46 Clark, *The Impossible Community*, 192.

47 See Clayton E. Cramer, "The Racist Roots of Gun Control," *Kansas Journal of Law and Public Policy*, Winter 1995, http://www.constitution.org/cmt/cramer/ racist_roots.htm, accessed June 25, 2017; Adam Winkler, "The Secret History of Guns," *The Atlantic*, July 24, 2011), http://www.theatlantic.com/magazine/ archive/2011/09/the-secret-history-of-guns/308608/, accessed June 25, 2017.

48 It's also safe to say that Ohio Open Carry isn't quite there yet with their analysis. See Heather Digby Parton, "Gun Nuts' Tragic Confusion: Why 'Open Carry' Groups Don't Get Police Brutality," *Salon*, October 1, 2014, http://www. salon.com/2014/10/01/gun_nuts_tragic_confusion_why_open_carry_groups_ misunderstand_police_brutality/, accessed June 25, 2017; Shane Dixon Kavanaugh, "Shameless Open-Carry Activists Co-opt Racially Charged Shooting," *Vocativ*, October 7, 2015, http://www.vocativ.com/culture/society/i-am-john-crawford/2/, accessed June 25, 2017.

49 Aaron Lake Smith, "The Revolutionary Gun Clubs Patrolling the Black Neighborhoods of Dallas," *Vice*, January 5, 2015, http://www.vice.com/read/huey-does-dallas-0000552-v22n1, accessed June 25, 2017.

50 Alice Speri, "KKK Missouri Chapter Threatens Ferguson Protesters with 'Lethal Force,'" *Vice News*, November 13, 2014, https://news.vice.com/article/kkk-missouri-chapter-threatens-ferguson-protesters-with-lethal-force, accessed June 26, 2017.

51 See Wesley Lowery, "The Brown Family's Pastor Tries to Make Sense of the Fire that Gutted His Church," *Washington Post*, November 28, 2014, http:// www.washingtonpost.com/national/the-brown-familys-pastor-tries-to-make-sense-of-fire-that-gutted-his-church/2014/11/28/15520f3e-7711-11e4-a755-e32227229e7b_story.html, accessed June 26, 2017; Steven D., "Michael Brown Family's Church Burned to the Ground—Arson Investigated by ATF (UPDATED)," *Daily Kos*, November 29, 2014, http://www.dailykos.com/ story/2014/11/29/1348212/-Michael-Brown-Family-s-Church-Burned-to-the-Ground-Arson-Investigation-by-ATF, accessed June 26, 2017.

52 Brian Heffernan, "In Ferguson, Oath Keepers Draw Both Suspicion and Gratitude," Al Jazeera America, December 14, 2014, http://america.aljazeera.com/ articles/2014/12/14/oath-keepers-fergusonprotests.html, accessed June 26, 2017.

53 Justine Sharrock, "Oath Keepers and the Age of Treason," *Mother Jones*, March–April 2010, http://www.motherjones.com/politics/2010/03/oath-keepers, accessed June 26, 2017.

54 Mark Hay, "The Leader of Oath Keepers Says the Right-Wing Group Is in Ferguson to 'Protect the Weak,'" *Vice*, December 1, 2014, http://www.vice.com/read/leader-of-oath-keepers-says-the-group-is-in-ferguson-to-protect-the-weak-1201, accessed June 26, 2017.

The Liberation Gun: Symbolic Aspects of the Black Panther Party

Ashanti Alston

> Blessed are those who struggle
> Oppression is worst than the grave
> Better to die for a noble cause
> Than to live and die a slave ...
>
> —The Last Poets,
> "Blessed Are Those Who Struggle"

Chickens Come Home to Roost

Resistance is the natural reaction of any people who have for so long suffered. Those of us who had accepted the *no compromise* position back in the 1960s and '70s stepped up, armed up—in the biblical sense, with the power of belief—and marched into the fray. In doing so, our lives were transformed.

For those of us who experienced what Frantz Fanon described as "gun in hand" we would always remember the most hidden secret of our captive existence: that to stand up, to confront our oppressors with guns was a magical psychic, maybe even spiritual, liberation.[1] Because we experienced the power of the people to inject fear into the oppressor and make them do as we command. It dawned on us that we *did* have the power to bring an end to our suffering.

We were always catching hell, fighting against our own self-doubt. Maybe this is it, this is how it always will be. A few of us noticed out of the corners of our eyes a rainbow—a ray of hope. We made our way toward it. A diversion from the path of struggle, but somehow very connected.

We were all collecting knowledge, wisdom with a community of like-minded souls who were becoming increasingly convinced of the rightness of our desire for freedom and dignity.

The Empire continued to assassinate, to imprison, to pull strings that caused us to lose jobs and homes—all to discourage resistance. Others from our Black communities watched scared and wavering but hopeful still. They may join us someday. But we couldn't wait.

Black Panther Party

> I am talking of millions of men who have been skillfully injected with fear, inferiority complexes, trepidation, servility, despair, abasement.
>
> —Frantz Fanon quoting Aimé Césaire's
> "Discourse on Colonialism"

The scene starts off with Huey P. Newton and a crew of Black Panthers in a car checking out the neighborhood. But this ain't just the neighborhood, it's where folks hang out at night to have a good time. In the alley two "pigs" are, as usual, whooping on some defenseless Black man. Then here comes the Panther-mobile pulling up. The Panthers get out the car and move into formation. There is discipline. They are armed, the whole crew. The pigs notice, but so do Black folks around, some folks coming out of the Cocktail Lounge and others who may have been just walking home.

The scene itself is powerful. It is loaded with layers of significance and teachable moments. In what is now a standoff, the police, addicted to nigger hatred and routine, let their victim go and turn their full attention now to the NWG (Niggas with Gunz). More people come to see what's going on. This is like nothing they have ever, ever seen before in their lives. NWG ain't running, they're confronting the police, the most terrifying force of white supremacy we have immediate contact with. NWG ain't running and ain't gazing *down* at these pigs' *feet*.

In the back and forth dialogue, Huey Newton takes the lead. People are listening. You can't help but listen when armed Black folks are talking free, dignified people shit to the police. Not a slavish drawl, not a slavish whisper. Huey states clearly, with a touch of arrogance and righteous hostility, what's up, and gives sharp responses to every query and directive that this "pig" spits in his way. This scene has enraptured an audience. *Enraptured.* The people maybe don't know whether to be terrified or awestruck, and so they just say *fuck it, I might never live to see such a thing again.* The moments pass quickly and the standstill reaches its limit; there's gotta be a climax. The pig leader orders his boys to stand down! And ... they leave.

They leave? Yes, they have been defeated by NWG. The dream of the Oppressed. This is a moment of authentic collective joy, happiness. This sets the stage for the cultural mechanism of folklore.

The next scene shows the morning after, around that same spot, and people are talking. They are talking it up. The Word is spreading. You'd have thought Jesus just rose from the dead. Or that Joshua had just blew the trumpet and the walls of Jericho came crumbling down. Communication back then wasn't through corporate social media. It was by word of mouth! And then amplified by 1960s technology, like the telephone, the mimeographed flier, the newspaper.

What We Have to Overcome

Whatever we do in resistance *against* Hell and *for* Liberation should try to psychologically overcome:

> *Learned helplessness*: the state of passivity developed in response to repeated experiences of failure.
> *Surplus powerlessness*: feelings of personal impotence beyond and above the actual limitations placed on the individual by the social context. (It is why people do not object to oppression, even when they might have an opportunity to alleviate it.)
> *Internalization* of hegemonic images of inferiority, including "useless," "incapable," "lazy," "unlovable," and "stupid"; and, finally: *Obedience to authority.*

The Panthers' challenge to police power inspired all who witnessed it, to overcome *each* of the points of internalized oppression *just in this one action.* Watch the scene again and again. Listen to the encounter, listen to the "bystanders" who no longer remain passive. Huey says to them, *Stay there! You ain't got to go nowhere!* And they stay. They are now a vital, self-acting part of this phenomenon. Subjects coming into their own—not objects, slaves forever at the mercy of white supremacy. What message did the image of the "Black Panther" give to a defeated, conquered *living* witness longing for a dignified, free existence? What did it mean to create temporary liberated spaces that were also invitations to step out of your comfort zones, your social caskets, to dare to embrace life through the activity of the revolutionaries? That seemingly impenetrable culture of alienation, trepidation, and servility is now beginning to look shaky, to feel shaky.

Black Liberation Army

> You do not have to be me in order for us to fight alongside each other. I do not have to be you to recognize that our wars are the same. What we must do is commit ourselves to some future that can include each other and to work toward that future with the particular strengths of our individual identities. And in order to do this, we must allow each other our differences at the same time as we recognize our sameness.
>
> —Audre Lorde, *Sister Outsider: Essays and Speeches*

As a Black Liberation Army (BLA) soldier I remember as if it were yesterday what it was like to go on my first armed mission: a small expropriation leading up to something bigger.[2] I experienced Fanon in my body. What does it feel like? Leading up to the action, it felt like nerves on end. But with my comrades, when it went down, I felt weirdly calm as our armed presence told the powers in this location what to do and to do it—*now*.

Wow. We'd been scared of them for so damn long. Look how easy that was. All the readings and all the experiences and all the remembrances of humiliation, dismissal and discrimination, and all the desires and imaginings of us acting on our own and for our selves personally and communally, thus becoming new beings—it's all there in this first mission.

Something powerful came over me. Maybe ancestral spirits. Maybe just a knowing that the time had come to take a stand and trust in the promise of—what? deliverance? liberation?

The action is definitely personal, but it is also communal, historical, and even existential. And maybe the weapon—in our case, the liberation gun—is the object infused with all this meaning. This thing that can ring a loud report of *No!*—metaphorically and in actuality. With our Panther orientations, we knew that the times called for more. Especially in the face of the civil rights movement's failure to halt the violence of oppression, while we constantly compromised. It took beatings, lynchings, being fired from jobs, kicked out of homes, spit on, etc. Too much to name. But as the saying goes, the dead shall open the eyes of the living. It opened the eyes of the United Negro Improvement Association and African Blood Brotherhood. It opened the eyes of Robert Williams and of the Deacons for Defense in the South. Cuz we remembered that the dead didn't live full lives, but half lives, butchered lives at the hands of racists, bigots, and police. And we know that they were simply folks who only wanted simple, dignified lives for themselves and their progeny and for the racist oppression to stop.

I think all of this has to go into an understanding of what we are up against as revolutionaries, liberators, defenders of the community. What will you face and how will you deal with it? If your idea of self-defense stems from your broader understanding of the intransigence of the U.S. Empire, then you know that it is useless to have any faith that this five-hundred-year project will give you "civil rights," "human rights," "democratic rights," reparations, whatever. But if you are coming to the idea of resistance as a resolute *no* to the Empire, then armed self-defense is as much a *yes* to liberated life as the *yes* of community gardens.

Killing Fear

We must always be careful and vigilant. The gun can be a stumbling block. The mind-set that reinforces Racist Imperialist Patriarchy created around guns is so deep within us, our beings, and this country, that we shudder to think that we can be armed in defense of our dreamwork to be free.

Today, when I join a march or demonstration where the police are also present, I try to encourage people to do what, symbolically, that gun allowed us to do: to exercise the courage to look your oppressor *in the face, square in the eyes*. An act of guerrilla counterterrorism. It is the act of killing your own fear. It is that act of accepting and finally embracing your own agency and taking back your lives, laying the *nigger* in you to rest. This was one of our first lessons as Panthers when we studied the anarchist Sergey Nechayev's *Revolutionary Catechism*. This was further developed when Huey Newton wrote *Revolutionary Suicide*. And then, Jamil Al-Amin's *Die Nigger Die*. In order to be able to *do*, to *act* for liberation, you have to let go of fears, accept death, and now live for the revolution. It's not about having *no* fears. It's as former Black Liberation Army member and U.S. revolutionary living in political exile Assata Shakur said a long time ago: It's having no fears *that control you*.

Now, go out and work your own Free Children's Breakfast program, set up them self-defense trainings. Police the police! You will discover that this same psychic challenge allows you to actually transform your own fears into new human ventures, as erotic as they are political.

Notes

1 This refers to Frantz Fanon's important concept of self-defense: "When the peasants lay hands on a gun, the old myths fade, and one by one the taboos are overturned: a fighter's weapon is his humanity." See Frantz Fanon, *The Wretched of the Earth* (New York: Grove Press, 1963), lv.

2 Here the term "expropriation" refers to taking either state or corporate private property for a purpose deemed to be in the public interest or public good through armed bank robberies to fund revolutionary engagements.

Desire Armed: An Introduction to Armed Resistance and Revolution

Western Unit Tactical Defense Caucus

Demystifying the Gun

Nothing has been a source of more debate within anarchist circles as the topic of "violence." At the heart of this debate has always been the topic of armed struggle. Nothing is more key to armed struggle than the firearm.

Firearms are an inherent part of a culture of death and have been used to kill, maim, subdue, and enslave. Since the invention of gunpowder, the firearm has been a useful tool for the Dominant Classes because of the fear instilled with these tools. We do not wish to embrace the methods of the Dominant Classes. However, it is futile to believe that any resistance or revolutionary movement can succeed against an armed ruling class without at least having a knowledge of the weapons that the ruling class will use against them.

This is not a call for every revolutionary to immediately rush out and obtain a firearm or to start indiscriminately targeting cops, soldiers, or members of the ruling class. Instead, we urge every revolutionary to, at the very least, become knowledgeable of the culture, use, and function of firearms. This means knowing how firearms work, how to disable them and those that use them, and how to evade them. That being said, we believe that it is important and a plus for revolutionaries to be proficient with firearms as part of our overall mass organizing.

How many anarchist posters and newspapers contain graphics that depict anarchists armed with rifles, explosives, or incendiary devices? Yet how many anarchists have actually even held any of these weapons, let alone used them? We believe that the time for fetishization of armed violence without a knowledge base is over. We must be able to back up our empty slogans and graphics with actual education and training in the workings of guns and armed revolution.

Tools of Revolution

As an old FARC member once put it: "Guns are like forks. You may not believe in forks, but that doesn't mean they don't exist and aren't a useful tool for the revolutionary. Guns, like forks, have a use and a purpose within the revolution." Quite simply put, guns are tools.

Guns alone are not power. Guns alone do not take the place of strategy. Guns are not the revolution. Guns are made of wood, metal, and plastic and are bound to the limitations of these materials.

The power of our movement comes from community organizing and empowerment. Without a social program and a social movement, all the guns in the world cannot lead to revolution. Our goal should not be to create an "armed revolutionary movement," but rather to arm the already existing "social revolutionary movement" with whatever means we can. Armed self-defense must be but one part of a much larger social campaign of liberation.

One of the greatest defeats for the revolutionary movements of the 1970s was their abandonment of the social program and their willingness to go underground as an armed revolutionary wing. This did nothing but alienate "the People," the group the vanguards wished to rally to the revolution. The fact that the Black Panther Party was armed was not reason enough for it to be considered a threat. The real threat came from their development of a social movement based around free food programs, prisoner organizing, and community empowerment.

If we are to be successful, we must view training with weapons in the same way we would view training union organizers or doing door to door campaigns: with the same degree of revolutionary zeal. If anything, it is the authors' belief that if you feel that the choice is between social organizing and armed training, that armed training should be what is abandoned. The social program is what we're fighting for and learning to use firearms in the first place.

Vanguardism and the "Armed Wing"

As anarchists, quite simply put, we do not believe in the Vanguard. The revolution must come from the People and not from the armed wings or elite groups of a governing party or cadre. We do not intend to create an armed vanguard. We intend to educate and inform individuals that seek to empower themselves and give that knowledge to others. Historically, armed revolutions have been subdued by parties and vanguards that have deprived arms and the knowledge to use them from the People. We want all members of a community to be able to use guns to defend themselves and their communities, not just an elite few.

We believe that the people must know why they are fighting and why they are putting their lives on the line. This must be an individual choice. A revolution cannot have draftees or forced combatants. Just as we don't believe that those that adhere to nonviolence have a right to inhibit those of us that don't, we don't have any right to force some one to use a weapon or to fight against their will. This pamphlet is intended not to convince others to use weapons, but to act as a guide for those that are interested in such tactics.

Privilege and Armed Struggle

All around the world, movements against capitalism and the state continue to organize and to attack capital in many different ways. One thing is shiningly clear when examining the differences between movements in the United States and their contemporary movements in other countries: Second and Third World uprisings are almost always armed, or include the use of arms. Revolutionaries in the United States have yet to arm their movements, and instead energy is spent debating whether "violence" is even a legitimate tactic.

Our first world (and in most cases, white skin) privilege has allowed us the luxury of even having these debates. We feel that these debates are healthy, and indeed necessary, but that the facts remain clear: our privilege allows us to question violence.

Some would argue that because our very lives aren't seemingly at risk right now, that that is the reason we should not be arming ourselves: it's unnecessary. This obviously overlooks the facts that women, people of color, queers, and other oppressed people face life and death situations daily because of their social status (yes, even here in the United States). This line of thinking also negates all the credibility of any of the rhetoric that movements like ours hold so dear. We all understand that capitalism is a deadly force and that the heart of global capitalism is here in the United States. Why then should people all the world over be fighting and dying in the battles against global capitalism, while we sit here in the belly of the beast with passivity? Is revolution a game? Is it just "angst and rebellion"? Do we really believe half of the theory that is spewed from our lips? When Emma Goldman said, "If they don't give you bread, take bread," she made it very clear that the struggle against capitalism is a very real and very serious struggle. What good do our chants of "Stop the War!" do for a person who feels compelled to fight and die against the U.S. occupation in Iraq? Shouldn't they expect that if we truly mean what we say, then we too would be willing to fight and die to stop this war and all capitalist wars?

How can our actions only be symbolic? As a friend once put it, "Do people starving to death just symbolically starve?"

Revolution vs. Activism

The current elements of the anti-capitalist movement in the United Stated have very little experience with revolutionary organizing. The current role of much of the anti-capitalist movement has been one of "weekend warrior" activism, in which the movement survives from one protest to another, one "campaign" to another. Largely, members of our movement continue to divide their "political lives" from their "social lives."

We must come to an understanding that if we really envision revolution, we must be revolutionaries. Every aspect of our lives is an extension of our "political work." The very way we live our lives is an expression of our desires to see a new egalitarian world. And this isn't about "consumer politics" or whether you buy "fair trade." This is about developing a mentality where our desire for a new world enters in every interaction, every facet of our lives.

This also isn't a call for all of us to become mindless drones with no sense of humor and no recreation or joy. The mentality is what is really the defining characteristic of the revolutionary, not the humorless and boring political life. Do we want transformation of our society? Or do we want an endless string of Reclaim the Streets parties and demos (not that these tactics are useless or even bad)? So how do we get there?

That's the point. The authors of this pamphlet have ideas and visions of how we can achieve that world. But it is not our place in this context to give you those ideas (yet). We have our own community to organize with and help empower. A foundation for a revolutionary mind-set is built once you start to ask these questions of yourself, and actually come up with real, tangible answers. The rest of the development then comes from action. You must fathom a social program and then build it. And this program must punctuate every aspect of your life.

Notes

This essay originally appeared in a pamphlet called *Desire Armed* released in 2006.

Mischievous Elves: Defending a Broader Concept of the Self

Leslie James Pickering

Survival is a necessity of life; self-defense is an inherent right of all living beings. Nations grant or deny their citizens this right in various ways, but it is not actually the state's to give or to take away. Malcolm X went to great lengths to draw a distinction between civil rights and human rights: a civil right is granted by a nation to its citizens, but a human right is inherent to all people regardless of their nationality. He famously argued that if your human rights were being violated you are justified to act in self-defense "by any means necessary."

If you're under direct violent attack, self-defense is a relatively straightforward concept. Much of the time, however, what threatens people is just as deadly, but a bit more complicated. It may seem that threats to air, water, food, climate, habitat, etc. are remote, but that depends on where you happen sit in history and on the global social spectrum.

Countless peoples have faced very real threats against their necessities of life, often coupled with direct violent attacks. Withholding necessities, killing off animal populations, burning crops, and destroying habitats on which targets are dependent are all well established methods of warfare that have been employed by invaders around the world for centuries. European settlers, for example, systematically slaughtered the buffalo as a means of attacking the indigenous nations that depended on the herds. More recently, the U.S. and other global powers have used international sanctions to starve the citizens of enemy nations.

For many land-based indigenous peoples, the distinction between defending against direct violent attacks and defending against attacks on habitat and shared natural resources is trivial. Often, indigenous peoples are violently attacked as a means to acquire the natural resources on their land, or to seize their land altogether, so there is really not much of a distinction to be made. At times, the American Indian Movement argued that it was not engaging in a revolution to overthrow the U.S. government, but simply defending their people against European invasion. The more you are a part of the land, the more threatening the attacks on the land are to you. Defending the land is necessary for survival and can only be viewed as an act of self-defense.

We are dependent on nature in many ways. The closer you live to the land, the more obvious this is, but it ultimately holds true for everyone. Some of these dependencies are actually rather direct: without air, you would die in a matter of minutes; without water, you would die in days; and without food, you would die in weeks. We are dependent on the sun, the climate, the seasons, gravity, and many other aspects of our natural environment that are typically taken for granted.

The systematic destruction of the earth's limited resources is now a growing ecological catastrophe. Pollution, deforestation, species extinction, resource extraction, ocean acidification, and of course, climate change, threaten us all in very real ways.

Since the 1990s, the underground Earth Liberation Front (ELF) has used arson against corporate and government polluters as a tactic for defending the environment and, by extension, all of us living here on Earth. Because we depend on the natural world, threats against the environment amount to threats against us all. The armed ecological resistance struggles can be understood as part of a struggle for the survival of our planet and are therefore taken in defense of a broad definition of the self.

The first ELF actions torched Forest Service offices and equipment in response to deforestation. Others burned down research facilities developing genetically engineered crops, SUV dealerships increasing oil consumption, and luxury housing developments encroaching on wilderness areas. The $24.5 million arson of the Vail ski resort was intended to prevent its expansion into some of the last territory of the endangered Canadian Lynx. With over three dozen large-scale arson attacks during the ELF's first half-decade, it became increasingly clear that there was a potential extralegal consequence to plundering nature. At times, ELF supporters embraced an ecocentric folklore, claiming that "mischievous elves" were striking back to defend the natural world.

The Earth Liberation Front started as an armed propaganda campaign for environmental defense. When corporations and government agencies wouldn't stop destroying the planet in response to the environmental movement's petitioning and protesting, the ELF raised the stakes and inspired the movement to fight harder. As it matured, the ELF grew increasingly anti-capitalist and revolutionary. The earth is being destroyed because capitalism is making its destruction very profitable. Addressing this profit motive linked the ELF's fight to other freedom struggles around the world and throughout history. The group looked to past tactics and strategies of armed self-defense and adapted them to its circumstances. Its range of targets broadened, actions became more frequent and severe, and the FBI internally expressed concerns about a new generation "being mentored" through "association with former members of leftist revolutionary groups" resulting in "the creation of a new armed self-defense force modeled after those organizations."[1]

The ELF helped to produce a generation of radicals and revolutionaries, because rather than simply decrying environmental destruction, the group engaged in a high-profile, multimillion-dollar arson spree, proclaiming its commitment to self-defense of the earth: "If you build it, we will burn it."

Notes

1   Author's own FBI file, entry dated July 2, 2003, regarding 2003 Break the Chains conference.

Antagonistic Violence: Approaches to the Armed Struggle in Urban Environments from an Anarchist Perspective

Gustavo Rodríguez

> Violence is only justifiable when it is necessary to defend oneself
> and others against violence. . . . The slave is always in a state
> of legitimate self-defense and so his violence against the boss,
> against the oppressor, is always morally justifiable and should
> only be adjusted by the criterion of utility and economy of
> human effort and human suffering.
> —Errico Malatesta, "Umanità Nova," August 25, 1921

Defense of Armed Struggle

Before starting, we consider it necessary to make a "statement"
affirming our compromise with antagonistic struggles. So it is worth-
while to reaffirm that, on the issue of "armed struggle," we are not,
nor can we be, neutral, because neither the "official History" nor the
means of massive alienation are neutral. So-called historical objectivity and journalistic objectivity do not exist. In the particular case
of the anarchist struggle, the distortion and alienation by historians
is constant. It really does not matter if we speak about conservative
and right-wing historians or leftist and "progressive" ones, the result
is the same: premeditated distortion and reduction to "irrational
violence" or banal "nonviolence." We will avoid ambiguities and will

take sides with what we understand as just and necessary: antagonistic violence.

We understand critique as an indispensable weapon and as an inescapable part of the struggle. To us, a critique that does not end in a concrete proposal is not an antagonistic position. To learn from the "armed critique" is to not repeat mistakes; it is the vehicle that feeds the antagonistic project; it is the path that will allow us the development of the refractory conscience through the transformation of apathy into antagonistic rage. Only in such a way will we make concrete the self-management of generalized insurrection.

Now that we've made our positions clear, we can start with our consequent defense of the armed struggle, of antagonistic violence, of direct action as an effective means of struggle. Sterile "nonviolence"—that innocuous militancy of idealist pacifism—does not match our general values. It comes at first from a Christian intoxication and from a certain "radical" liberalism that serves the ideology of citizenship, that amorphous mass subjected to the State that reclaims a more elevated level of interlocution with Papa State. Anarchists, by principle, are "anti-militarists," and, by consequence, we are "anti-war," which means that we openly and with all our strength oppose the institution of the military, identifying it with all the different repressive corporations as agents of the system of domination.

In speaking about armed struggle, we defend and support its effectiveness as a necessary vehicle to combat domination, and we do so starting from our ethical foundations of liberty and the radical critique of Power. Which doesn't mean "irrational" violence, which expresses itself usually in qualifying the "unexplainable" violent deeds using false dichotomies of "insecurity-security," or "violence-nonviolence." We underline that anarchists fight for the elimination of violence against the present brutal force in the social relations. We fight against systemic violence, or what is the same, we fight for the eradication of capitalist violence and State terrorism. Logically, the only way to fight systemic violence is to use antagonistic violence. Thus, our critique is not against guns, per se, but the cult of arms that is encouraged by certain armed groups. For this reason, our discussion is not centered in the use of guns but what is to be achieved through their use. The arms are not the problem but who carries them and for what purpose—for the organization of vanguard party structure (by consequence authoritarian) or the informal, horizontal, and autonomous configuration (anti-authoritarian).

We fight for total liberation. We fight against everything that dominates us. Our struggle is not the struggle for the State's power but for the total destruction of the State; it is not for the implementation of "another possible capitalism" but for the total destruction of capital. Therefore, we identify in the struggle against the institutional power another instituting power that generates within it the same evils that we fight against.

The Origin of the Urban Guerrilla

To begin with, it is necessary to highlight that the origins of the so-called urban guerrilla are 100 percent anarchist as a concept, an organizational model, and a strategy. It should be pointed out that the subject of armed struggle was elaborated in 1965 by the anarchist Abraham Guillén during his exile in Uruguay, under the title *Estratégia de guerrilla urbana* (Urban Guerrilla Strategy)—four years before Carlos Marighella, inspired by the works of Guillén, wrote the *Minimanual of the Urban Guerrilla*.

The ones who built the bases for the development of the "urban guerrilla," with their tireless and consequent action against domination, were the nineteenth century's "illegal" anarchists. Among these comrades' basic principles were "direct action" and "autonomy," which is to say, action without intermediaries or hierarchies and with the absolute freedom and independence of groups and individuals involved. Some of the methods used have been called "propaganda of the deed," "retaliations," and "expropriation." The majority of times, these actions would interrelate with each other in a complementary fashion. Besides, these actions were almost always done (and are done) by the same affinity groups, although not all the groups necessarily concur on all practices.

Sometimes there are groups more dedicated to expropriation or to the propaganda by the deed or to attacks. But going a bit deeper in the interaction between these methods of struggle, there are groups and individuals that, although dedicated solely to expropriation activities, are in solidarity with the armed action groups through the donation of their expropriations' proceeds, destined to the acquisition of primary material needed for the fabrication of explosives or to buy ammunition, etc.

Besides, we would have to insist, this way of acting was not cir-cumscribed to the nineteenth century but kept on as modus operandi throughout the twentieth century, and still continues as an anarchist practice. The profusion of armed anarchist groups had its zenith at the dawn of the twentieth century in Europe, the United States, and all over Latin America, especially in Argentina, Chile, Cuba, Uruguay, and Mexico, At the end of the nineteenth century the big urban zones had been converted into the natural center of capitalist development, concentrating the industries and banks, as well as the different power institutions. In their streets would grow the contradictions between the opulent bourgeoisie and the exploited and oppressed workers, a situation that would facilitate social confrontation. This allowed the development of antagonistic structures formed by small cells based on affinity among comrades. On the other hand, these small cells of between five and ten comrades would coordinate in an informal way with other affinity groups when it came time for joint actions, reach-ing a certain irregular strength without sacrificing their autonomy. Such ways of acting would give them mobility and would allow them to insure a maximum of effectiveness and a minimum of risk, which makes impossible an "efficient" repression on the part of domination, as was pointed out recently by the Mexican insurrectionist and eco-anarchist groups in a collective communiqué. This way of acting and organizing would serve as a paradigm for the Federación Anarquista Ibérica (Iberian Anarchist Federation), a group that pushed forward the conditions of social revolution during the Spanish Second Republic.

The defeat of anarcho-syndicalism in 1939 would create space to put into practice the urban guerrilla strategy against the national-ist military dictatorship. The anarchists in the Spanish State would combat Francoism, organizing the first urban guerrillas in Madrid, Barcelona, Málaga, Granada, Valencia, and Zaragoza. For almost two decades, from 1939 to 1957, the cells of the anarchist urban guerrilla would put in check the Francoist dictatorship. In Catalonia, the cells coordinated by Quico Sabaté and José Luis Facerías would stand out. In Málaga, Córdoba, and even Madrid, the war was being carried out by the anarchist group of Antonio Raya, who had found refuge in the mountains. In Granada, it was the spectacular actions of the Quero brothers' group. However, a pronounced diminishing of anarchist revolutionary action would come about through Francoist repression and the obscene negotiations between the "anarcho"-syndicalists of Madrid's CNT and the vertical unions.

The New Generation

At the beginning of the '60s, a new generation of anarchists residing in Spain and in exile would continue the struggle. In July 1965, the Federación Ibérica de Juventudes Libertarias (Iberian Federation of Libertarian Youth—FIJL) would release a communiqué promoting "a more general, more concrete, more urgent and more positive demand: FREEDOM FOR ALL POLITICAL PRISONERS." On April 30, 1966, the Italian media informed the public of the "mysterious disappearance of Monseigneur Marcos Ussía, church counsellor at the Spanish embassy at the Vatican." Four days later, a communiqué signed by the Grupo Primero de Mayo (Sacco y Vanzetti) would be published in the newspaper *Avanti*: "We are a group of Spanish anarchists forced to use this form of action in order to make the Spanish ambassador in the *'Santa Sede'* petition the Pope with this ultimate, public demand to General Franco's government: the freedom to all Spanish democrats (workers, intellectuals, and young students) condemned to different sentences in the Francoist prisons." With Grupo Primero de Mayo's action, anarchists would restart the antagonistic action in the Spanish State under the flag of direct solidarity with the imprisoned comrades.

On the August 20, 1967, the Movimiento de Solidaridad Revolucionária Internacional (International Revolutionary Solidarity Movement—MSRI) would make its presence public, with the Grupo Primero de Mayo as one of the most active components. That day, the American embassy would be strafed in London, an action claimed by MSRI. On November 12, 1967, eight embassies and two governmental offices were completely destroyed by very strong explosive devices in an action coordinated in different European cities and claimed by MSRI. In Paris, at the end of 1967, the Movimiento 22 de Marzo (22nd of March Movement), released several reflections that established a theoretical basis for the differentiation between anti-authoritarian action and "focoism": "It is imperative to abandon the theory of a 'leading vanguard' and to adopt the much more honest concept of an active minority that ... promotes action without wanting to direct it." In the first days of April 1968, the Grupo Primero de Mayo sent a document to all the anarchist groups titled "For an International Anarchist

Practice," pointing to a rebellious attitude of permanent conflict and the critique of authoritarianism.

These ideas influenced countless new groups. In Germany, the Zentralrat der umherschweifenden Haschrebellen (Central Council of the Roaming Hash Rebels) radicalized a year and a half after the assassination of a student at the hands of police during the protests against the visit of the Shah in 1967, forming the Bewegung 2. Juni (2nd of June Movement) with other anti-authoritarian groups—the most determined "anarchist guerrilla" in West Germany. In Great Britain at around the same time, the popular Angry Brigade appeared and would harass the system of domination for over a decade. In most cases, condemnation came from leftist social organizations, from unions, and from the "communist" parties, based on what they labeled the "anarchist syndrome." In effect, by following to the letter the suggestions of Guillén's manual, as was done even by the "anti-imperialist" urban guerrillas, they inscribed their action within the anarchist logic.

They returned to expropriation, to documents forgery, to retaliation, to propaganda by the deed, to police executions, etc. That's how groups like RAF, Red Brigades, the SLA, even—here in Mexico—the Liga Comunista 23 Septiembre (23rd of September Communist League) would be cataloged by the "specialists" on the issue: as "anarchist" groups.

From this side of the puddle, around these same years, I would highlight in Uruguay the Organización Popular Revolucionaria 33 Orientales and the armed wing of the Federación Anarquista Uruguaya (FAU), which made its presence public in 1966 as countermeasure to the focoism of the Movimiento de Liberación Nacional–Tupamaros. Leninist contamination and nationalist inclinations would not only provoke the FAU, but as time passed would lead to the formation of a vanguard party structure, the Partido de la Victoria del Pueblo, as a logical consequence of Bolshevik deviation. Something similar would happen with the anarchist urban guerrilla in Germany. The legendary 2nd of June Movement would finish its days in 1980 with many of its members joining the RAF. If, on the one hand, their presence imposed a lightly libertarian stamp that would lead the RAF to a prolonged process of rethinking, culminating in its self-dissolution, on the other hand, the fusion with this Leninist group closed the possibilities of anarchist armed groups in Germany.

The Critique of Revolutionary Action

The anarchist etiology of the "urban guerrilla" continues to provoke a deep discussion about the very concept of the "guerrilla" and the methodology that inheres within it. In the last years of the '70s and beginnings of the '80s of the last century a decrease of the "classical" urban guerrilla gave rise to a "new type" of urban guerrilla that problematized adherence to the strategy of irregular war. The year of 1976, the Italian spring of '77, and the "days of reflection" of January 1978 marked the deepening of the critique of the guerrilla issue. The emergence of Azione Rivoluzionaria (AR) and its feminist structure Azione Rivoluzionaria—Autonomia Femminista would recontextualize the issue in Italy. These structures analyzed the leadership role that was deployed by vanguardists like the Red Brigades and put forward a different organizational proposal based on informal coordination and affinity groups where "the traditional link is substituted by relations based in sympathy, characterized by a maximum of reciprocal intimacy, conscience and trust between its members."

In the same text, they would reaffirm that "the new movement not only rejects the historical Soviet Marxist monsters and hybrid Italian Marxism" but also "rejects the myth of proletarian as a revolutionary class, a myth that has conducted the movement into a dead-end alley from 1968 until now." Azione Rivoluzionaria would affirm in this "first theoretical document" that the new movement doesn't relegate combat to "the classes" but "assumes it in the first person," underlining the fact that "direct action returns to individuals' consciousness of themselves as individuals who can transform their destiny and take back the control of their own lives." As if they had written their document this morning, Azione Rivoluzionaria correctly observes that a "critical, constructive, and utopian presence is a necessary condition, but is not enough. Such presence cannot be hegemonic nowadays. In parallel it is necessary to develop a negative critical presence, destructive of the ongoing processes. The destructive critique, the armed critique, is, nowadays, the only force capable of realizing any credible and reliable emancipatory project."

As if this categorical critique of the first days of 1978 was not enough, Azione Rivoluzionaria would disseminate a piece during the Third Congress of IAF (International of Anarchist Federations), celebrated March 23–26 of that same year in the city of Carrara:

Comrades, let's revive ourselves once again, let's march side by side with the times or, even better, lets try to stand against the times. How can we pretend to be incisive if our methods of intervention, our small amount of theoretical propaganda, turned out to be obsolete and exhausted, reducing anarchism to a sterile and fruitless opinion movement only capable of acting in the defensive terrain each time that power throws its repressive arrows? . . . Comrades, let's abandon the politics of slogans, of schemes, of information generated, in fact, a hundred years ago.

Toward Armed Joy

Despite the adverse interests of "anarchist" officialism, those approaches of the late 1970s would generate an intense polemic that would shape the insurrectionist tendency. The article "Appointments for an Internal and External Discussion" would synthesize the concerns and reflections of the first moment of the debate and would be published in its entirety in *Anarchismo* and *Contrainformazione*. These reflections inevitably led to questioning, from an anarchist perspective, the pertinence of the "guerrilla" as a concept and method of struggle. The term "guerrilla" refers to the "small war." It started to be used as tactic in Spain during the Napoleonic invasion, forming small groups of civilians trained and commanded by experienced military men to assure the constant attack against the occupying French troops. Since then, guerrilla warfare has been used to fight any asymmetrical war. Contrary to conventional wars, "guerrilla warfare" is flexible, less geometrical, and much more mobile.

In the particular case of the "urban guerrilla," this strategy is centered in the attack at the heart of State and capital: the city. All attacks are planned against repressive institutions (police, judiciary, military), combining the gathering of arms and ammunition and expropriations with the sabotage of the productive apparatus, the destruction of commodities, solidarity with the prisoners, and the attack against the centers of massive alienation. This combination of attacks seeks their extension and reproduction, deploying on the surface combat against domination to develop "revolutionary consciousness" among the alienated multitude. According to this strategy, the "common people" would abandon their usual passivity and would join the insurrection once they realized the vulnerability of the system of domination. Nevertheless, the practice of the classic "urban guerrilla" requires the use of "specialists," of specialized "technicians," which brings the acceptance of the denominated "professional revolutionary," the cult of the arms, and a series of particular "necessities" (the safe houses, the intelligence and counterintelligence systems, the hierarchies, etc.), eventually abandoning anarchist ideas.

In this sense, Alfredo Bonanno reminds us in *Armed Joy* that the traditional guerrilla organizations inevitably fall into the technocratic danger, because they impose their "technicians." In this pamphlet, he points out that the insurrectionist structure that finds joy in action directed to the destruction of domination

> considers the means used to carry out such destruction as instruments, as means. The ones who use those instruments shouldn't be converted into their slaves. And the ones that don't know how to use them should not be transformed into slaves of those who know how to use them. The dictatorship of the means is the worst of the dictatorships. . . . It is necessary to develop a critique of arms. We have seen too much worshipping of the machine gun and of military efficiency. The armed struggle is not something that only concerns arms. Arms cannot represent, by themselves, the revolutionary dimension. . . . It is dangerous to reduce the complex reality to only one dimension and to only one object. In fact, the game has the risk of reducing the vital experiment to a toy, converting it into something magical and absolute. It is not by chance that the machine gun appears as a symbol of many combatant revolutionary organizations. We should advance toward an understanding of the deep meaning of struggle as pleasure, escaping from the illusions and traps of the representation of the commodified spectacle by mythical or mythified objects.

So he suggests that we refuse all roles, including the one of "professional revolutionary," with the objective of "breaking the magical siege of the commodity's dramaturgy," conscious that the armed struggle has to avoid the division of tasks and the assignment of roles imposed by the ideology of production, refusing "professionalism."

The "moral" that underlies this reflection centralizes the type of structure that is developed and the role of the insurrectionist minorities. The obsolescence of the classical "urban guerrilla" is its "technical specialization," the preponderant role that is given to knowledge of arms, their worship, and the role of the "professional revolutionary," together with all infrastructure required. This reflection makes clear that it is not enough to spread the struggle everywhere. It must be spread to each aspect of our daily life. That is where the self-organization of the struggle and the development of antagonistic "factions" of the active minorities are rooted. From the side of anarchist reflection, based on the experience of struggle, we have reaffirmed our values of direct action to face the inflexible schemes of "professionalization" of the struggle, invalidated beforehand in the contemporary social war against renovated domination.

The social war will impose the need for an organization that is the true advance of the real movement. The permanent antagonism of the active minorities is the proposal of attack, here and now, against the structures of domination, to highlight, in the first place, that the enemy is vulnerable and to show that the comrades kidnapped by the State are not alone—that they can count on our solidarity. The specific weight of antagonistic minorities, of affinity groups in permanent conflict, is neither shown by the number of attacks nor by the damages that stronger blows give to the enemy. The gravitation of these active minorities lies in the geometrical expansion of the struggle and the rise of anti-authoritarian consciousness. So behind every explosion, every bullet, every expropriation—behind putting into practice any manifestation of antagonistic violence—our ideal has to be present, ensuring that our struggle is for total liberation, for the definitive destruction of the system of domination, for Anarchy.

Notes
This is excerpted from an introductory text for a debate at the Center of Anarchist Information (CEDIA), Mexico City, October 8, 2011.

Ten Ways to Advance Liberatory Community Armed Self-Defense

North Carolina Piece Corps

Here are a few concrete things we can do to advance our own self-defense, exert our communities' autonomy, and change the current dialogue that surrounds gun ownership.

- Support voluntary, non-State-initiated peace work in communities that regularly deal with gun violence.
- Work against sexually and emotionally abusive relationship patterns that so often result in violence against women and children.
- Support all oppressed people's right to defend themselves, regardless of whether or not their attackers work for the government.
- Organize community forums and neighborhood assemblies that deal with problems locally rather than going to the police and courts.
- Organize anti-racist, queer-positive, and women-positive self-defense patrols that can defend folks from racist attacks and police brutality.
- Organize our own comfortable, safe environments where we can train with firearms safely and effectively. Buy ammunition in bulk to save money!

- Be clear that gun ownership does not mean support for the arms industry, the military, or sport hunting.
- Support efforts by rank-and-file soldiers to speak and act out against the military hierarchy.
- Defend gun ownership in the face of legislative attacks, on principle.
- Show up to gun shows as a visibly queer-positive, anti-racist, feminist, and anti-capitalist presence. These are great places to learn about weapons and their uses from knowledgeable people.

Notes

This list was originally taken from the North Carolina Piece Corps pamphlet *Politicians Love Gun Control*, published circa 2008.

HISTORIES
OF THE TWENTIETH AND
TWENTY-FIRST CENTURIES

Russian Anarchists and the Civil War, 1917–1922

Paul Avrich

When the first shots of the Russian Civil War were fired, the anarchists, in common with the other left-wing opposition parties, were faced with a serious dilemma. Which side were they to support? As staunch libertarians, they held no brief for the dictatorial policies of Lenin's government, but the prospect of a White victory seemed even worse. Active opposition to the Soviet regime might tip the balance in favor of the counterrevolutionaries. On the other hand, support for the Bolsheviks might serve to entrench them too deeply to be ousted from power once the danger of reaction had passed. It was a quandary with no simple solutions. After much soul-searching and debate, the anarchists adopted a variety of positions, ranging from active resistance to the Bolsheviks through passive neutrality to eager collaboration. A majority, however, cast their lot with the beleaguered Soviet regime. By August 1919, at the climax of the Civil War, Lenin was impressed with the zeal and courage of the "Soviet anarchists," as their anti-Bolshevik comrades contemptuously dubbed them, that he counted them among "the most dedicated supporters of Soviet power."[1]

An outstanding case in point was Bill Shatov, a former Industrial Workers of the World (IWW) agitator in the United States who had returned to his native Russia after the February Revolution. As an officer in the Tenth Red Army during the autumn of 1919, Shatov threw his energies into the defense of Petrograd (Saint Petersburg) against the advance of General Yudenich. The following year he was summoned to Chita to become minister of transport in the Far Eastern Republic. Before he left, Shatov tried to justify his collaborationist position to his fellow libertarians, Emma Goldman and Alexander Berkman. The anarchists, said Shatov, were "the romanticists of the Revolution," but one could not fight with ideals alone. At the moment, the chief task was to defeat the reactionaries. "We anarchists should remain true to our ideals, but we should not criticize at this time. We must work and help to build."[2]

Shatov was one of a small army of anarchists who took up weapons against the White Army during the Civil War.[3] Others accepted minor posts within the Soviet government and urged their comrades to do likewise, or at least to refrain from activities which were hostile to the Bolshevik cause. Yuda Roshchin, a former Black Banner terrorist and a foe of the Marxists, now surprised everyone by hailing Lenin as one of the great figures of the modern age. According to Victor Serge, he even tried to work out an "anarchist theory of the dictatorship of the proletariat."

But listeners were not impressed, they wrote him off as another loss to "Soviet anarchism" and a traitor to the cause of Bakunin and Kropotkin. For even in these precarious circumstances a large and militant segment of the anarchist movement would deny their Bolshevik adversaries any quarter. The Briansk Federation of Anarchists, for example, called for the immediate overthrow of the "Social Vampires" in the Kremlin who sucked the blood of the people. Translating this appeal into action, a terrorist organization in Moscow known as the Underground Anarchists joined forces with the Left Socialist Revolutionaries and bombed the headquarters of the Communist Party Committee, killing twelve of its members and wounding fifty-five others, Bukharin among them.

In the south, where the authority of the state was completely disrupted, anarchist violence found its most fertile soil. Bands of armed marauders, operating under such names as "Hurricane" and "Death," sprang up in every quarter, ready to swoop down on town or village whenever the opportunity presented itself. The Bakunin Partisans of Ekaterinoslav sang of a new "era of dynamite" which would greet oppressors of every stripe, Red and White alike.

And in Kharkov a circle of Anarcho-Futurists proclaimed "Death to world civilization!" and urged the dark masses to take up their axes and destroy everything in sight.

Anarchists of a more pacifistic bent denounced these groups as "bandits" who used the cloak of anarchism to conceal the predatory nature of their activities. For the moderates, robbery and terrorism were grotesque caricatures of anarchist doctrines, which served only to demoralize the movement's true adherents and to discredit anarchism in the eyes of the public. Renouncing violent action, the milder anarchists armed themselves with nothing more lethal than pen and ink, and mounted a verbal attack on the Soviet dictatorship. A major theme of their criticism was that the Bolshevik Revolution had merely substituted "state capitalism" for private capitalism. In their view, what had taken place in Russia closely resembled the earlier revolutions in Western Europe: no sooner had the oppressed farmers and craftsmen of England and France removed the landed aristocracy from power than the ambitious middle class stepped into the breach and erected a new class structure with itself at the top; in a similar manner, the privileges and authority once shared by the Russian nobility and bourgeoisie had passed into the hands of a new ruling class composed of party officials, governments bureaucrats, and technical specialists.

As the Civil War deepened, the government grew less tolerant of such criticisms and started clamping down on anarchist groups in Moscow and Petrograd. As a result, there began an exodus of anarchists to the Ukraine, the perennial haven of fugitives from the persecutions of the central government. In the city of Kharkov a new anarchist organization, the Nabat Confederation, sprang up in 1918 and soon could boast of flourishing branches in all the major cities of the south. As might be expected, Nabat's adherents were extremely critical of the Soviet dictatorship, yet they believed that the most pressing task of the anarchist movement was to defend the revolution against the White Army onslaught, even if this should mean a temporary alliance with the Communists. To save the revolution, they pinned their hopes on a "partisan army" organized spontaneously by the revolutionary masses themselves.

As the most likely nucleus of such an army the Nabat leaders looked to the guerrilla band led by Nestor Makhno, whose followers believed he would realize their ancient dream of land and liberty. Travelling on

99

horseback and in light peasant carts (*tachanki*) on which machine guns were mounted, Makhno and his men moved swiftly back and forth across the open steppe between the Dnieper and the Sea of Azov, swelling into a small army and inspiring terror in the hearts of their adversaries as they went. Hitherto independent guerrilla bands accepted Makhno's command and rallied to his black banner. Villagers willingly provided food and fresh horses, enabling the *Makhnovtsy* to travel long distances with little difficulty. Suddenly they would turn up where least expected, attack the gentry and military garrisons, then vanish as quickly as they had come. In captured uniforms they infiltrated the enemy's ranks to learn their plans or to fire on them at point-blank range. When cornered, the Makhnovtsy would bury their weapons, make their way singly back to their villages, and take up work in the fields, awaiting the next signal to unearth a new cache of arms and spring up again in an unexpected quarter. Makhno's insurgents, in the words of Victor Serge, revealed "a truly epic capacity for organization and combat."[4] In September 1918, when Makhno's insurgents defeated a much superior force of Austrians at the village of Dibrivki, his men bestowed on him the affectionate title of *batko*, their "little father."[5]

For a time, Makhno's dealings with the Bolsheviks remained reasonably friendly. The Soviet press extolled him as a "courageous partisan" and a great revolutionary leader. Relations were at their best in March 1919, when Makhno and the Communists concluded a pact for joint military action against the White Army of General Denikin. Such gestures of harmony, however, could not conceal the basic hostility between the two groups. The Communists had little taste for the autonomous status of Makhno's insurgent army or for the powerful attraction which it exerted on their own peasant recruits; the Makhnovtsy, on their side, feared that the Red Army would attempt to bring their movement to heel. As friction increased, the Soviet newspapers abandoned their eulogies of the Makhnovtsy and began to attack them as "kulaks" and "anarcho-bandits." In May, two Cheka[6] agents sent to assassinate Makhno were caught and executed. The following month, Leon Trotsky, commander in chief of the Bolshevik forces, outlawed Makhno, and Communist troops carried out a lightning raid on his headquarters at Gulyai-Polye.

That summer, however, the shaky alliance was hastily resumed with the White Army's massive drive toward Moscow sent both the Communists and the Makhnovtsy to action. Makhno suddenly launched a successful counterattack at the village of Peregonovka, near the town of Uman, cutting the White Army's supply lines and creating panic and disorder in the rear. This was their first serious reverse in this dramatic advance into the Russian heartland and a major factor in halting his drive toward the Bolshevik capital. By the end of the year a counteroffensive by the Red Army had forced them to beat a swift retreat to the shores of the Black Sea.

The *Makhnovshchina* reached its crest in the months following the victory at Peregonovka. During October and November, Makhno occupied Ekaterinoslav and Aleksandrovsk for several weeks and obtained his first chance to apply the concepts of anarchism to city life. Makhno's aim was to throw off domination of every type and to encourage economic and social self-determination. Furthermore, the peasants and artisans could barter the products of their labor, whereas the urban workers depended on regular wages for their survival. Makhno, moreover, compounded the confusion when he recognized all paper money issued by his predecessors—Ukrainian nationalists, Whites, and Bolsheviks alike. He never understood the complexities of an urban economy, nor did he care to understand them. He detested the "poison" of the cities, and cherished the natural simplicity of the peasant environment into which he had been born. In any event, Makhno found very little time to implement his ill-defined economic programs. The Makhnovshchina, on the words of one of the his associates, was a "republic on *tachanki*. ...As always, the instability of the situation prevented positive work."[7]

At the end of 1919, Makhno received instructions from the Red Command to transfer his army forthwith to the Polish front, to draw the Makhnovtsy away from their home territory and leave it open to the establishment of Bolshevik rule. Makhno refused to budge. Trotsky's response was firm and unhesitating: he outlawed the Makhnovtsy and sent his troops against them. There ensued eight months of bitter struggle with losses high on both sides. A severe typhus epidemic augmented the toll of victims. Badly outnumbered, Makhno's partisans avoided pitched battles and relied on the guerrilla tactics they had perfected in more than two years of Civil War.

Hostilities were broken off in October 1920, when the Whites in the south launched a major offensive, striking northward from the

Crimean peninsula. Once more, the Red Army enlisted Makhno's aid. In return, the Communists agreed to amnesty for all anarchists in Russian prisons and guaranteed the anarchists freedom of propaganda on condition that they refrain from calling for the violent overthrow of the Soviet government. Barely a month later, however, the Red Army had made sufficient gains to assure victory in the Civil War and the Soviet leaders tore up their agreement with Makhno. Not only had the Makhnovtsy outlived their usefulness as a military partner, but as long as he was left at large the spirit of primitive anarchism and the danger of a peasant revolt would remain to haunt the unsteady Bolshevik regime. Thus, Makhno's commanders in the Crimea, fresh from their victories over the White Army, were seized by the Red Army and immediately shot. The next day Trotsky ordered an attack on Makhno's headquarters in Gulyai-Polye, while the Cheka simultaneously arrested the members of the Nabat Confederation in Kharkov and carried out raids on anarchist clubs and organizations throughout the country. During the attack on Gulyai-Polye, most of Makhno's staff were captured and imprisoned or simply shot on the spot. Makhno himself, however, together with a battered remnant of an army that had once numbered in the tens of thousands, managed to elude his pursuers. After wandering over the Ukraine for the better part of a year, the partisan leader, exhausted and still suffering from unhealed wounds, crossed the Dniester River into Rumania and eventually found his way to Paris.

The downfall of Makhno marked the beginning of the end for Russian anarchism. Three months later, in February 1921, the movement suffered another major blow when Peter Kropotkin, nearly eighty years old, fell ill and died. Emma Goldman spoke at Kropotkin's graveside, and students and workers placed flowers by his tomb.

At Kropotkin's funeral the black flag of anarchism was paraded through Moscow for the last time. Two weeks later the Kronstadt rebellion[8] broke out and a new wave of political arrests swept the country. Anarchist bookstores, printing offices, and clubs were closed and the few remaining anarchist circles broken up. Even the pacifist followers of Tolstoy—a number of whom had been shot during the Civil War for refusing to serve in the Red Army—were imprisoned or banished. In Moscow a circle of leading "Soviet anarchists" known as the Universalists were arrested on trumped-up charges of "banditry and underground activities," and their organization was replaced by a new group called the "Anarcho-Biocosmists," who pledged unwavering support of the Soviet government and solemnly declared their intention to launch a social revolution "in interplanetary space but not upon Soviet territory."[9]

Repression continued unabated as the months advanced. In September 1921, the Cheka executed two well-known anarchists without a trial and without bringing formal charges against them. Emma Goldman was so outraged that she considered making a scene in the manner of the English suffragettes by chaining herself to a bench in the hall where the Third Comintern Congress was meeting and shouting her protests to the delegates. She was dissuaded from doing so by her Russian friends, but soon afterward she and Berkman, profoundly disheartened by the turn the revolution had taken, made up their minds to leave the country. "Grey are the passing days," Berkman recorded in his diary. "One by one the embers of hope have died out. Terror and despotism have crushed the life born in October. The slogans of the Revolution are foresworn, its ideals stifled in the blood of the people. The breath of yesterday is dooming millions to death; the shadow of today hangs like a black pall over the country. Dictatorship is trampling the masses under foot. The Revolution is dead; its spirit cries in the wilderness. . . . I have decided to leave Russia."[10]

Notes

This is an excerpt from an essay that first appeared in *Russian Review* 27, no. 3 (July 1968).

1   V.I. Lenin, "Sochineniya," in *Collected Works*, Vol. 24 (Moscow: Progress Publishers, 1974 [2nd edition]), 437.

2   Emma Goldman, *Living My Life* (New York: Alfred A. Knopf, 1931), 729; Alexander Berkman, *The Bolshevik Myth (Diary 1920–1922)* (New York: Boni and Liveright, 1925), 35–36.

3   The 'White Army' was a loose confederation of nationalist, pro-Tsarist anti-communist forces that fought the Bolsheviks in the Russian Civil War.

4   Victor Serge, *Memoirs of a Revolutionary 1901–1941*, trans. and ed. Peter Sedgwick, (London: Oxford University Press, 1963), 135

5   P. Arshinov, *Istoriia makhnovskogo dvizheniia (1918–1921 gg.)* (Berlin: Izd. Gruppy russkikh anarkhistov v Germanii, 1923), 57–58.

6   Created in 1917, it was the first Soviet state security organization, similar to the FBI in the U.S.

7   Voline, *La révolution inconnue (1917–1921)* (Paris, 1943), 578, 603.

8   A major, yet unsuccessful, anarchist uprising against the *Bolsheviks* in the later years of the Russian Civil War.

9   Gregory Petrovich Maximoff, *The Guillotine at Work* (Chicago: Alexander Berkman Fund, 1940), 362.

10 Alexander Berkman, *The Bolshevik Myth: Diary 1920–1922* (New York: Boni and Liveright, 1925), 319.

Not Only a Right but a Duty: The Industrial Workers of the World Take Up the Gun in Centralia, Washington, 1919

Shawn Stevenson

> The Industrial Workers of the World (IWW) in Centralia, Washington who fired upon the men who were attempting to raid the IWW headquarters were fully justified in their act.... Mob rule in this country must be stopped, and when mobs attack the home of a millionaire, or of a laborer, or of the IWW, it is not only the right, but the duty of the occupants to resist with every means in their power. If the officers of the law cannot stop these raids, perhaps the resistance of the raiders may have that effect.
>
> —Edward F. Bassett, commanding officer,
> American Legion Silver Bow Post #1[1]

The events of Armistice Day, November 11, 1919, in Centralia, Washington, and their aftermath are often referred to as a "massacre" or a "tragedy." What really happened was more like a pitched battle in an intense class war that had been escalating for over a decade. Union members took up arms to defend their right to organize, striking a blow against the bosses despite great personal sacrifice.

The Wobblies, as IWW members were known, began organizing in the Pacific Northwest within a year of the union's formation, and they found a fertile recruiting ground among the region's loggers and harvest workers. Conditions in the woods were particularly horrible:

> The loggers up in the state of Washington were working 11 hours a day. They were sleeping 40 men in the bunkhouse, double-deck bunks on the wall. Just one little window—just one sash—not really a window, but half a window, for a bunkhouse. You'd open the door and open the one sash and that's all the ventilation you got. You worked all day in the rain, you came in at night and hung your soggy clothes up around the one stove in the center with wires going out from it like a spider web, and they hung and steamed all night. And you slept there in the steam. That's the only bath you got.[2]

The loggers had to provide their own bedding and the camps quickly became infested with lice and bedbugs. The job was extremely dangerous, pay was poor, and workers were subject to the venal system of exploitative "job shark" employment agencies.

The IWW tended to follow a policy of what would today be called nonviolent direct action. Its most common tactics were work slowdowns, strikes, occasional sabotage of equipment, and "free speech fights" that clogged up the legal system. Two-fisted loggers might brawl with strikebreakers and scabs, but firearms were not something they normally resorted to. Guns had been used in a showdown with sheriff's deputies and vigilantes at the end of the Everett, Washington, free speech fight in 1916. The Wobblies also organized armed "flying squads" to protect itinerant laborers riding the rails from being robbed.

Still, the leaders of the lumber industry were completely unwilling to compromise on issues such as the eight-hour day, job sharks, or better conditions in the camps. They responded to IWW organizing with a brutal campaign using influence at all levels of government, as well as extralegal means. Free speech was regularly suppressed to keep Wobblies from agitating from the soapbox or at street meetings. Police and armed vigilantes raided and smashed up Wobbly halls. IWW organizers were kidnapped, beaten, and tarred and feathered. Wobblies were jailed without charge. While in jail they were subjected to beatings, "sweated" in overheated cells, and forced to spend days in unheated cells without blankets. Food was wretched. Wobblies died in jail on hunger strike against bad food and rough treatment.

Armed vigilantes or "special police" would stop working men on the street and forcibly search them. Those found with the IWW's red membership card would be forced to leave town. Often they would be loaded on trucks and forced to run the gauntlet between two lines of men who would beat them with blackjacks, clubs, and revolver butts.

When the U.S. entered the First World War, things got worse. Violence and lynchings targeting Wobbly organizers and membership became common. Federalized National Guard and army troops were used to arrest Wobblies. Makeshift detention camps had to be set up to house prisoners in Pasco, Wenatchee, Cle Elum, Ellensburg, and other towns. Immigration agents began to initiate the deportation of radicals born abroad. States throughout the region passed syndicalism laws that made mere membership in the IWW a crime. Twenty-five thousand men were conscripted into a military organization called the Spruce Production Division and put to work in the woods under military discipline. Loggers throughout the region were pressured to join a government-backed company union, the Loyal Legion of Loggers and Lumbermen.

Centralia was a regional hub for the timber industry. The IWW had opened a hall in March 1917. This enraged the local business community. During a Red Cross parade in May 1918, members of the Home Guard and the Elks Lodge broke ranks and stormed the hall. The furniture was dragged into the streets and set ablaze. A Victrola and a desk were auctioned off to businessmen in the crowd. The Wobblies in the hall were "lifted by their ears" into waiting trucks and taken outside of town where they were forced to run a gauntlet of vigilantes who beat them with sticks and ax handles.

The Wobblies were not easily deterred. They opened a new hall at Second and Tower in 1919. In response, the Centralia Citizen's Protective Association was formed by the business community to combat the IWW in the area. A committee chaired by Warren Grimm, William Scales, and local lumber baron F.B. Hubbard was formed to pursue "alternative solutions" to the Wobbly problem.[3]

The Wobblies were aware something was afoot. They took various steps to head off a raid without violence. A written appeal was printed calling for the citizens of Centralia to take a stand against mob violence. Mrs. McCallister, the Wobblies landlady, appealed to local law enforcement. The Wobblies' attorney wrote the governor about the situation. None of these efforts met any success in heading off the raid.

The Wobblies had thoroughly exhausted all their avenues of recourse within the system. They had only two choices. They could submit to the mob or they could resist. They were brave men committed to bringing about a better world for working people—part of an organization with an anarchistic commitment to the ethos of direct action, believing that the working class had to safeguard its own interests. They unanimously chose to resist, although they don't seem to have thought much past stopping the initial attack. There is some suggestion that they approached the defense with a sense of determined fatalism, understanding that they were most likely to face jail or death as a result of their actions.

The day of the battle was Armistice Day, November 11, 1919. Three Wobblies lay prone around a large stump in a cold gray mist atop Seminary Hill on the edge of Centralia. They peered through rifle sights at men in military garb marching on a road below, nearly 150 yards away. One turned to the others and said, "I hope to Jesus there won't be any trouble." Then there was.

On the street below, a patriotic parade was in progress. Veterans marched down Tower Street. The largest contingent was the American Legion men of Centralia's Grant Hodge post. Most of them had recently returned from service in France and Siberia. As they approached Second Street, their leader, Lt. Warren Grimm, called out, "Halt, close up ranks!" On horseback, Lt. Frank Cormier gave the order, "Bunch up men!" and rode to the rear of the formation.[4]

To their right was the union hall of the Centralia local of the International Workers of the World. Most of the Legion men were businessmen or professionals and they despised the IWW members for their tireless organizing in pursuit of the eight-hour day, better conditions in the region's logging camps, and industrial democracy. Inside the hall, Wobblies looked on nervously. They saw a local minister and the postmaster at the head of the parade carrying nooses. Men in ranks outside carried lengths of gas pipe and rubber hose. Two army trucks were parked across the street. A small crowd had gathered and looked on expectantly. There was tension in the air. One man in the formation was crouched like a runner on second base waiting for a hit to send him home. Every time a command was given, he made a false start toward the hall.[5]

The IWW was prepared to defend its hall. Bert Bland, Loren Roberts, and Ole Hansen had positioned themselves with rifles on top of Seminary Hill. O.C. Bland and John Lamb were upstairs in the Arnold Hotel on the other side of the street with a rifle between the two of them. Further down the far side of Tower Street, Jim Davis was on the second floor of the Avalon Hotel also armed with a rifle.[6] Few of these men had formal training with firearms, but they came from what was still a frontier culture where hunting and shooting were commonplace. The legionnaires had no idea that the Wobblies were armed.

Frank Cormier blew a shrill blast on his whistle. There were shouts of, "Let's get them! Grab them! At them!" The legionnaires charged the hall in a wedge formation.[7] Their soldiers—Warren Grimm, Dr. Eldon Roberts, and Dutch Pfitzer—hit the door and kicked it in. Arthur McElfresh, a sergeant who had seen heavy fighting in the Meuse-Argonne, drove his elbow through the window and jumped through the opening. As the glass shattered and hit the floor, the men inside began shooting.

Standing near the window of the hall, Wobbly Bert Faulkner felt a bullet pass through his coat sleeve as the men behind him opened up. The Wobblies on the hill opened fire at the sound of gunshots from below, letting off perhaps twenty rounds. Jim Davis leaned out the window of the Avalon and started firing. O.C. Bland drove the butt of his rifle through the window of his room. The breaking glass cut his hand so badly that his comrade Lamb was sickened. He was too badly wounded to use the rifle.[8]

The legionnaires took heavy losses. McElfresh was hit in the head and dropped dead on the floor of the hall. Pfitzer was shot in the arm. Warren Grimm took a bullet in the stomach in the doorway, and stumbled away toward the corner of the street, trailing blood down the sidewalk. A bullet passed through the body of soldier Ben Casagranda as he broke away from the gunfire. John Watt, another legionnaire, was also badly hit in the stomach, and dropped to the ground.[9]

Chaos ensued. Some of the raiders, combat hardened in France, regrouped and continued their charge into the hall. Other men with guns and an ax materialized next door in the lobby of the Roderick and pushed into the back of the hotel to force their way into the hall through an interior entrance.

The Wobblies inside escaped through the broken front windows and the back door of the hall. Around a dozen made their getaway. Some hid out. Others were not so lucky.[10]

As Wesley Everest ran out the back of the hall and down the alley to the north, he was spotted by legionnaires. One of them shouted, "Look out, he's going to shoot!" Everest fired a single shot, which missed, and continued running. The chase made its way six blocks through a maze of houses, vacant lots, stables, sheds, and alleys. Everest reached the banks of the Skookumchuck River and followed it until he neared its confluence with the Chehalis River. He made his way through the trees and underbrush to the river and attempted to cross. He was encumbered with heavy logger's clothes and work boots. The river proved too deep and the current too strong. He waded back, and took cover behind a stump at the water's edge, gun in hand, ready to meet his rapidly approaching pursuers.

Dale Hubbard, George Barner, and Joseph Cole were the first to approach, followed closely by five other legionnaires. Hubbard began to approach, a pistol leveled at Everest. The Wobbly shouted, "If there's a bull in the crowd, I'll submit to arrest, otherwise stand back." Hubbard continued to advance. Everest shot him once, but he kept coming. Everest shot him twice more, and he dropped. The Wobbly's gun was empty. Seeing him frantically trying to reload, the mob charged, so he dropped the pistol and went for a belt knife at his back. At least eight men were on him before he could get it out. He fought fiercely with his fists but was badly outnumbered. Barner pinioned his arms and threw him to the ground. Another man kicked him in the face hard enough to draw blood. A sharp stick was jammed through both of Everest's cheeks. Everest fought on. One of his captors took off his belt and put it around the battered Wobbly's neck, dragging him toward the jail over a mile away.

Hubbard was loaded into a car and rushed to the hospital, where he would die of his wounds.[11] Grimm was helped into a car next to Casagranda, who was dying or already dead. When they arrived at the hospital Grimm was able to walk in under his own power, but he had serious internal bleeding and quickly bled to death.

A "White Terror" followed. Any working person with an association to the IWW was rounded up by vigilantes, their homes searched without warrant and vandalized. Many were arrested. That night, Wesley Everest was taken out of the jail, castrated, and hanged from a bridge. He seemed to still be alive, so the lynch mob hoisted him up and hanged him a second time. His body was riddled with bullets. It is quite likely that Everest was targeted because he had infiltrated the public meeting in which the raid was planned and could have testified to a conspiracy to raid the hall.

Jim McInerney was also taken from the jail, very nearly hanged, and badly beaten. According to Joe Murphy, a young Wobbly who was brought to the jail shortly after Everest was lynched, some ten other Wobblies were taken out that night and never seen again. Persistent rumor suggested they were burned alive in the incinerator at a nearby sawmill. Years later, Jim McInerney would relate that he had seen Jim Davis killed in the jail and that he had seen who did it. Loggers at the Saginaw Camp said they saw the body being covered with ashes and cinders later that night.

In the aftermath of the raid, ten Wobblies and their lawyer Elmer Smith, whose only crime was to advise them of their right to self-defense, were tried for capital murder. This included Eugene Barnett, who was not party to the plan to defend the hall but had witnessed the whole thing. Rather than allowing Barnett to be a star witness for the defense, the prosecution indicted him with the others, going so far as accusing him of being the man who fatally shot Warren Grimm—a crime for which they hoped to see him hang with the others.

The trial took place in a very hostile environment and was over-seen by an unsympathetic judge. Eight of the eleven men were ulti-mately found guilty of second-degree murder. The law called for a sen-tence of "not less than ten years." The judge handed down sentences of twenty-five to forty years.

Armistice Day 1919 in Centralia was the first time that the union men of the IWW took up the gun to defend one of their halls from a vigilante raid. It would also be the last time an armed mob attacked a Wobbly hall. A message had been sent that the Wobblies would not always submit to beatings and the destruction of their property peace-fully, and few would-be vigilantes appear to have been willing to put their lives at risk in face of the example set in Centralia.

Over time the Centralia defendants helped bring attention to the oppression targeted at radical labor and clearly played a role in making the most extreme abuses more difficult to employ. They also did their part in the struggle that paid off with the eight-hour day, better conditions for people on the job, and social programs that gave many working people some small measure of security. Many victories had been achieved by the time the Centralia defendants were released from prison. Of all the goals the Wobblies articulated, only the democratization of the economic system has not yet been achieved.

The men that made the bold step to pick up the gun and face the mob in Centralia paid a horrible price, along with their families. The eight men convicted all served more than ten years in the penitentiary. Four would later die under questionable circumstances. It would be easy to simply portray these people as victims, but that would discount the broader historical context. When viewed in that light they emerge as brave men and women who took a principled stand in the fight for the rights of working people under attack by lumber interests and the state.

Notes

1   Esther Barnett Goffinet, *Ripples of a Lie: A Biographical/Labor History of Eugene Barnett, A Victim of the Centralia, Washington Conspiracy of 1919* (Lewiston, ID: lulu.com, 2011), 295.
2   Eugene Barnett, recorded by Ben Legere, 1940.
3   Affidavit of D.E. Burrell, Raymond Becker Papers, Oregon State Historical Society.
4   John McClelland Jr., *Wobbly War: The Centralia Story* (Tacoma: Washington State Historical Society, 1987); Goffinet, *Ripples of a Lie*, 114.
5   Goffinet, *Ripples of a Lie*, 114, 132; McClelland, *Wobbly War*, 143.
6   Goffinet, *Ripples of a Lie*, 126–27; McClelland, *Wobbly War*, 70–71.
7   This is telling—Warren Grimm had earned the nickname "Wedge" as a freshman at the University of Washington when he used the formation to overcome upperclassmen during a hazing skirmish.
8   Goffinet, *Ripples of a Lie*, 128–29.
9   Ibid., 128.
10 Ibid., 129; McClelland, *Wobbly War*, 74–77.
11 Goffinet, *Ripples of a Lie*, 129–30; McClelland, *Wobbly War*, 75–76.

The People Armed: Women in the 1930s Spanish Revolution

Anti-Fascist Action UK

The events of 1936–1939 brought massive upheavals to the daily lives of Spanish people. Working-class women, in particular, participated in and witnessed great changes as the old order of Church and domestic culture were swept away by social revolution and war. Thousands of ordinary women were propelled by necessity into revolutionary events, from frontline fighting and organizing community defense to collectivizing and running farmland and factories. When the revolution was crushed in 1939, the memories and bonds formed in the revolutionary period sustained them through long years of the fascist dictatorship, in prison, exile, or continuing the struggle in the resistance movements.

The July Uprising

Workers, unions, and working-class communities were swift to react to the fascists' attempted coup on July 17–18, 1936. Men and women in Barcelona slept in union halls during the week before the uprising, expecting a call to arms. In Catalonia, Madrid, and Asturias, men and women both young and old stormed the armories to grab the weapons that the government had refused to provide. Cristina Piera entered the armory at San Andreas at dawn on the 19th with her son and his friends in the FIJL (libertarian youth organization) and was caught up in the excitement: "I woke up in the morning and heard that people were in the armory ... so I went there.... Everybody went.... I took a pistol and two ramrods (for rifles)....They had gunpowder there too.... Even me, with the little I knew and could do, I was there. People took arms and ammunition, and I took what I could."

Enriqueta Rovira, a young woman of twenty, jumped the first train back to Barcelona when she heard the news: "Most of the action was in the center of Barcelona. I had a pistol ... and I was prepared to use it. But they soon said no.... I didn't know how to use it and there were *compañeros* without arms. So they sent me—and all the women, all families—to build barricades. We also took care of provisions. Women in each barrio [district] organized that to make sure that there would be food for the men.... Everyone did something." Women were at a disadvantage in having no experience of weapons handling. In the heat of the battle and with limited arms, it was only logical that guns went to those who already knew how to use them. But in building the barricades women continued to play a vital role. A group of five or six militant women set about fortifying one of the city's most elegant buildings. "When the (CNT) compañeros returned—victorious, of course—(from storming the military barracks at Atarazanas, at the foot of the Ramblas) and saw how beautiful it was, they took it over as the casa CNT-FAI" (Soleded Estorach). Other women took to the rooftops with loudspeakers, calling on the soldiers to take off their uniforms and join the people.

The fascist uprising was crushed in Barcelona, but the workers knew that this was only the beginning. While the government urged people to stay at home rather than actively defend the city, Miguel García and others were involved in efforts to organize a people's army:

> But by this time every man and woman in Barcelona knew that we had stormed the heavens. The generals would never forgive us for what we had done. We had humiliated and defeated the Army, we—an "unorganized, undisciplined rabble." We had altered the course of history. If fascism won, we knew that we would not be spared. Mothers trembled for their small children. When the news came from the South that the invading rebels were using Moorish troops to put whole towns to the sword, many of these women, even elderly ones, struggled and fought

to obtain a rifle so that they could take part in the defense of their homes. Indomitable, inscrutable, they sat together in pairs, chatting among cronies, with a rifle across their lap, ready for Franco and his Moors "and if Hitler comes, him too."

While some women headed for the front with the newly formed militia columns, others were widely involved in the social revolution back home, requisitioning buildings for communal eating halls, schools, or hospitals, or collecting and distributing food and other supplies. Women took manufactured goods to barter with farmers in rural areas in exchange for food. Taxis and trams were repainted with revolutionary insignia, as communities brought local services back under their control. "The feelings we had then were very special. It was very beautiful. There was a feeling of—how shall I say it?—of power, not in the sense of domination, but in the sense of things being under our control, if under anyone's. Of possibility. A feeling that we could together really do something" (Enriqueta Rovira).

Mujeres Libres

In late 1934, a group of Barcelona women met to overcome these problems and encourage greater activism among existing CNT women: "What would happen is that women would come once, maybe even join. But they would never be seen again. So many compañeras came to the conclusion that it might be a good idea to start a separate group for these women.... We got concerned about all the women we were losing.... In 1935, we sent out a call to all women in the libertarian movement." (Soleded Estorach). They organized *guarderías volantes* (flying daycare centers), offering childcare to women wanting to serve as union delegates and attend evening meetings.

Meanwhile, Madrid women, calling themselves Mujeres Libres ("Free Women"), were trying to develop women's social consciousness, skills, and creative abilities. Toward the end of 1936, the two groups merged as Agrupación Mujeres Libres. "The intention that underlay our activities was much broader: to serve a doctrine, not a party, to empower women to make of themselves individuals capable of contributing to the structuring of the future society, individuals who have learned to be self-determining, not to follow blindly the dictates of any organization" (Federación Nacional [M.L.], Barcelona, 1938).

Spanish anarchists from the Mujeres Libres (Free Women) organization on the war front, 1932. Credit: unknown.

These were women who had as their goal a complete social and political revolution. Their means of achieving this was to ensure that women were included and preparing to be included at every step. By July 1936, a network of anarchist women activists had been established for some time, ready and able to participate in the July events and encourage other women to take part in creating the new society.

In the Front Line

Despite traditional disadvantages women continued to take part in actual combat against the fascists. Mujeres Libres supported them in Madrid by setting up a shooting range and target practice for women "disposed to defend the capital," while the Catalonia group's "War Sports" section offered "preliminary preparation for women so that, if it should be necessary, they could intervene effectively, even on the battlefield." It was.

Armed women were always most noticeable in urban defense, when the fascists threatened cities like Madrid. But during the first year of the war, women also served as frontline combatants with the militia columns, in addition to nursing and, in the usual militia system, working alongside the rural population to ensure a common food supply. Their bravery at the front cannot be overstated, because, if captured alive, they inevitably faced rape, mutilation, and death. It was only after the battle of Guadalajara, in May 1937, that women were asked to leave the front, as the government demanded incorporation of the militia into regular army units.

Donald Renton, an English volunteer with the International Brigades in Figueras in November 1936 recalls the impact of seeing militia women: "While we had often talked about the role to be played by women in the general struggle, there for the first time we saw the militia women, comrades who like ourselves were either going to have or already had had, first line experience in the battle against the fascist enemy. These were wonderful comrades, people who had—so far as I was concerned at least—a very, very powerful inspirational effect on arriving inside Spain itself."

Foreign women also served in the international sections of the columns. Abel Paz refers to four women "nurses" in the "International Group" of the Durruti Column. They were captured by Moors in a fierce encounter at Perdiguera. As prisoners of the fascists they were as good as dead:

> Georgette, militant of the *Revue Anarchiste*, Gertrude, a young German woman of the POUM who liked to fight with the anarchists, and two young girls whose names haven't been recorded in the war chronicles. Durruti was very close to all of them...and he was deeply moved by these deaths. The death of Georgette, who was a sort of mascot of the Column, filled the militiamen with rage, particularly the "Sons of Night." She had carried out many surprise attacks on the enemy rearguard with the latter. They vowed to avenge her and during a number of nights made fierce attacks against the Francoists.

The "Sons of the Night" were a specialized group operating behind enemy lines—women were not just at the front as nurses.

In the defense of Madrid in early November 1936, women were also prominent in the fighting. The Women's Battalion fought before Segovia Bridge. At Gestafe, in the center of the Northern Front, women were under fire all morning and were among the last to leave. Fighting with the Italians of the International Column in Madrid was a sixteen-year-old girl from Ciudad Real, who had joined up after her father and brother were killed. She had the same duties as the men, shared their way of life, and was said to be a crack shot.

Back in Madrid itself, women were organizing in defense of the city, building barricades, providing communication services, and organizing the distribution of food and ammunition to the barricades and throughout the city through local committees. Women also played a major role in antiaircraft observation and surveillance of suspected fascist sympathizers.

An International Brigade volunteer, Walter Gregory, who fought in Madrid in July 1937 recalls:

> A frequent sight in the area of Las Cibeles was of the women's militia coming on and off duty. In twos and threes they would make their way down the Gran Via which ultimately led to the University City and the Madrid front line. The Gran Via was too often shelled to be used by vehicles, nor would the women have risked marching down its length in formation. In small groups

and chattering away to each other, they looked very like women the world over, and only their disheveled khaki uniforms after several nights in the trenches marked them out as being something special. Yet Madrid remained the only place in Spain where I saw women in the front line.

During the bitter battle at Jarama in 1937, another International Brigader, Tom Clarke, described the courage of a small group of Spanish women: "I remember there was a bit of a retreat. There was a rumor went round ... and they started retreating. We'd gone back a bit, and some of them were actually running. And here we came across three women who were sitting behind a machine gun just past where we were, Spanish women. I saw them looking at us. I don't know whether it shamed us or what. But these women—they sat there.... We sort of stabilized the line."

They were certainly an eye-opener for foreign men! The Austrian writer Franz Borkenau describes a lone militia woman serving with a POUM column:

> She was not from Barcelona, but a native of Galicia [who had] ... followed her lover to the front. She was very good looking, but no special attention was given to her by the militia men, for all of them knew that she was bound to her lover by a link, which is regarded among the revolutionaries as equal to marriage. Every single militiaman, however, was visibly proud of her for the courage she seems to have displayed in staying in an advanced position under fire with only two companions. "Was it an unpleasant experience?" I asked. "*No, solo me da el entusiasmo*" (to me it is only inspiring) replied the girl with shining eyes, and from her whole bearing I believed her. There was nothing awkward about her position among the men. One of them, who was playing an accordion, started la Cucaracha, and she immediately began the movements of the dance, the others joining in the song. When this interlude was over, she was again just a comrade amongst them.

By late December 1937, there were still women serving in the militias, but their numbers were diminishing fast. Orwell noticed that by this time male attitudes toward women had changed, citing an example of militiamen having to be kept out of the way while women were doing weapons drills, because they tended to laugh at the women and put them off. However, if women were becoming less active on the front line, this was not the case elsewhere.

Nationalist Repression

The nationalists were well aware of the opposition they faced from women. General Queipo de Llano, in his radio broadcasts from Seville, raved against and threatened the "wives of anarchists and communists." As they consolidated their power, the fascists wasted no time in reversing the liberalization of divorce and introducing strict dress codes for women—including the banning of bare legs. The repression, of course, was much more terrible, with up to a third of Spain's population ending up behind bars and countless men, women, and children massacred in fascist reprisals. In 1945, there were still eight jails for women political prisoners in Madrid alone. A Falange newspaper reports a baptism ceremony in Madrid in 1940 for 280 children born in prison. Many Spanish women fled to the French refugee camps, where they pooled food and established communal kitchens. Others joined the Resistance.

In their struggle against fascism and for a radical political and social alternative, the "Free Women" of Spain provide an example that is still relevant today: "To be an anti-fascist is too little; one is an anti-fascist, because one is already something else. We have an affirmation to set up against this negation . . . the rational organization of life on the basis of work, equality, and social justice. If it weren't for this, anti-fascism would be, for us, a meaningless word."

Notes

This essay originally appeared in Anti-Fascist Action's magazine *Fighting Talk*, August 29, 2015.

Schwarze Scharen: Anarcho-Syndicalist Militias in Germany, 1929–1933

Helge Döhring and Gabriel Kuhn

Historical Background

The roots of the anarcho-syndicalist movement in Germany date back to the union movement of the nineteenth century. As opposed to the big centralist unions under the influence of the Social Democratic Party (SPD), anarcho-syndicalists were strongly based in class struggle, antimilitarism, and federalism. During World War I, the anarcho-syndicalists were the first union activists to speak out against the war. After 1918, they recruited many new members, and important anarcho-syndicalist unions emerged in Berlin, Saxony, Thuringia, Rhineland, and the Ruhr Valley. Soon, they united in the Freie Arbeiter-Union Deutschlands (Free Workers' Union of Germany, FAUD). At its peak in the early 1920s, the FAUD had about 150,000 members. Many of them were unemployed, and there was a lot of agitation on the streets, mainly outside of government offices. This led to an activism that was very different from that of the regular union movement.

The growing popularity of the FAUD led the centralist unions, which were organized in the Allgemeine Deutscher Gewerkschaftsbund (ADGB), to actively undermine the FAUD's organizing efforts. Workers were forced to join social democratic unions under the threat of being denounced to bosses or the police otherwise. ADGB-affiliated workers even went on strike to have management lay off their anarcho-syndicalist colleagues. As a result, FAUD membership had dropped to ten thousand by the end of the 1920s, when anarcho-syndicalists were faced with an even more worrisome development: the rise of the National Socialist movement.

Schwarze Scharen

In light of the increasing Nazi threat, different workers' militias for self-defense were formed. The largely social democratic Reichsbanner Schwarz-Rot-Gold (The Banner of the Reich: Black, Red, and Gold) and the communist Rote Frontkämpferbund (League of Red Front Fighters) were founded in 1924. In 1929, they were joined by little-known anarcho-syndicalist militias, which called themselves the *Schwarze Scharen* (roughly, Black Droves).[1]

Members of the Schwarze Scharen wore arms and uniforms consisting of black boots, black pants, black shirts, and black berets. They engaged with Nazis in street fights and provided security at meetings and events, mainly of the FAUD and the Syndikalistisch-Anarchistische Jugend Deutschlands (Syndicalist-Anarchist Youth of Germany, SAJD). The FAUD cofounder and famed anarcho-syndicalist Rudolf Rocker was looked after by Schwarze Scharen more than once. Some groups also prepared for prolonged armed confrontations with the Nazis.

Those who joined the Schwarze Scharen saw fascism as a serious threat, not least to the working class; they tried to mobilize fellow workers to join their ranks. In July 1930, the Schwarze Scharen of Berlin-Brandenburg issued the following appeal:

> Are you aware of the consequences of your passivity? Comrade, don't get us wrong! We do not fear for the Schwarze Scharen. We are well established and our organizational structure is strong. We will not disappear. But think about the following: many workers act in the same way as you. But by being passive you sabotage our work; you get in the way of an effort that counts on your solidarity. As a class-conscious proletarian, can you with a clear conscience let a promising movement, equipped with the most useful of weapons, advance by itself? Can you with a clear conscience join this movement only when it has become a mass movement and done its deeds? Come on, comrade, make an effort yourself![2]

The Schwarze Scharen were founded on anarcho-syndicalist principles and they were close to the FAUD, but they organized autonomously. While in some regions, especially in Upper Silesia, local FAUD groups often overlapped with the Schwarze Scharen, there were stronger divisions in other places. Some groups of the Schwarze Scharen also had members without an anarcho-syndicalist—or any union—background. Many members were young, which is why the Schwarze Scharen were often referred to as a "youth organization," yet the average age was almost thirty.

The only Schwarze Scharen charter that survived the Nazi regime—ironically, at the Prussian Secret State Archives—was the one issued by the Berlin-Brandenburg group. It read as follows:

1. The Schwarze Scharen are an anti-fascist association of revolutionary workers.
2. Without reservation, they stand behind the principles of syndicalism and its organizations, that is, the FAUD and the SAJD.
3. They see themselves as a supplement to the named movements and as a protective force against fascism and the enemies of anarcho-syndicalism.
4. First and foremost, they consider it their duty to rally against fascism and to propagate libertarian socialism by means of education.
5. Any worker can become a member of the Schwarze Scharen.
6. The Schwarze Scharen have a federal structure. Individual groups consist of eight members. They form the basis of the federation. Any four additional members constitute a new group. Each group has a leader and an assistant leader. Three groups form a section. Each section elects a leader from the membership. Four sections form a Hundertschaft.[3] The leader of a Hundertschaft must be elected from the section leaders. The Hundertschaft leaders in one district form an administrative board.
7. Any leader can be dismissed at any time by a simple majority vote in the respective group, section, or Hundertschaft.
8. Each member pays a fee of fifty pfennig a month. The fee has to be paid to the group leader during the first week of

the month. Each new member must pay an admission fee of twenty-five pfennig.

9. If a member violates a group's principles, guidelines, or resolutions, or if he engages in behavior that harms the organization or his comrades, he can be expelled.

10. The organization can only be dissolved by a general assembly that has to be announced to all members fourteen days in advance and only by a two-thirds majority vote. In the case of dissolution, all assets of the organization will be transferred to the FAUD and SAJD.[4]

The relationship between the FAUD and the Schwarze Scharen was not without tensions. These can be summarized as follows:

1. For the FAUD, the revolution could only start with a general strike. In the opinion of the Schwarze Scharen, a general strike had to be accompanied by an armed struggle extending beyond workplace disputes and industrial centers.

2. Some FAUD members criticized the Schwarze Scharen for their martial appearance and violent behavior.

3. Some FAUD members feared that the Schwarze Scharen would turn into a vanguard-type rival anarcho-syndicalist organization, in the worst case replicating Bolshevism.

However, there was also widespread support for the Schwarze Scharen within the FAUD, as the following leaflet handed out in Berlin in 1930 reveals:

Comrade, what is *your* take on the Schwarze Scharen?

Not long ago, FAUD comrades in Upper Silesia founded an *anti-fascist association*. It took only a short time for this organization, which calls itself Schwarze Scharen, to recruit a much wider circle of active comrades than the local FAUD chapter. In Southern and Central Germany and in the Rhineland similar groups have emerged. Also in Berlin-Brandenburg. Do we believe that the existence of armed organizations is justified? Our answer is yes. We feel that, especially at a time when National Socialism is on the rise, we have to answer this question in the affirmative.

In the FAUD, we have so far not been able to reach bigger masses of workers because we have no solid circle of active comrades who, well versed in the politics of the day, are able to recruit in workers' quarters.

We, who are sincerely trying to promote the FAUD, have realized that it is mandatory to be active where workers live, to use modern means of propaganda (bands, theater groups, posters, wall newspapers, and, in rural areas, sound trucks), and to organize the self-protection of the proletariat.

Join the Schwarze Scharen![5]

Support came also from prominent figures in the radical milieu. In his journal *Fanal*, the well-known anarchist writer and agitator Erich Mühsam said the following about the Schwarze Scharen in November 1930:

In response to concerns that have been raised: if, almost at the same time and independently from one another, antiauthoritarian youth in Silesia, Kassel, and Berlin—and probably other places as well—form "Schwarze Scharen" in order to turn the "defense" of the working class against fascism into *physical* defense, then there must be a reason for it. *Fanal* has no cause to give the young anarchist comrades of the Schwarze Scharen a moral lecture; we can only send our regards and encourage them.[6]

Although the charter of the Schwarze Scharen group of Berlin-Brandenburg is the only one that survived, the group itself was short-lived. It encountered more than the usual resistance from the local FAUD chapter. In general, it was easier for the Schwarze Scharen to establish themselves in places where FAUD groups were small. Therefore, the most influential groups of Schwarze Scharen hailed from Upper Silesia (the center of the movement), Wuppertal in the Ruhr Valley, and Kassel in Hesse.

Upper Silesia

Upper Silesia—today a part of Poland—was one of the historically most reactionary regions of Germany. This also meant that workers' organizations were forced to develop particularly militant forms of action, which, in turn, helped the formation of the Schwarze Scharen in the

Schwarze Scharen in Ratibor, 1929. The banner, calling for a rally, reads: "The proletarian revolution will restore the unity of Upper Silesia. Workers of all countries, liberate yourselves from the oppressors!" Credit: German Anarcho-Syndicalist Archive.

late 1920s. Another factor working in favor of the Schwarze Scharen was that many militant workers were fed up with the authoritarian structures of the communist parties; they were looking for more flexible organizations.

The first group of Schwarze Scharen was founded in the town of Ratibor (Racibórz) in October 1929. It had about forty members and was always the most active Schwarze Scharen group. One of its main activities was to embark on tours in the region to inspire new groups. Ratibor's Schwarze Scharen would appear on the back of trucks in small towns and, according to a police report, wave banners proclaiming "Down with the State."[7] They also seemed to have a talent for agitprop. At an anti-war protest in August 1930, a carriage was equipped with self-made drawings, including a figure of Jesus Christ with a gas mask, and with a puppet representing Paul von Hindenburg, the German president, smoking a long pipe and wearing a nightgown and slippers. The artworks were confiscated by the police and charges were filed.

The significance of the Upper Silesia Schwarze Scharen for militant anti-fascist resistance rivaled that of the regional Rote Frontkämpferbund. In Ratibor, Schwarze Scharen outnumbered Communist Party members at a joint anti-fascist demonstration in April 1930. In Beuthen (Bytom), one of the region's major towns, the militant anarcho-syndicalists were at times the most powerful anti-fascist force. And in Katscher (Kietrz), a small town of only ten thousand people, the mayor complained in 1932: "On every occasion—especially when bans on demonstrations, marches, and meetings are lifted—communists and, in particular, syndicalists terrorize Katscher in a way that probably only few towns of its size experience."[8]

In fact, the Schwarze Scharen became so popular that the communists started to turn against them as well, especially since many former Communist Party members were filling their ranks. In 1931, the FAUD journal *Der Syndikalist* published a report under the headline "The Struggle for Upper Silesia." It included the following lines:

> Our comrades are repeatedly attacked while demonstrating outside the unemployment office. Sometimes, they are outnumbered twenty to one. When, on one occasion, nine drunken thugs were repelled in a rougher manner by two Schwarze Scharen members, the nine proceeded to attack a FAUD members' meeting with knives. It is only thanks to the Schwarze Scharen that the FAUD in Upper Silesia is able to defend itself against these fascist-like terror attacks.[9]

However, the Nazis remained the biggest threat, and since the Schwarze Scharen in Upper Silesia wanted to be prepared for the Nazi Party seizing power, they began to store explosives. In May 1932, based on an informant's tip, the police made several house searches in the region, confiscating dynamite cartridges, blasting caps, and fuses. The material came from sympathetic miners who had stolen it at work. Some Schwarze Scharen members escaped to foreign countries, others were convicted in court. It was the beginning of the end of the organization in Upper Silesia.

Wuppertal

In Wuppertal in the Ruhr Valley, the Schwarze Scharen regularly got into armed confrontations with Nazis. A November 1931 incident was described in *Der Syndikalist*:

> On Friday, November 13, at about 11 p.m., these [Nazi] brutes attacked without any reason members of the Reichsbanner. When, right at that moment, five of our comrades passed by,

the bandits let go and, under loud threats, turned on our comrades instead. Comrade Huhn suffered a deep cut from brass knuckles right above his eye. When more thugs arrived from the nearby SA barracks, the nineteen-year-old comrade Eugen Benner fired four shots. This put an end to the rowdiness and the warlike ballyhoo of the SA minions. Instantly, they backed off, and eighty "Hitler guards" ran in panic from an advancing nineteen-year-old anarchist. Eventually, Benner was arrested by a police patrol.[10]

Benner was put on trial and sentenced to three months in prison. The judge conceded that he had acted in self-defense but charged him for carrying an illegal weapon. Eventually, the sentence was reduced to three weeks. A year later, another Wuppertal Schwarze Scharen member, Helmut Kirschey, was sentenced for injuring a Nazi. Kirschey, who had also acted in self-defense, had shot a Nazi attacker in the leg. He was sentenced to four months in prison.

The status of the Schwarze Scharen in Wuppertal was unique in terms of their militancy. They prevented many fascist attacks on meetings and working-class neighborhoods. What they lacked in numbers, they made up in dedication. Their bold acts also served as a psychological weapon. As an activist remembered: "The SA took us for stronger than we were; they were afraid of us."[11]

Kassel

The Schwarze Scharen in Kassel, Hesse, distinguished themselves by publishing influential anarcho-syndicalist propaganda material, producing two periodicals. *Die proletarische Front—Kampforgan der Schwarzen Schar* (The Proletarian Front—Militant Publication by the Schwarze Schar) was their main journal; it appeared from 1930 to 1933. In 1930, a smaller journal titled *Die schwarze Horde* (The Black Horde) was also released. The journals were produced under difficult circumstances, as a 1931 article in *Der Syndikalist* reveals:

> Since the founding of our anti-fascist and revolutionary Schwarze Scharen group, we have been harassed without end by the police and the courts. Our journal *Die proletarische Front* has been banned, so we can only distribute it with enormous trouble.

Issues are confiscated, distributors arrested, fines handed out....
The machinery of the justice system is coming at us with full
steam.[12]

Eventually, a prosecutor in Kassel, calling *Die proletarische Front*
a "demagogic publication full of defamations of the republic and its
servants," demanded prison terms of several months for the editors
Willy Paul and Hermann Hannibal. However, he failed to convince
a jury of laymen, who apparently didn't consider phrases such as "a
republic of fat cats and money bags" to be libel. Willy Paul propagated
anarchist principles throughout the trial. Anarcho-syndicalists across
the country felt giddy about a jury in Kassel ruling in two anarchists'
favor.[13] It was a small victory in a battle doomed to fail.

Conclusion

In comparison to the Reichsbanner Schwarz-Rot-Gold and the Rote
Frontkämpferbund, the federation of the Schwarze Scharen was
small. It never had more than a few hundred members. There was no
common administrative body, and there were no common charters or
congresses. Contact between groups was loose and no group existed
for more than four years. After the Nazis took power in March 1933, no
group was able to withstand the repression and the brutality of the
regime. Even before the Nazi Party's rise to power, many members
of the Schwarze Scharen had already been arrested, not least in the
wake of the discovery of explosives in Upper Silesia. Yet the Schwarze
Scharen occupy an important place in the history of militant anarcho-syndicalist anti-fascism. Many Schwarze Scharen made a difference, and they raised important and timeless questions for militant
anti-fascist organizing: How to unite different tactics? How to keep a
common line? What is the role of the unions? What is the role of the
working class? Which are the sites of anarcho-syndicalist struggle?

Even if the Schwarze Scharen didn't exist long enough to provide
any answers to these questions, there can't be any doubt about the
genuineness of their anti-fascist convictions. Many former members
continued the anti-fascist struggle in the underground resistance
against the Nazis or as volunteers in the Spanish Civil War.

Regardless of the historical circumstances people find themselves
in, the need for militant anti-fascism always remains.

Notes

1 *Scharen* is plural. One "drove" is a *Schar*.
2 *Mitteilungsblatt der Schwarzen Scharen* (Bulletin of the S.S.), no. 3, July 1930. All translations from German by Gabriel Kuhn.
3 *Hundertschaft* is an old German military term for units of about a hundred men.
4 Geheimes Staatsarchiv—Preußischer Kulturbesitz (GStA), Bestand I HA, Rep. 219, Nr. 72, Bl. 26–27.
5 GStA, Bestand I HA, Rep. 219, Nr. 72, Bl. 37.
6 *Fanal*, no. 2, 1930, 48.
7 GStA, Bestand I HA, Rep. 219, Nr. 140.
8 Quoted from Helge Döhring, "Syndikalismus in Katscher/Schlesien," *Mitteilungen des Instituts für Syndikalismusforschung*, no. 3, 2013, 92.
9 *Der Syndikalist*, no. 40, 1931.
10 *Der Syndikalist*, no. 48, 1931.
11 Ulrich Linse, "Die 'Schwarzen Scharen'—eine antifaschistische Kampforganisation deutscher Anarchisten," in *Archiv für die Geschichte des Widerstandes und der Arbeit*, no. 9, 1989, 56.
12 *Der Syndikalist*, no. 12, 1931.
13 *Der Syndikalist*, no. 33, 1931.

Other Stories from the Civil Rights Movement: A Spectrum of Community Defense

Lamont Carter and scott crow

From the time of Reconstruction, there has been violence visited upon black people's homes and businesses by whites. Throughout the South, sanctioned white racist terror was an omnipresent fact of life, with vigilante lynchings of black people who challenged the racial status quo in any form. For many rural black people, the only protection against white racist violence was to protect themselves, including with guns if necessary. Rural southern blacks and whites owned guns to protect their property or to hunt. Many also had guns because it was necessary to protect themselves from white people. These conditions created a material basis for an armed black response of self-defense in the South before and during the civil rights era of the 1950s–60s.

In the dominant civil rights era narrative there is the popular conception of the civil rights movement as a peaceful and nonviolent expression of civil disobedience that aimed to integrate black people into civil society. Martin Luther King Jr. and the Southern Christian Leadership Conference's version of pacifism is generally accepted as the moral and ideological foundations of the civil rights movement. But the movement was more than one person or one movement, and it was more than just nonviolence and civil disobedience. This understanding of the civil rights era simplifies the variety of tactics and strategies present during those times. While nonviolent protests (sit-ins, marches, boycotts, civil disobedience) were certainly used, the existence and tactical use of weapons cannot be overlooked, especially in the southern United States. The people who advocated for armed self-defense were not fringe elements of the civil rights movement. Instead, they were part and parcel of the mainstream of the movement.

People like Medgar Evers and Robert F. Williams, as well as groups like the Deacons for Defense and Justice, were members and leaders in civil rights groups throughout the South that practiced armed self-defense in their communities. Additionally there were scores of black civilians, who were not members of any formal organization and who fought back with arms to protect organizers, their neighbors, and themselves. An understanding of armed self-defense and its role in the civil rights era allows us to analyze our own current political moments and the strategic questions facing us currently.

Before Mississippi Summer: Medgar Evers

Medgar Evers's work and outlook was inspired by his time fighting in World War II. Like many leaders of the civil rights movement, fighting for supposed freedoms abroad that black people did not possess in their own country fueled in Evers a desire to see change once he returned. Additionally, the much better treatment they received in France and other European countries gave black veterans a hope for different future. After returning home to Mississippi, he enrolled in college and started his work with the NAACP.

Evers and his brother Charles registered to vote with four other black men. When the election time came, they were threatened with attempts to keep them from voting. As they tried to cast their ballots, they were stopped by an armed mob of white people. They turned back, armed themselves, and again attempted to vote. Again they were stopped. Without resorting to their weapons, they left that day, but Evers determined to not allow that to happen again. The next year he voted without hassle.[1]

Medgar Evers had a fascination with the 1950s Mau Mau Rebellion in Kenya.[2] He looked at the guerrilla tactics of the Mau Mau and wondered if they could be applied to the United States. At the very beginning of his work with the NAACP, he believed there would be a race war in the United States and considered forming an underground guerrilla group. This fascination did not persist as Evers came to believe that this strategy would not come to pass. Instead, he continued his legal and fieldwork with the NAACP.

Part of his fieldwork was to gather evidence in towns and cities to build cases for the NAACP. He would drive across the state to interview witnesses and encourage people to come forward to tell their stories. During his travels, Evers would always be armed. He would sit on a pillow that covered a pistol so that he could have it at the ready should it be needed. Additionally, Evers would keep rifles in the trunk of his vehicle for added protection.[2]

Sadly though, Medgar Evers' habit of keeping weapons with him on his travels did not protect him from an assassin's bullet. In 1963, Byron De La Beckwith, a member of the White Citizens' Council, shot Evers in the back as he exited his car in the driveway of his house.[3] He would not be the last activist murdered in Mississippi either.[4] Slightly over a year later, three unarmed activists, from the organization Congress of Racial Equality (CORE) were murdered by the Ku Klux Klan at the beginning of the Mississippi Freedom Summer. Their deaths inspired a member of the Student Nonviolent Coordinating Committee (SNCC) to buy a gun for her protection. In a violent, racist state like Mississippi, a gun didn't guarantee you would not be murdered, but people embraced it as a method to protect themselves regardless.[5]

1950s North Carolina: Robert F. and Mabel Williams

Robert F. Williams was another veteran turned NAACP leader. Inspired by his time in the military where he faced discrimination, he and his wife Mabel Williams joined the Monroe, North Carolina, chapter of the NAACP upon his return home after leaving the military. Robert was voted as chapter president in 1955. He and Mabel worked with Albert Perry, a newcomer to Monroe and chapter vice president. They worked hard recruiting black veterans to their chapter, which gained the reputation of being very militant.

Perry and the Williamses worked to desegregate the town's public libraries and public swimming pools and for equal rights for blacks. Their efforts in these areas were not easy, as Monroe's Ku Klux Klan was thriving with support from the racist local sheriffs and city council. To protect civil rights activists and citizens in Monroe, Williams established a National Rifle Association–endorsed gun club.[6] The gun club, called the Black Guard, openly advocated for black armed self-defense. It was an outlet for members to learn gun safety, how to shoot, and to protect themselves and their community against racist violence.

In an anecdote shared in his seminal book *Negroes with Guns*, Robert Williams describes a situation in which the local police would not protect him or the passengers in his vehicle from white mob violence in a picket line in broad daylight. As the mob surged closer he pulled out his rifle and pointed at the crowd to keep them at bay while a passenger in the car pulled another handgun, halting a surprise attack from behind.

In another incident, Albert Perry had been receiving threats from the KKK. Knowing that there might be an attack, the members of the Black Guard fortified the positions around his house. During the night a KKK motorcade came through, shooting at the Perry residence. The Black Guard, numbering about fifty men, returned fire, forcing the Klansmen to retreat.[7] After that, the KKK night rides stopped happening in the neighborhood.[8] These defensive measures were the only way to ensure the safety of activists and himself in Monroe.

In 1959, after a Monroe jury acquitted a local white man charged with the attempted rape of a pregnant black woman, Williams told reporters that as a deterrent to white racist violence, that violence would be met with black violence. This sparked a clash between the national organization and the Monroe chapter. Williams was suspended for six months. During his suspension, Williams's wife Mabel served as chapter president. After his suspension was over, he continued on as president, having received a unanimous reinstatement vote.[9]

Williams continued to push self-defense as a tactic while in the NAACP. In *Negroes with Guns*, he writes that at his town's sit-in demonstrations, "There was less violence ... than in any other sit-ins in the South. In other communities there were Negroes who had their skulls fractured, but not a single demonstrator was even spat upon during our sit-ins. We had less violence because we had shown the willingness and readiness to fight and defend ourselves."[10]

Robert Williams's support of armed self-defense pulled Martin Luther King Jr. into a debate on the merits of the tactics in 1959 at a NAACP conference. King, despite a popular understanding to the contrary, was not entirely a dedicated pacifist. Under constant death threats, there was a time when King was surrounded by armed supporters. He also applied for a gun permit in the 1950s but was rejected.[11] While King may have moved toward a fuller pacifism later in life, in his debate with Williams, he was not too far removed from a life of armed self-defense. After the conference debate between them, Williams wrote an article titled "Can Negroes Afford to be Pacifists?" decrying the violence to which he and his community had been subject and the lack of action by "cringing negro ministers." In one of the final sections, Williams demands that black people stop lynching with violence and demands a recognition of the right to armed self-defense. He criticizes King's hypocrisy based on his support of the black soldiers and the U.S. role in World War II. He ends his piece saying, "Some Negro leaders have cautioned me that if Negroes fight back, the racists will have cause to exterminate the race. How asinine can one get? This government is in no position to allow mass violence to erupt, let alone allow twenty million Negroes to be exterminated. I am not half so worried about being exterminated as I am about my children's growing up under oppression and being mentally twisted out of human proportions."[12]

King's side of the debate, "The Social Organization of Nonviolence," mischaracterized Williams's position in support of armed self-defense as one that advocated for black armed insurrection against white supremacy. But while making this point, King shored up the argument for armed self-defense, saying, "When the Negro uses force in self-defense he does not forfeit support—he may even win it, by the courage and self-respect it reflects."[13]

Mississippi: Freedom Rider Supporters

It would be a complete oversight to not include the community armed self-defense that happened outside of any formal organizations. While groups like the SNCC and CORE debated over their non-violent approaches to change, the people whose houses they stayed in, both white and black, did not need to debate it. For them, a rifle or a handgun was the protection they needed to do their jobs or protect their loved ones when the Klan came to attack them.

One such individual was E.W. Steptoe, a black farmer in Mississippi. A fierce presence in the town of Amite, Mississippi, Steptoe housed the SNCC organizers who came to that small town. He also housed a large supply of weapons and often kept a gun on him wherever he went.

When Bob Moses, a SNCC organizer, asked him not to carry a weapon to a meeting, Steptoe just hid it from sight.

Laura McGhee, also a Mississippi native, was another proponent of armed self-defense. McGhee housed SNCC organizers on her property and also allowed voter registration classes, meetings, and rallies to be held there. She and her sons protected the property from night rider shootings.[14]

In 1964, Janie Brewer and her sons attempted to register to vote. On their way home after being denied, they noticed vehicles following them. One of Brewer's sons radioed to neighbors on her property and they set up an ambush for the racist caravan. When the Brewers pulled up to the property, the vigilantes saw the dozens of black folks waiting with guns and quickly turned around.[15]

More than just providing security for SNCC organizers, they provided a new perspective on tactics. The nonviolent portion of SNCC's name was taken seriously early on, but as time and the brutal beatings wore on, organizers grew disillusioned with the tactic. In the communities they worked in they saw the positives of weapons as protective measures. Many even began to use weapons to assist in patrols and to protect the "Freedom Houses" they lived in. This escalated into an organization-wide debate on nonviolence and the role of armed self-defense in their struggle. The strength of armed self-defense prevailed to allow the defense of Freedom Houses, with concessions to the nonviolent faction in that weapons would not be carried in public.[16]

These individuals were an addition to the informal networks of community defense that existed before the civil rights era, where it often took the entire community to protect a single home from night rider attacks. These defense networks were necessary to protect organizers and community members from violent retaliation for the work they were doing. These informal networks precipitated the formalized network of the Deacons for Defense and Justice that formed in the 1960s.

Louisiana Steps toward Liberation: Deacons for Defense

By the time the Deacons of Defense developed in 1964, lynching had given way from the public spectacle of violence against black bodies into more clandestine affairs including shooting and firebombing black people's homes with relative impunity from law enforcement.

The Deacons for Defense and Justice was a southern regional organization formed in Jonesboro, Louisiana, by Earnest "Chilly Willy" Thomas and Frederick Douglass Kirkpatrick. The Deacons, as they were referred to, were dedicated to defending communities and civil rights organizers from Klan and racist violence with arms. It was the first group of its kind. Where previous groups tended to stay anonymous, informal, and underground, the Deacons gave themselves a name and opened twenty-one chapters in Louisiana, Mississippi, and Alabama, with a few in the northern states.

The Deacons had their origins in protecting and defending the Freedom Houses that Congress of Racial Equality (CORE) organizers were housed in. They often had ongoing debates with CORE members over their armed stances.[17]

Earnest Thomas, like Evers and Williams, was a veteran. When he returned to the South, his experiences propelled him into the civil rights movement. But unlike the organizers he was meeting, he did not believe in nonviolence. He would not allow himself and others to be beaten by white cops and civilians in the streets, but he felt that he and others could participate in protecting CORE organizers.

CORE, like many other civil rights organizations at the time, was an explicitly nonviolent organization. The presence of guns was a major challenge for many of the activists just arriving from the North. Although guns were a deterrent to white racists, it clashed with the deeply held moral convictions of CORE's nonviolent pacifism. To the Deacons, allowing themselves or communities to be brutally beaten or killed at the hands of the police and the Klan was added humiliation to what they already experienced in the white, racist society they lived in. Some chose to sit out of demonstrations completely rather than have to watch the brutality unfold and do nothing.[18]

Some black community leaders attempted to stem the brutality of the demonstrations in the town of Jonesboro by appealing to official channels. Local black community members were officially deputized as members of the police force, which was armed and expected by the sheriff to intervene on the side of the white establishment in conflicts between racist mobs and demonstrators. The sheriff wanted the black police to stop the demonstrations altogether. Black deputies were caught in a tough position: to do their duty as black men and stand up against racist violence, or to do their duty as policemen and enforce laws restricting demonstrations. When the demonstrations died down, the Jonesboro sheriff disbanded the black police squad entirely. The limitations of black policing were bared as hypocrisy.[19]

After this failure, black men and women in Jonesboro supported a black community armed defense force. The Deacons led a desegregation action against a local restaurant. Like earlier desegregation efforts in Monroe, North Carolina, the presence of armed men in the action dissuaded violence from occurring and the restaurant served the demonstrators. From there, the desegregation campaign expanded. At the same time, the Deacons used domestic workers in white neighborhoods to put fear into white supremacists. The workers distributed a leaflet threatening to kill anyone burning a cross in the black part of town.[20]

In March 1965, black students at a Jonesboro high school went on strike. They picketed the school and the offices of the district's administration. The students demanded improvements to the school and expansion of the library. As the strike went on, the police and Klan members were eager to shut it down. The fire department was called in to hose the striking students. The Deacons showed up with shotguns, threatening to shoot the firemen if they didn't turn off their hose. After a tense standoff, the firemen backed down. The end of the strike occurred when the governor of Louisiana came to negotiate with the students. Not only were the Deacons successful in preventing racist violence during the strike, but they also allowed the students to continue, forcing the hand of the government.

The Deacons' biggest growth continued between 1964 and 1966.[21] In 1967, civil rights activist James Meredith was shot by a white Klansman during an attempted pilgrimage for voter registration from Memphis, Tennessee, to Jackson, Mississippi, called the March Against Fear. After the shooting, the Deacons went to Mississippi to act as guards of the march held to finish Meredith's abandoned walk.[22] SNCC, led by newly elected chairman Stokely Carmichael, welcomed the Deacons. Many in SNCC were tiring of the movement's rigid adherence to nonviolence.[23] As the March Against Fear grew after Meredith's shooting, Roy Wilkins of the NAACP balked at the inclusion of the Deacons. Martin Luther King Jr., while hesitant, agreed to their presence. This march marked the beginning of the slogan "Black Power." Though some of the marchers were arrested, prompting Carmichael's chants for "Black Power," the Deacons were able to march without weapons, but some members rode armed in vehicles at the front and rear of the march.

The growing disillusionment with lack of material gains from the Civil Rights Act and the subsequent assassination of Dr. King in 1968 led to rebellions and uprisings across the U.S. The rallying cries for liberation and Black Power emerged from those who had earlier only wanted equal rights. The influence of groups like the Deacons and people like the Williamses, who had once been a vanguard calling for blacks to stand up on their own terms within the laws, gave way to newer groups calling for revolution. In this atmosphere, although the Deacons had been a catalyst, they slowly dissolved around 1968, much like other groups of the era. The Williamses went into exile, first in Cuba and then in China.[24]

Reconsidering the Past to Make New Futures

The taking up of arms in self-defense by black individuals and communities during the civil rights era, as we have seen, was born out of necessity for survival and as steps toward self-determination. Despite the unfounded fears of the time by the white establishment, armed black communities never used guns for armed insurrections, retribution against whites, or in "overthrowing" the U.S. government. These defensive tactics, in addition to providing protection, allowed spaces for individuals and communities, forced into subservience through racist Jim Crow laws and vigilante violence, to assert their dignity and power on equal footing with those they feared.

Histories of community armed defense during this era were rarely written about until more recently. Instead, the prevailing narrative within school classrooms and commemorations celebrates those who embraced Gandhi's style of pacifism as if the other tactics had never existed or were wrong. The civil rights movement participants always employed diverse tactics in overcoming violent racism, often hidden from view. The nonviolence codes were often touted because they played into the palatable narratives of northern liberal supporters and the religious organizations that funded the campaigns. This often left the nonviolent strategy of the movement's leaders clashing internally with the daily survival tactics of its rank-and-file members who were challenged at every turn with violence and intimidation.

The self-defense histories have largely been written out or ignored due to many factors—from movement leaders who went on to be career politicians and pacifists who follow the code of nonviolence like a religion to individuals and groups who did not record their actions for decades, due to fear of government and white establishment reprisals. Additionally governments have embraced nonviolent resistance as the only "legitimate" alternative for people to air their grievances outside of voting because its seen as a "respectable."[25] Black people using force against white-initiated violence is unsettling in a society where racism continues as a structural norm. Instead the nonviolent protests and movements overshadow the other narratives, in a way similar to the "recognized" history of Gandhi's nonviolent movements overshadowing the armed struggles that took place for India's independence. Armed struggle against state-sanctioned violence is always a challenge to the state itself.

The narrative of strict nonviolence promotes unequal power and privilege, and often delegitimizes the difficult struggles that traditionally oppressed people have engaged in for survival and beyond. Today, when black youths are gunned down in the street, the only solution provided by established black leadership, who often promote their civil rights bona fides, is to dress nicer and softly petition governments for fewer black deaths. They exhort people to be more like Dr. King, neglecting to mention that Dr. King owned guns, and over the years had armed bodyguards too.

Lessons learned from the past are still applicable today. At this current juncture, we have an increasingly radicalizing movement of black people protesting police brutality, for the end of solitary confinement within prisons, and for the abolition of prisons themselves. At the same time, we have a leadership class that is doing what it can to clamp down on that radicalism and filter it through nonprofits and the Democratic Party. What we can learn from the civil rights movement is the necessity of a diversity of tactics.

It is necessary to understand this diversity of tactics as we look to the horizon of contemporary struggles. Today, in the early decades of the new millennium, we face a renewed reactionary Far Right and a continuation of police brutality backed by unjust and selectively enforced laws much like the struggles in the 1950s and '60s. We also see social and political movements with leadership that stresses nonviolence over everything else while marginalized people continue to exist in a white supremacist society facing renewed racial and ethnic violence. This survival tactic is at once limited and also holds the seed of possibilities.

This renewed right, with paramilitary groupings that threaten the lives of black people and recent immigrants, cannot be met with only nonviolent tactics. When Dylann Roof entered a black Charleston church, killing nine churchgoers in 2015, it harkened back to the Birmingham church bombings that killed four black girls on a church Sunday in 1963.[26] The only method by which people can defend themselves is to develop communities that are capable of taking their defense into their own hands as part of larger struggles for autonomy and liberation.

Notes

1   Myrlie Evers-Williams and Manning Marable, *The Autobiography of Medgar Evers: A Hero's Life and Legacy Revealed through His Writings, Letters, and Speeches* (New York: Basic Civitas Books, 2006), 7.
2   Jennie Brown, *Medgar Evers* (Los Angeles: Holloway House Publishing, 1994), 74.
3   Evers-Williams and Marable, *The Autobiography of Medgar Evers*, 40.
4   White Citizens' Councils were an associated network of white supremacist organizations in the Southern U.S. founded primarily to oppose racial integration.
5   Adam Nossiter, *Of Long Memory: Mississippi and the Murder of Medgar Evers* (Cambridge, MA: Da Capo Press, 2002).
6   Charles E. Cobb Jr., *This Nonviolent Stuff'll Get You Killed: How Guns Made the Civil Rights Movement Possible* (New York: Basic Books, 2014).
7   The NRA did not know upon the Black Guard's formation that they were a black organization. The NRA would later support gun control laws in 1967 in order to disarm the Black Panthers.
8   Cobb, *This Nonviolent Stuff'll Get You Killed*, 10.
9   Ibid., 129–30.
10 Robert F. Williams, *Negroes with Guns* (Mansfield Centre, CT: Martino Pub., 2013), 30.
11 Cobb, *This Nonviolent Stuff'll Get You Killed*, 7.
12 Robert F. Williams, "Can Negroes Afford to Be Pacifists?" *Liberation* 4, no. 6, (1959): 4–7, available online at http://kingencyclopedia.stanford.edu/encyclopedia/documentsentry/the_social_organization_of_nonviolence.1.html, accessed June 27, 2017.
13 Martin Luther King Jr., "The Social Organization of Nonviolence," *Liberation* 4, no. 6, (1959): 4–7, available online at http://kingencyclopedia.stanford.edu/encyclopedia/documentsentry/the_social_organization_of_nonviolence.1.html, accessed June 27, 2017.

14 Akinyele Omowale Umoja, *We Will Shoot Back: Armed Resistance in the Mississippi Freedom Movement* (New York: New York University Press, 2013), 49.
15 Ibid., 109–11.
16 Ibid., 86–89.
17 Lance Hill, *The Deacons for Defense: Armed Resistance and the Civil Rights Movement* (Chapel Hill: University of North Carolina Press, 2006), 25.
18 Ibid., 27–29.
19 Ibid., 36–38.
20 Ibid., 56.
21 Ibid., 167.
22 Ibid., 246.
23 With Carmichael as chairman, SNCC moved away from nonviolence (and would soon remove "Nonviolent" from its official name, becoming the Student National Coordinating Committee) and oriented itself more with the Deacons for Defense and the burgeoning Black Power movement.
24 Hill, *The Deacons for Defense*, 237–38, 254.
25 Peter Gelderloos, *How Nonviolence Protects the State* (Cambridge, MA: South End Press, 2007).
26 United Press International, "Six Dead after Church Bombing," *Washington Post*, September 16, 1963, http://www.washingtonpost.com/wp-srv/national/longterm/churches/archives1.htm, accessed June 27, 2017.

Negroes with Guns: Oral History Interview with Mabel Williams

David Cecelski

Mabel Williams (MW): It was early on after Robert became the president of the NAACP. He was becoming known in town as the president of the NAACP. Other people who were on jobs and who were members of the NAACP would tell us that these folks were saying, They're going to do this to you. They're going to do that to you. They're going to wipe out the family. They're going to kill Rob, and all that kind of stuff. And then we began to get telephone threats. And at that time I started to realize that this is serious business. These folks mean business.

David Cecelski (DC): They would call and talk to Rob or—?

MW: They would call and talk to whomever answered the phone and threaten to do us harm. They would talk to the children, or Daddy John, or me, or whomever.

DC: And they'd say, "If Rob keeps doing this we're going to kill you or do you—."

MW: We're going to kill you, or blow up your house, and all that kind of stuff. So Daddy John, who was Rob's father, always kept a twelve-gauge shotgun in his house at the door. I remember one day when he pulled that twelve-gauge shotgun out and said, "We're going to keep this at the front door because if the bastards come over here after us, we may have to use it." By that time Robert was going down to help protect

Dr. Albert E. Perry's house, whom they had threatened that they were coming in and going to blow him away.[1] Because he had been convicted of doing an abortion on a white woman even without a fetus to prove that there was an abortion. Even though he was a Catholic who had refused to do abortions for local black people, and usually did not even serve white customers. But because this woman had so little money and needed medical attention, he let down his guard and let her in there. They were able to use her as a tool against him and against our struggle.

DC: Why would they go after Robert because of Perry?

MW: Rob was the president of the NAACP, and Dr. Perry was the vice president. So whenever official protests went out to the city council or whomever, it went out with both their names on it. Most of the white people thought that because Dr. Perry was a doctor he was the one who was the brains behind the protest movement. At one time, a man wrote a letter to the editor in the Monroe *Enquirer-Journal*, and said, "What we ought to do is get that Robert Williams, bring him downtown, lock him up, and make him write something," because they didn't believe Robert had the capability of writing the articles with the depth that he was writing. They saw the two of them as a threat.

DC: That's when y'all started to take up defense.

MW: Yes. The Klan made a run or two past Dr. Perry's house and some shots were fired. And that's what made the men organize to defend his home. They dug trenches—and in the trenches they had sandbags. And our friend, Father MacAvoy would come and stay all night. He'd say, "You all do the shooting and I'll do the praying." And he'd stay up all night, read scripture, walk around, and bring coffee to the fellows. This went on for weeks on end.

DC: Dug trenches?

MW: Yeah. They had trenches and sandbags. And made Molotov cocktails that they were going to use against any vehicles.

DC: And the Klan was fairly strong in Monroe?

MW: Oh, yes. The Klan was very strong. The Klan was having rallies all over. One rally they reported that they had five thousand people at it. Rob and a few of the other fellows went out to some of those Klan rallies and were there on the scene. I think it kind of unnerved the Klansmen, but that was what kind of brought on the rifle club. We organized a rifle club and got an affiliated charter through the National Rifle Association.

DC: What did the rifle club do?

MW: We practiced shooting. We were all members. We taught the kids how to shoot. We'd have our little meetings. That was the backbone of our defense group. The NRA didn't know for sure because when Robert sent off for the charter he had himself as an author. He had Dr. Perry as a doctor. He had one of our officers, McDowell, as a businessman, he put down "construction contractor" for the construction workers, and the women he put down "housewives." We got our first charter like that! I'm sure when we joined, and the years after then, had they known we were a black group, they would have revoked our charter.

DC: I think they would have too.

MW: I'm sure they would have. But in the later years when they were under such attack for guns, they came up with the fact that they were proud of the fact that, "Well, if it hadn't been for guns in North Carolina, that man would have been dead," you know. [Laughter] And that's true. But the ironic part that I want people to know is that, although we had an association with guns, we knew how to use guns. We trained other people how to use guns, our children included. We never had the occasion to have to shoot anybody. That's remarkable because a lot of people, when they think about having guns, they think about killing folks. And Robert, always the ultimate teacher, taught us all that a gun is a weapon that can do terrible damage to people. And the only reason you would ever pick up a gun is for self-defense and not for anything aggressive or not to scare off anybody and not to play with anybody. It was serious business when you really had to pick up a gun.

DC: Why would it upset white southerners so much for blacks to have a rifle? I mean the right to bear arms and that kind of thing. Why was that so upsetting in 1956 or 1959?

MW: Because they knew that black people were at the point where they were demanding their equal rights. They knew much better than we did that all of that political power had to be backed up. They were backing their political power up with guns. And the only thing that was going to take it away from them, or threaten it, was if black people took up guns, too. I think that was the reason they were so afraid. So they were going to nip that in the bud if they possibly could and keep black people from even thinking about resorting to resistance. They had control of the police department, the state troopers and the National Guard. They didn't intend to release that power.

DC: Do you think that men were more threatened by those guns than by the nonviolent protest?

MW: Oh yes.

DC: There was something about blacks and guns that—

MW: That's right. They felt more threatened by that because that would mean that they would have to meet black men on an equal basis because that gun would equalize you. And they weren't ready to face that on an equal basis, no. So, yes, they were much more threatened by that than they were by the nonviolent protests.

Notes

This is an excerpted, edited, and annotated version of an interview with Mabel Williams originally conducted in August 1999. Interview K-0266, August 20, 1999, Southern Oral History Program Collection, Southern Historical Collection, Wilson Library, University of North Carolina at Chapel Hill, http://docsouth.unc.edu/sohp/K-0266/excerpts/excerpt_8789.html#citing, accessed June 27, 2017.

1   Dr. Albert E. Perry was a radical, black medical doctor and ex-college professor living in Monroe and fighting for civil rights in the 1940s–1960s.

Self-Respect, Self-Defense, and Self-Determination: A Presentation

**Kathleen Cleaver and Mabel Williams
with an introduction by Angela Y. Davis**

Introduction

Angela Y. Davis: We often trace the civil rights movement beginning with the 1955 Montgomery Bus Boycott and the subsequent develop-ment of the nonviolent strategies we associate with the civil rights movement. But as that movement was emerging, Mabel and Robert Williams in Monroe, North Carolina, directed an NAACP chapter, which decided that they would stand up and fight back against the Ku Klux Klan. This work, which led to their subsequent exile to Cuba and China, inspired black people all over the South to participate in similar efforts. There were the Deacons for Defense and Justice in Louisiana [applause].

I remember growing up in Birmingham, Alabama—the most seg-regated city in the South—and the black armed patrols that nobody talked about that prevented figures like Bull Connor urging the Klan to bomb and burn homes in the black community. People gathered every evening and patrolled the community. I remember my father taking out his gun when it was his turn to participate in the patrol.

This evening we'll hear about some of that subjugated history of self-defense that enabled the emergence of organizations like the Black Panther Party and the ideas of community armed self-reliance.

Kathleen Cleaver (KC): I'd like to comment on the book *Negroes with Guns* [cowritten by Mabel and Robert Williams], because I saw it when I first came out to the Bay Area in July 1967 in Eldridge Cleaver's apartment. He had a whole case of them he was handing out. Anybody that came into the Black Panther Party had to get a copy of *Negroes with Guns*, they had to read it, and we had to discuss it. This notion of self-defense in the book was very effective, because Robert and Mabel Williams pointed out that if there's a violent Klansman who believed fervently in white supremacy, they will come to take your life. But if you're armed, they have to make a calculation: Are they willing to risk their superior life to take your inferior life? So there was an important role to be armed that in this discussion reduced the level of violence.

In the community that I was accustomed to being in in the South, all the black people had guns. It was not even discussed. There would be a call that would go out if they heard the Klan was going to ride, everybody would be prepared. In fact, I thought it was odd when I came to Oakland that people were walking around displaying and parading guns around. You wouldn't do it in Alabama, but everybody had the guns. But as far as the concept: in '67 there were huge rebellions. In this country they tried to call them riots. There were uprisings in Detroit in which the U.S. Army in tanks were shooting house-to-house and sniper fighting. There were uprisings and rebellions in Newark that thousands of people were arrested, and millions of dollars of property damage. And so we, the Black Power revolutionaries, thought this was the beginning. It was moving from insurrection to revolution. Our concept of self-defense was not merely, we will have weapons so when the terrorists or the police come we'll be defended. That was definitely a core, but also, the notion of violence that was so pervasive. The black community was subjected to the violence of horrible education, the violence of bad housing, the violence of insult, the violence of the inability to get jobs that are sufficient for your livelihood. Being subjected to trials by juries that were against you from the get-go. Being sent to prison not having a fair trial. Being sent into the military to fight against people on the other side of the world who had done nothing to us. So we in the BPP considered many forms of violence against which we had to defend ourselves. The notion of self-defense was broader than weapons, but it did not at all exclude weapons, and that was fundamental—the notion that people had to accept the responsibility of standing up for themselves.

Mabel Williams (MW): In Monroe, North Carolina, we knew that the power structure in the local town was against us. But we didn't know when we started fighting that the FBI was supporting the power structure, that the federal government was supporting the power structure.

We were asking for what we thought were simple things like the right to have a job in a plant being supported by tax dollars and government contracts. But they wouldn't give us that, and Robert was one trying to go through channels, asking the federal government to come in and intervene. They were oppressing us terribly. When the Klan would come out, people would be afraid. That had been our history. The people would go in the houses and close the door and pull down the blinds. They had the guns in there but they still would be afraid of the Klan.

Robert said, "We should not be afraid of the Klan, because if they're going to invade our communities, we should protect ourselves." The law said you could carry a gun as long as it wasn't concealed, so he walked around with a Luger on one side. When we drove our cars around, even during our civil rights movement, we had a gun on the seat of the car. He was trying to stay within the legalities of what the law said.

What he knew but did not accept was that the law was not meant for us, but he was going to make it be for us. He said he would rather die just five minutes standing up like a man than crawling at the feet of his oppressors. Fortunately, he never had to kill anybody. I witnessed three attempts on his life while the authorities stood there and watched and pretended that they just didn't see.

We were in Monroe and we used the tactical demonstrations of nonviolence: trying to sit down on a lunch stool reserved for white people. As we would go around to the different drug stores—they would sell us the medicine but we couldn't sit down. So we'd picket. We picketed a swimming pool. We asked for one day of the week in the pool if they could not build one in our community. They said, "Oh no, we can't do that. We'd have to wash out the pool after you used it." That's what spurred us to continue picketing for the right to swim in a tax-supported swimming pool.

The Freedom Riders, who were down in Alabama, asked if we would accept them to come in and demonstrate in our hometown. They wanted to prove that nonviolence worked. Robert said, "You can come in and we will protect you as long as you're in our community,

Black Panther Party Communications Secretary Kathleen Cleaver circa 1969.
Credit: Alan Copeland.

but I'm not going out there because they know I'm not going to allow anybody to spit in my face and live." So the Freedom Riders came in and supported us with the pickets. The officials, determined to crush our movement, were calling for support from the Klan and everybody else. We told the Riders we didn't think they should demonstrate on Saturday or Sunday, because that's when folks are off work and they're going to be getting their beer and stuff; it's gonna be pretty bad. But they chose to go ahead anyway. The city officials sprayed insecticide on the picketers.

James Forman [of SNCC] was there on the picket line. When they got ready to leave, Robert sent the groups of armed men in to bring them out because thousands of racists were surrounding the picketers, shouting, kicking, and spitting at them, and the police were on the side of the rioters. We were in our community protecting it but all hell had broken loose. People were really upset about what was happening to the young people on the demonstration line.

A white couple came into our community. Though Rob kept them from being killed, they said that they had been kidnapped. Then Rob got a telephone call saying, "You caused a lot of trouble. In thirty minutes you're going to be hanging from the courthouse square." So he said, "Come on, get the children," and we had to leave. And we left thinking that we would go to New York, let things cool off, and then come on back home. When we got to New York there was a FBI all-points bulletin saying that Rob was armed and dangerous, schizo-phrenic, and should be apprehended. And then at the end it said he's traveling in the company of his family. He was on the Ten Most Wanted list. His poster was tacked up in post offices all over.

Anyway, we went to Canada, then to Cuba; our family had to split up. I didn't see our two boys or Rob again until after we all got to Cuba. We were able to survive through a network of friends that we had created all over and eventually end up in Cuba.

KC: Things were heating up while you and Robert were in Cuba. A lot happened in the Bay Area. Huey Newton, cofounder of the BPP, was on trial for the shooting of an Oakland policeman and the wounding of another one. The very small local group that had been called the Black Panther Party for Self-Defense was basically in a state of collapse when I got here. I said, "You want to get attention on this case? You should have demonstrations." We started having them in front of the courthouse and getting press.

The BPP built itself again around the case of freeing Huey, because we felt this issue was self-defense, and the murder that we were subjected to was central to what was going on in the whole country, as far as black people were concerned. We could take it from there, and we were organizing a movement to build a party around the 10-Point Platform and the basic principles of human rights and social justice, but the focus was on that trial.

The trial was scheduled to start in mid-April 1968. On April 4, Martin Luther King was murdered in Memphis and the whole country changed. There were uprisings and riots starting in the South. Two hundred cities went up in flames. People were jamming the Black Panther Party office asking for guns. They wanted to go out and start shooting.

Two days later there was an encounter between about fifty Oakland police and eight Black Panthers in Oakland that ended up in a ninety-minute gun battle with Eldridge Cleaver and Bobby Hutton, who was [seventeen]. They came out to surrender when Bobby Hutton came out with his hands up and was shot and killed. They just riddled his body with bullets. Eldridge had been shot in the leg and he couldn't stand up, so he was trying to come out. Neighbors in that area had seen what was going on and they said "Don't shoot!" He was arrested and taken off to prison for parole violation. That's the same weekend, that of April 6, that King was killed.

In June, Eldridge was released because parole authorities had not proved that he had violated his parole. They let him out on bail. This was right around the time Robert Kennedy was murdered in Los Angeles. So this country was kind of off the hinges. Nobody knew what was going on. It was insane. Everybody seemed to be frightened except those people who were too young to know how frightening it was. Eldridge was ordered to go back to prison after his appeal was overturned. He was ordered to turn himself in, and he said he was afraid he'd be killed. He disappeared, eventually ending up in Cuba in 1968. I tried to go to Cuba to join him. It never happened. I discovered after he left that I was pregnant. I wanted to be with my husband, and the only way was to go where he was. We finally ended up meeting in Algiers. We stayed for four years.

MW: Because of our difficulties in the U.S. we were able to build bridges of friendship with people from one end of Africa to the other, all over Asia and Europe as well.

KC: By the time the Black Panther Party came along, the notion of international solidarity was happening around the same time as the Organization of Solidarity with the People of Asia, Africa, and Latin America (OSPAAAL) Conference in Havana. OSPAAAL had established a day of solidarity with African American people. There was an international consciousness and dimension and recognition within the BPP of how our liberation struggles were not isolated from the rest of the world. Now there was also in existence in the world networks of solidarity for black radicals that continued. There were countries that had a sense of solidarity with our struggle. We wanted to maintain our struggle and ask for recognition as a liberation movement.

The U.S. State Department had a document I found out many years later stating that it was imperative that the black militants in the United States do not make links with the Arab and African revolutionaries, which is exactly what we were doing over there.

MW: Someone asked me, "Do you believe nonviolent revolution is possible in the United States or around the world?" Do you think "the man" is gonna give it up? Do you think that that one percent that is controlling 99 percent of the world's resources is going to say, "Oh, you know, let's just stop what we're doing here"? I don't think so.

Notes

This is an excerpted, edited, and annotated version of a talk presented by these three women in Oakland in 2004. See the full version from FreedomArchives.org /AK Press. org at http://vimeo.com/87520418, accessed June 27, 2017.

Repression Breeds Resistance: The Black Liberation Army and the Radical Legacy of the Black Panther Party

Akinyele Omowale Umoja

Introduction

The Black Panther Party (BPP) was one of the most significant radical movements in American history. As an organized political organization, the BPP existed from 1966 to 1982. Many activists and scholars argue that the BPP only existed as a revolutionary organization from 1966 until 1971, in the initial period of its existence. In this period, the BPP emphasized armed resistance as a primary means of achieving social change. After 1971, historians of the BPP argue the organization dropped its revolutionary, pro–armed resistance agenda to pursue reformist politics.[1] While governmental repression led to the ascendancy of a reformist agenda for one faction of the BPP, it was not the only organizational response. Some BPP members committed themselves to involvement in or support of clandestine military resistance that accelerated the development of the armed movement called the Black Liberation Army (BLA).

"The Black Liberation Army," Assata Shakur informs us, "was not a centralized, organized group with a common leadership and chain of command. Instead there were various organizations and collectives working together out of various cities, and in some larger cities there were often several groups working independently of each other."[2]

Given this multiple and decentralized character it is unsurprising that there are different accounts of its origins and composition. Some scholars see the BLA as a result of the split within the Panthers.[3] However, former political prisoner and Black revolutionary Geronimo ji-Jaga suggests that several Black revolutionary organizations contributed to the ranks of a Black underground that was collectively known as the Black Liberation Army.[4] Since the BPP was the largest revolutionary nationalist organization of the Black liberation movement of the 1960s and '70s, its membership contributed greatly to the BLA's numbers. The nature of that relationship—especially the influence and participation of BPP members and supporters in the Black Liberation Army—constitutes the focus of this study.[5]

RAM Proposes War

Before the Panthers, there was the Revolutionary Action Movement. Founded in 1962 by "revolutionary Black nationalists" seeking to win freedom for the "colonized Black nation,"[6] RAM served for years as a radical clandestine organization within the Black liberation movement. For example, RAM worked with SNCC field staff to develop armed self-defense units to protect their organizing projects in the Mississippi delta.

In the spring of 1964, RAM chairman Robert Williams, a political exile in Cuba, published an article titled "The USA: The Potential for a Minority Revolt." Williams stated that in order to be free, Black people "must prepare to wage an urban guerrilla war."[7] That same year, RAM organizers presented a twelve-point program at a National Afro-American Student Conference in Nashville, advocating the "development of Liberation Army (Guerrilla Youth Force)."[8] In 1967, RAM began to organize Black urban youth into a paramilitary force called the Black Guards. A RAM document, titled "On Organization of Ghetto Youth," urged: "In the early stages of the mobilization of Black ghetto youth we must prepare for the ultimate stage, a protracted war of national liberation; therefore the type of organization that must be established is a paramilitary organization." This document referred to the paramilitary organization as the Black Liberation Army, or BLA.[9]

The Black Panthers and the Black Underground

Before he helped to start the Black Panther Party for Self-Defense, Bobby Seale was a member of the Revolutionary Action Movement.

Seale and BPP cofounder Huey P. Newton disagreed with RAM's secretive approach, but the question of clandestine military action was a principal issue for the Panthers from the start. The BPP organized an underground from its earliest days, as a precaution in case the party's political activities would not be allowed to function in the public arena. In this context, the BPP envisioned a clandestine guerrilla force that would serve as the vanguard of the revolution. In 1968, Newton stated:

> When the people learn that it is no longer advantageous for them to resist by going into the streets in large numbers, and when they see the advantage in the activities of the guerrilla warfare method, they will quickly follow this example.... When the vanguard group destroys the machinery of the oppressor by dealing with him in small groups of three and four, and then escapes the might of the oppressor, the masses will be overjoyed and will adhere to this correct strategy.[10]

Still, the Panther underground was not openly referred to or publicly acknowledged. It was organized as a series of decentralized cells, with some large cities hosting several autonomous units. Besides serving as an urban guerrilla force, the network included an underground railroad to conceal comrades sought by police and clandestine medical units to provide care to revolutionaries wounded in combat.[11] These underground units were all part of a movement concept called the Black Liberation Army. The BLA was broader than the BPP, representing the underground military forces of the revolutionary nationalist Black movement as a whole.[12]

The Southern California chapter of the BPP had an underground almost from its inception. Former Los Angeles gang leader Alprentice "Bunchy" Carter virtually brought a military force into the BPP when he joined in 1967. Carter was the leader of the Renegades, the hardcore of the Slausons, the largest street gang in the city. During a stay in prison, Carter joined the Nation of Islam and met Eldridge Cleaver, who taught Soledad's African American History and Culture class. Cleaver and Carter made plans to form a revolutionary nationalist organization, including an underground military wing. Upon leaving prison, Bunchy Carter worked to move loyal members of his street organizations, ex-inmates, and other Los Angeles street gangs from the criminal mentality to revolutionary consciousness. When Carter joined the BPP, he brought with him an autonomous collective of radicalized street forces.[13]

In his role as Southern California minister of defense, Carter made it his responsibility to organize an underground Panther cadre. His most trusted comrades formed the Southern California Panther underground, often referred to as the "Wolves." Working without the knowledge of the aboveground rank-and-file Panthers, Carter's Wolves carried out secret operations to support the work of the BPP.[14]

Probably Carter's most significant recruit was Geronimo ji-Jaga (then known as Geronimo Pratt), a former Special Forces commando with combat experience in Vietnam. Ji-Jaga proved invaluable in the development of the underground. After Carter was murdered in an FBI-provoked clash between the Panthers and the US Organization in 1969, ji-Jaga was appointed the Southern California minister of defense. With national Minister of Defense Huey Newton in prison, ji-Jaga assumed responsibility for organizing the military wing of the entire BPP. He helped to develop new chapters in places like Atlanta, Dallas, New Orleans, Memphis, and Winston-Salem, North Carolina; and he visited existing chapters to offer his expertise in establishing their clandestine cadre.[15] He saw it as his duty to utilize his military skills to develop the Panther underground and to build a cooperative relationship with other clandestine military forces in the Black liberation movement acting together under the banner of the Black Liberation Army.[16]

In December 1969, police raided the BPP offices in Los Angeles and Chicago. In the Chicago raid, Panther leaders Fred Hampton and Mark Clark were murdered. In contrast, the Los Angeles BPP office, staffed mainly by teenagers, was able to survive a five-hour predawn siege that included the use of SWAT forces. While ji-Jaga was not present during the raid, the preparations and military training he had provided were decisive to the survival of his comrades.[17] Ji-Jaga's stature within the party increased as repression did.

But then, when Newton was released from prison in 1970, he inherited a national organization and a military force that had been created largely in his absence. While the BPP always envisioned an underground military wing to complement the party's aboveground activities, Newton was uncomfortable with the direction the party was going, and became particularly suspicious of ji-Jaga. In due time, government operatives and ambitious party members convinced Newton that ji-Jaga was a threat to his leadership and thus to the organization and the movement.[18]

The Panther Split and the Black Liberation Army

In 1968, the national BPP leadership had announced a policy to expel any members involved in "unauthorized" military and clandestine activity.[19] Simultaneously, increased political repression convinced many Panthers that it was time to develop the underground vanguard. But the new policy put those going underground in a precarious position. Newton and Party Chief of Staff David Hilliard were viewed as abandoning the clandestine vanguard at the very moment repression was forcing members of the Party underground.

One of those was Geronimo ji-Jaga. In August 1970, ji-Jaga went underground to further develop the BLA. Based upon his assessment of the counterinsurgency assault on the Black liberation movement, ji-Jaga concluded that the "establishment of guerrilla bases" was "an integral necessary part of the overall freedom movement." His strategy was to strengthen the revolutionary nationalist clandestine network throughout the United States, particularly in the historic Black belt in the southeast.[20]

On December 8, 1970, ji-Jaga and his comrades Will Stanford, Will "Crutch" Holiday, and George Lloyd were arrested in Dallas. After the arrests, high-ranking Party members (including some government infiltrators) urged Newton to expel ji-Jaga. A month later, Newton publicly denounced ji-Jaga, his wife Nsondi ji-Jaga (Sandra Pratt), and their codefendants for exhibiting "counterrevolutionary behavior." Newton's directive also implied that ji-Jaga was a government operative loyal to the CIA: "He is as dedicated to that Pig Agency as he was in Vietnam."[21] Needless to say, this attack caused major division and confusion in the BPP.

Tensions within the party increased after incarcerated members of the New York chapter (aka the Panther 21) published an open letter to the Weather Underground. "Weatherman," a white organization engaged in a bombing campaign against targets involved in the Vietnam War, had officially recognized the Black Panther Party as the vanguard of the revolution in North America. The Panther 21 reciprocated, addressing Weatherman as part of the vanguard while criticizing the national leadership of the BPP. The letter called for an underground guerrilla offensive because "racism, colonialism, sexism and all other pig 'isms' . . . can only be ended by revolution . . . ARMED STRUGGLE."[22] They believed the Weather Underground was going in the direction the BPP should be going. For their open criticism, the Panther 21 were expelled from the party.[23]

Recognizing the confusion created by these various expulsions, the FBI determined to "more fully exploit" the ideological and factional differences in order to fatally divide the party. Government operatives were instructed to manipulate the ideological differences and exploit insecurities within the organization, with the aim of creating a split between Newton and Eldridge Cleaver, head of the International Section of the BPP.[24] These counterinsurgency efforts created an environment that made resolving internal contradictions within the party virtually impossible.

In February 1971, Panthers from northeastern chapters held a press conference calling for the expulsion of Newton and Hilliard. The "East Coast" Panthers named Eldridge Cleaver, Kathleen Cleaver, Donald Cox, and Bobby Seale as the legitimate leadership of the party. At the time, the Cleavers and Cox were political exiles in Algeria; Seale was incarcerated in Connecticut. New York would become the headquarters for this faction.[25] After the split, the "East Coast" Black Panther Party became the aboveground apparatus of BPP members who joined the BLA. Their newspaper *Right On!* became a public organ of the armed movement, publishing instructions for guerrilla warfare and news about airline hijackings and other military actions.

The exiles then entered the fray. The members of the International Section were deeply concerned about the recent expulsions and the lack of support for armed resistance.[26] Believing these developments signaled the ascendancy of authoritarian rule by Newton and Hilliard, the International Section accused them of "consciously set[ting] about to destroy the underground." Given the repression of the Black liberation movement, the exiled Panthers believed it was "necessary . . . to advance the armed struggle. . . . We need a people's army and the Black Panther vanguard will bring that about."[27] Ignoring his own previous position, Newton blamed Cleaver for the emergence of pro–armed struggle currents, and accused him of overemphasizing the "gun" and moving the party into military action without the support of the community.[28]

There were other forces that supported an underground military presence but nevertheless remained loyal to the Newton's Oakland faction. Within the California prison system, BPP Field Marshall George Jackson attempted to transform incarcerated Black men into revolutionary soldiers. Jackson's published prisons letters reveal his desire to develop a clandestine army to defend and complement the activity of the aboveground Black Panther Party under Newton's leadership. The murder of Jackson on August 21, 1971, and the disruption of his recruits by government forces would eliminate this potential clandestine army.[29]

A year later, the Oakland-based BPP created a security force (aka "the squad") to protect its leadership. In time Newton would use the security force as his personal "goon squad" to maintain internal discipline and to pressure local businesses to contribute finances to the party. Newton envisioned controlling legal and illegal activity throughout the city. While the BPP became involved in local electoral campaigns, the military elements loyal to Newton struggled for control of drugs and prostitution. More and more, Newton's squad would be used for intimidation and criminal activity.[30]

Meanwhile the government employed a "carrot and the stick" strategy. As the Oakland-based BPP moved in a more reformist direction, the harassment, police raids, and arrests subsided. Within four years, the Oakland-based BPP, then under the leadership of Elaine Brown, would receive federal and foundation funding. In 1976, Brown served as a delegate to the Democratic National Convention.[31] Panther members and supporters associated with the radical BPP factions, however, found themselves under greater police pressure. As a result, the aboveground radicals were reduced to organizing defense committees for captured BLA comrades and serving as propagandists for the underground. Within four years of the split, by 1975, the radical factions had no visible aboveground presence.

Defensive/Offensive

The BLA's declared purpose was to "defend Black people, to fight for Black people, and to organize Black people militarily, so they can defend themselves through a people's army and people's war."[32] Thus they waged a "defensive/offensive" campaign against police, retaliating against the agents of genocide in the Black community.

On May 19, 1971, the BLA claimed responsibility for shooting two New York police officers guarding the home of Frank Hogan, the district attorney in charge of prosecuting the Panther 21.[33] Two days later, BLA members killed two police officers in an ambush attack. In August 1971, BLA soldiers carried out several actions in San Francisco, including an attack on two police stations and one police car, resulting in the death of one officer and the wounding of several others. These actions were in retaliation for an FBI raid on the headquarters of the Provisional Government of the Republic of New Afrika on August 18, 1971, and the shooting death of BPP Field Marshall George Jackson on August 21.[34] Police also suspected the BLA of shooting a cop in Atlanta, Georgia, on November 3. On December 21, police accused the BLA of using a grenade to attack a police car in Atlanta, resulting in injuries to two officers.[35] In the two years after the BPP split, the U.S. government attributed the deaths of twenty police officers to the Black Liberation Army.[36]

In response, the FBI and local police initiated a national "search and destroy" mission. On May 3, 1973, BLA members Zayd Shakur, Sundiata Acoli (aka Clark Squire), and Assata Shakur (aka Joanne Chesimard) were stopped by police on the New Jersey Turnpike. A shoot-out ensued. When the smoke cleared, one of the police officers and Zayd Shakur were dead, and Assata Shakur was severely injured.[37] Police hailed the capture of Assata, calling her the "Black Joan of Arc" and the "high priestess" and "the soul" of the "cop-hating BLA." After separate trials, Assata and Acoli were both convicted by all-white juries for the murder of the New Jersey state trooper and of Zayd Shakur; they were sentenced to life plus thirty years.[38] Between 1971 and 1973, police claimed responsibility for the deaths of seven suspected BLA members and the capture of eighteen others believed to be "key figures in the movement."[39]

Then, on November 14, 1973, BLA member Twyman Meyers was ambushed by a joint force of FBI agents and New York police. As Meyers was leaving a Bronx apartment, he was surrounded by dozens of cops. Meyers responded with gunfire. According to witnesses, Meyers ran out of ammunition and was then killed by police.[40] New York Police Commissioner Donald Cawley announced that cops had "broken the back" of the Black Liberation Army.

But something unexpected happened six years later, on November 2, 1979. Members of the BLA conducted an armed action at Clinton

Correctional Institution for Women in New Jersey, resulting in the escape of Assata Shakur. Prison authorities described the action as "well planned and arranged."[41]

Three days later, on Black Solidarity Day in New York, a demonstration of five thousand marched from Harlem to the United Nations building under the slogan of "Human Rights and Self-Determination for the Black Nation." Hundreds of the marchers carried signs stating "Assata Shakur is welcome here." At the rally that day, a statement from the BLA was read to the crowd: "Comrade-Sister Assata Shakur was freed from racist captivity in anticipation of Black Solidarity Day, November 5th.... In freeing Comrade-Sister Assata we have made it clear that such treatment and the criminal 'guilt' or innocence of a Black freedom fighter is irrelevant when measured by our people's history of struggle against racist domination."[42] A statement written by Assata was also circulated at the rally. It condemned U.S. prison conditions and called for freedom for political prisoners, support for human rights, and an independent New Afrikan nation-state.[43]

Despite the cops' boast of breaking the back of the BLA six years prior, the BLA had certainly achieved a victory. One of their most well-known members escaped captivity through the actions of her comrades. The BLA was not dead.

The Continuation of Armed Struggle

On October 20, 1981, an incident occurred that would eventually reveal a significant resurgence of BLA activity. Four people—Judy Clark, David Gilbert, Kathy Boudin, and Solomon Brown—were arrested in the aftermath of an attempted holdup of a Brink's armored truck and a subsequent shoot-out at a police roadblock in Rockland County, New York. The episode resulted in the death of one Brink's guard and two police officers.[44] The FBI immediately followed a trail of physical evidence, which led them to members of the Black underground.

The Black Liberation Army later issued a communiqué to put these events into a political context. The holdup was described as an "expropriation" undertaken by the Revolutionary Armed Task Force (RATF), a "strategic alliance ... under the leadership of the Black Liberation Army" of "Black Freedom Fighters and North American (White) Anti-Imperialists."[45] This alliance, coming together in response to an escalation of white supremacist violence, was politically as well as racially diverse; it included revolutionary nationalists, Muslims, anarchists, and communists under the leadership of clandestine forces from the New Afrikan Independence movement.[46]

The FBI and federal prosecutors determined that the Rockland County incident was part of a series expropriations by the BLA and its white allies between 1976 and the end of 1981. The focus of the "revitalized" BLA during that period was different from that of the postsplit period (1971–1975). The emphasis in the earlier period seemed to be retaliation against police, the occupying army of the colonized nation. In the later period, the focus seemed to be the development of infrastructure for the armed clandestine movement and support for aboveground organizing. The RATF planned to "accumulate millions of dollars under the political control of ... revolutionary elements" for use establishing self-defense units and community cultural, health, and educational institutions in Black communities throughout the United States.

Because of the political character of the actions of the RATF, the communiqué stated, "The comrades who are in jail are not criminals. They are Prisoners of War.... They are heroes struggling against RACISM, FASCISM, AND IMPERIALISM."[47]

Conclusion

The Black Panther Party was one of the most significant radical groups in American history. As a political organization, the BPP existed from 1966 to 1982, but many scholars argue that it only existed as a *revolutionary* organization from 1966 until 1971. After 1971, its leadership officially dropped the revolutionary, pro–armed resistance agenda to pursue reformist politics.[48] But Panther participation in the BLA demonstrates that there were multiple responses to the repression the party faced. While one faction adopted a reformist agenda, others committed themselves to clandestine military resistance and accelerated the development of the armed movement called the Black Liberation Army.

The BLA is often presented as the product of the repression against the Panthers and the split within the party.[49] However, as Geronimo ji-Jaga makes clear, the BLA was a movement concept that both predated the Panthers and was broader than any one organization.[50]

Certainly, the role of the underground and the armed struggle was a critical issue in the 1971 split. But perhaps the most important issue was not whether the party emphasized a reformist or radical agenda but rather its inability to maintain its organizational unity and cohesiveness in the face of repression.

Notes

This is excerpted from Dr. Umoja's longer essay, which first appeared in *New Political Science* 21, no. 2, 1999.

1   Angela D. LeBIanc-Ernest, "The Most Qualified Person to Handle the Job: Black Panther Party Women, 1966–1982," in *The Black Panther Party [Reconsidered]*, ed. Charles E. Jones (Baltimore: Black Classic Press, 1998), 305; Ollie Johnson, "Explaining the Demise of the Black Panther Party: The Role of Internal Factors," in Jones, *The Black Panther Party [Reconsidered]*, 407; Kathleen Cleaver, "Back to Africa: The Evolution of the International Section of the Black Panther Party (1969–1972)," in *The Black Panther Party [Reconsidered]*, 239.

2   Assata Shakur, *Assata: An Autobiography* (Chicago: Lawrence Hill Books, 1987), 241.

3   Dhoruba Bin Wahad, "War Within: Prison Interview," in *Still Black, Still Strong: Survivors of the War Against Black Revolutionaries*, ed. Jim Fletcher et al. (New York: Semiotext(e), 1993), 13; Jalil Muntaqim, *On the Black Liberation Army* (Montreal: Anarchist Black Cross, 1997), 4; Sundiata Acoli's August 15, 1983 testimony in *United States v. Sekou Odinga et al.*, in the pamphlet *Sundiata Acoli's Brinks Trial Testimony* (Patterson, NJ: Black Anarchist Collective, 1994), 21.

4   Geronimo ji-Jaga interview with author (September 14, 1998), Morgan City, Louisiana.

5   Scholarly research on the BLA is a challenging endeavor. Most books that focus on this organization have been journalistic or biographic. The journalistic texts have primarily relied on police or prosecution records. American newspapers also reported on BLA activities based upon information offered to the media to support police investigations and prosecutions of Black radicals. The journalistic literature on the BLA is usually written from a perspective that is uncritical of American law enforcement and its counterinsurgency tactics. Since the BLA is a radical clandestine movement, its activities by their very nature are illegal, making it difficult for scholars to interview its members. Facts are often omitted from biographies and BLA statements to protect incarcerated or indicted members of the movement. The nature of the organization also does not provide the researcher with organizational archives. This study will utilize public documents of the BLA and other movement literature, statements and autobiographies from incarcerated BLA members, as well as from former BLA militants and supporters as a balance to police- and prosecutor-oriented literature and records.

6   Robert Brisbane, *Black Activism: Racial Revolution in the United States 1954–1970* (Valley Forge, PA: Judson Press, 1974), 182. Robert Williams quoted in Robert Earl Cohen, *Black Crusader: A Biography of Robert Franklin Williams* (Secaucus, NJ: Lyle Stuart, 1972), 271–72.

7   "USA: The Potential of a Minority Revolt" originally appeared in the May–June 1964 issue of Williams's newsletter *The Crusader*.

8   Maxwell C. Stanford, "Revolutionary Action Movement (RAM): A Case Study of a Urban Revolutionary Movement in Western Capitalist Society" (master's thesis, Atlanta University, 1986), 99. Available at http://www.ulib.csuohio.edu/research/portals/blackpower/stanford.pdf, accessed June 30, 2017

9   Revolutionary Action Movement, "On Organization of Black Ghetto Youth," in *Hearings before the Permanent Subcommittee Investigations of the Committee on Government Operations United States Senate, Ninety-First Congress, First Session, Riots, Civil, and Criminal Disorders, June 26 and 30, 1969, Part 20* (Washington, DC: U.S. Government Printing Office, 1969), 4221–24.

10 Huey Newton, "The Correct Handling of a Revolution," in *The Black Panthers Speak*, ed. Philip S. Foner (New York: Da Capo Press, 1995), 41–42.

11 Geronimo ji-Jaga, "A Soldier's Story," interview by Bakari Kitwana, *The Source*, February 1998, 132.

12 Ji-Jaga interview with author (September 14, 1998).

13 Ibid.; Earl Anthony, *Picking Up the Gun: A Report on the Black Panthers* (New York: Dial Press, 1970), 66–67.

14 Ji-Jaga interview with author (September 14, 1998).

15 Ji-Jaga, "A Soldier's Story," 132.

16 Ji-Jaga interview with author (September 14, 1998); ji-Jaga, "A Soldier's Story," 132; David Hilliard and Lewis Cole, *This Side of Glory: The Autobiography of David Hilliard and the Story of the Black Panther Party* (Boston: Little, Brown, 1993), 218.

17 "Chronology of the Black Panther Party," in *Still Black, Still Strong*, 233; Kathleen Cleaver, "Back to Africa: The Evolution of the International Section of the Black Panther Party (1969–1972)," in *The Black Panther Party [Reconsidered]*, 237.

18 Hilliard and Cole, *This Side of Glory*, 299–300, 304–12; ji-Jaga interview with author (September 14, 1998); Ward Churchill and Jim Vander Wall, *Agents of Repression: The FBI's Secret Wars Against the Black Panther Party and the American Indian Movement* (Boston: South End Press, 1988), 87.

19 Kit Kim Holder, "The History of the Black Panther Party, 1966–1971" (PhD dissertation, University of Massachusetts, 1990), 55–56.

20 Geronimo Pratt (ji-Jaga), "The New Urban Guerrilla," in *Humanity, Freedom, Peace* (Los Angeles: Revolutionary Peoples Communication, 1972), 26.

21 Huey Newton, "On the Expulsion of Geronimo from the Black Panther Party," *Black Panther*, January 23, 1971, 7.

22 "Open Letter to Weather Underground from Panther 21," *East Village Other* 8, January 19, 1971, 20.

23 Rod Such, "Newton Expels Panthers," *Guardian*, February 1971, 4; E. Tani and Kaé Sera, *False Nationalism, False Internationalism* (Chicago: Seeds Beneath the Snow, 1985), 209; Akinyele O. Umoja, "Set Our Warriors Free: The Legacy of the Black Panther Party and Political Prisoners," in *The Black Panther Party [Reconsidered]*, 421–22.

24 Huey P. Newton, *War Against the Panthers: A Study of Repression in America* (New York: Harlem River Press, 1996), 65–71.

25   Holder, "History of the Black Panther Party," 275–77; "A Call to Dissolve the Central Committee," *Right On! Black Community News Service*, April 3, 1971, 3.

26   Cleaver, "Back to Africa," 236–39.

27   Jack A. Smith, "Panther Rift Aired in Algiers," *Guardian*, April 17, 1971, 3.

28   Huey Newton, "On the Defection of Eldridge Cleaver from the Black Panther Party and the Defection of the Black Panther Party from the Black Community," in *The Black Panthers Speak*, 272–78.

29   George Jackson, *Blood in My Eye* (Baltimore: Black Classic Press, 1990), 11–72; Hilliard and Cole, *This Side of Glory*, 379–80.

30   Ollie Johnson, "Explaining the Demise of the Black Panther Party: The Role of Internal Factors," in *The Black Panther Party [Reconsidered]*, 407.

31   Charles Hopkins, "The Deradicalization of the Black Panther Party: 1967–1973" (PhD dissertation, University of North Carolina, 1978), 231.

32   Acoli, *Sundiata Acoli's Brinks Trial Testimony*, 21.

33   "By Any Means Necessary: Writings of the Black Liberation Army," *Breakthrough: The Political Journal of the Prairie Fire Organizing Committee* 2, no. 2 (Fall 1978): 50; United States Justice Department LEAA (Law Enforcement Assistance Act) document quoted in Muntaqim, *On the Black Liberation Army*, 5.

34   "By Any Means Necessary," 50; Muntaqim, *On the Black Liberation Army*, 5.

35   Muntaqim, *On the Black Liberation Army*, 6.

36   Evelyn Williams, *Inadmissible Evidence: The Story of the African-American Trial Lawyer Who Defended the Black Liberation Army* (New York: Lawrence Hill, 1993), 74.

37   "1 Panther Killed, Another Imprisoned," *Guardian*, May 16, 1973, 17.

38   Lennox Hinds, "Foreword," in *Assata*, xi.

39   Michael Kaufman, "Slaying of One of the Last Black Liberation Army Leaders Still at Large Ended a 7-Month Manhunt," *New York Times*, November 14, 1973, L-10

40   Ibid.; Williams, *Inadmissible Evidence*, 109; Owadi, "The Saga of Twyman Myers," *New Afrikan Freedom Fighters* 1, no. 1 (June 1982): 8.

41   Williams, *Inadmissible Evidence*, 171.

42   "To: The Black Community and the Black Movement, Special Communique (Joanne Chesimard), From: Coordinating Committee, B.L.A., Subject Freeing of Sister Assata Shakur on 2 November 79," *Breakthrough: Political Journal of the Prairie Fire Organizing Committee* 4, no. 1 (Winter 1980): 12.

43   Assata Shakur, "Statement from Assata Shakur," *Breakthrough: Political Journal of the Prairie Fire Organizing Committee* 4, no. 1 (Winter 1980): 13–15.

44   "A Chronology of Key Events, 1979–1982," *New Afrikan Freedom Fighter* 2, no.1 (1983): 6; John Castelluci, *The Big Dance: The Untold Story of Kathy Boudin and the Terrorist Family That Committed the Brinks Robbery Murders* (New York: Dodd, Mead, 1986), 3–21.

45   Black Liberation Army communiqué, "On Strategic Alliance of the Armed Military Forces of the Revolutionary Nationalist and Anti-Imperialist Movement," in *America, the Nation-State: The Politics of the United States from a State-Building Perspective*, ed. Imari Abubakari Obadele (Baton Rogue: The Malcolm Generation, 1998), 423.

46 "Freedom Fighters: Profiles of Struggle," *New Afrikan Freedom Fighter* 2, no. 1 (1983): 8. This article profiles BLA soldiers Sekou Odinga and Kuwasi Balagoon and RATF members Judy Clark and David Gilbert. It is an indication of the varied political perspectives in this armed alliance.

47 Black Liberation Army, "On Strategic Alliance," 423.

48 LeBlanc-Ernest, "The Most Qualified Person to Handle the Job," 305; Johnson, "Explaining the Demise of the Black Panther Party," 407; Cleaver, "Back to Africa," 239.

49 Dhoruba Bin Wahad, "War Within: Prison Interview," in *Still Black, Still Strong*, 13; Muntaqim, *On the Black Liberation Army*, 4; Acoli, *Sundiata Acoli's Brinks Trial Testimony*, 21.

50 Ji-Jaga interview with author (September 14, 1998).

Drifting from the Mainstream: A Chronicle of Early Anti-rape Organizing and WASP

Nikki Craft

1972–1975

New information was surfacing within the women's movement about the myths surrounding rape. Women were beginning to discuss rape in feminist consciousness-raising groups. For the first time women could benefit from the experience and knowledge of other women. Susan Brownmiller's eloquent historical analysis in *Against Our Will: Men, Women and Rape*, Diana Russell's *The Politics of Rape*, and Medea and Thompson's *Against Rape* laid the foundation for the changes that would sweep the country in the next decade.

Consciousness Raising

A small group of Dallas women left their consciousness-raising group[1] and began to organize specifically around the issue of rape. Each woman in the group, including myself, had been raped at one time in her life. Each was tired of talking about it and wanted to act. None of us were exactly sure of what to do. We began by educating ourselves. Part of that educational process was attending an anti-rape conference in Austin, Texas. It would change our lives.

Hundreds of women had come from across the country to convey their individual experiences about rape. We stood dumbfounded as, one after another, women went before the microphone sharing all-too-similar accounts. Women spoke of their interactions with the police, with doctors, judges, juries, and lawyers. Repeatedly they encountered hostile, insensitive, and blatantly suspicious questioning by the agencies appointed to uphold the "law and order." They spoke of being double victims, first by their rapist, and then by a judicial system secure in its two hundred years of patriarchal justice. Many women found the aftermath of their rape to be more traumatic and painful than the rape itself. We began to see rape not as a sexual crime but as a political crime against women.

The experiences gained from psychological humiliation to horrifying accounts of brutal torture. Several women showed gashes from knife wounds and scars from gunshots. As the hours wore on it became apparent that the scars pierced deeper than our flesh.

One woman cried for fifteen minutes before the microphone as other women held and comforted her. Finally she managed to calmly state, "During the whole rape I wondered: How can this man hate me so much without even knowing who I am? I am afraid of all men now. I am afraid to walk the streets. I am afraid to be alone in my apartment. I am afraid to be."

There were many tears that weekend, and then our tears turned to rage. There would be no more years of silent anger, guilt, anguish, and fear; no more acceptance that this is the way it must be. No longer would we exist in isolated cages being forced to deal with rape unprepared until the moment of crisis. There would be no more willing victims. There would be no turning back for us. *We must fight together or be attacked alone*" became our battle cry. We knew our only alternative was for all women to join in a common defense against male terrorism.

We were living in a state of siege, moving about in a war zone. Though no official declaration had been signed, statistics proved we were open to attack on all fronts: in our bedrooms, our cars, at bus stops, in our marriages, alleyways, in elevators. The wartime curfew had been set. Women were to be off the streets at sunset.

So much was still to be done. We realized that women must work at every level. We needed new laws. We needed new attitudes about sexuality. We needed the most fundamental changes in our culture. At the time however, the most crucial need was to open our communication with other victims of rape. Our group established a brief alliance with the newly formed Dallas Women Against Rape (DWAR). Their goal as a volunteer agency was to provide counseling and support for victims of sexual violence.

Working within the System

The phones began to ring; one woman after another called in. There were women who needed protection from their husbands because the police would not intervene; and women who needed companionship as they went through the ordeal at the hospital. There were those who needed to talk about rapes that had happened years before and others who had been raped only hours before. One woman called *minutes* after a rapist had left her house. She did not want to go to the police but only wanted to go to a place where she could feel safe. (Dear God, I thought, there is nowhere for us to be really safe. But I did not tell her that.)

There was a seminar held with the Dallas Police Department, an effort to sensitize the police officers and change their methods of dealing with rape victims. The officers surely learned something, but I am sure we must have learned more. We discovered how little progress the anti-rape movement had made. Our optimistic enthusiasm dwindled with the realization that we had underestimated the task before us. This would be a movement years in the making; a lifetime commitment.

We began to wonder how long we could continue counseling women who had been victims of male rage. We were exhausting ourselves doing what women have traditionally done, volunteering our time, our energy, and our lives to apply band-aids to a system that required major reconstructive surgery.

There were weekly meetings that drained our energy. There were personality conflicts and trivial infighting over issues which blinded us from seeing our committed goal. And as always there were financial strains. Where would we get our money? From individuals? From foundations? Or would we be co-opted into a county-run, county-funded, nonpolitical social service agency? The more establishment-oriented faction of DWAR began to hint that being too vocal in our criticism of the police might hamper our ability to get funding. This began the first rumblings of what was to end in a major split within DWAR.

Women Armed for Self-Protection shooting practice outside of Dallas, Texas, 1975. Credit: Nikki Craft.

Falling from Grace

We were young and naive. We were primarily politically oriented and made better activists than counselors, but we were learning. Several of us had never worked within a group and it was difficult for all involved. We were dogmatic and arrogant. We had no patience; the task ahead was too awesome and urgent. We were overflowing with anger, and

DWAR no longer met our needs. In retrospect, the group was probably relieved when we packed up one evening and left their organization.

A Walk on the Wild Side

Suddenly we were individuals; six women, free to move, unhampered by the burdensome group process that existed at DWAR. We were excited. We were as angry as we could have been and survived it. We contemplated retaliation. There are some violent offenders who do not realize how close they did come to dying.

We had all-night brainstorming sessions. Our plan was to seek out less traditional avenues of expression where we would perhaps work more effectively. The sky was the limit. In a world where we saw no justice, it was no longer useful to restrict our work to the confines of the law. We were infiltrated by the police. Our phones were tapped, our houses invaded, and a few threats were made against our lives.

Our split from DWAR; our impatience and anger, the realizations we had come to, separated and isolated us from many of Dallas's liberal and academic women, who exerted lots of control over the larger women's movements.

The more isolated we were, the more radical we became. We sensed our own power. We began learning to use guns. We fantasized and even planned how to accomplish actual justice against men who violently abused women with impunity and tacit protection from the police, law enforcement, and the courts. At that time no sex offenders were even identified, and in the court it was most often women put on trial instead of the perpetrator. When it came to rape, in the '70s discussions of "rights" and protections were reserved for violent offenders, not so for victims. It was infuriating. We became WASP—Women Armed for Self-Protection—and we were willing to kill rapists before they killed us.

Our first leaflet ended:

WE ARE WOMEN ... WE ARE ARMED. WE REPEAT ... WE ARE WASP.
WE ARE PREPARED TO STING.
WE SUPPORT IMMEDIATE AND DRASTIC RETALIATION AGAINST
ALL RAPISTS.

In Texas the right to bear arms is not only a constitutional one, but it's a God-given one. This applies to everyone except blacks and women. The authorities were none too pleased to have angry feminists advising women to arm themselves. Many women already had guns— we advised them to learn how to use them. "Women must perceive themselves as being worth defending. In a life threatening situation there must be no hesitation to pull the trigger," read our statement of purpose. Police intelligence officers began paying "friendly" visits to our instructors and friends, our phones were tapped. Paranoia set in. Were there infiltrators among us?[2] We drifted even further from the mainstream.

Posters appeared in Dallas reading, "*Men and women were created equal ... and Smith & Wesson makes damn sure it stays that way.*" A woman was depicted in a militant stance with rifle resting across her chest. Graffiti appeared on the side of a building at a busy intersection reading, "*Women—castrate your rapist—let him know women don't enjoy being raped.*"

We urged lawyers to refuse to defend rapists as an expression of solidarity with women. We publicly praised women who had killed rapists in self-defense or even after the fact, as in the case of Inez García.

Amid much criticism we began getting letters of support from women across the country. Many women were ready for defiance. They wanted to channel their anger and were ready to hear what we had to say, even if it was rhetorical and rigid. Four women came from Chicago to meet with us, share ideas, and discuss strategy. National communication became important. A network began that would be used in actions over the next seven years.

In the end of 1974, in addition to arms training we began observing at rape trials. During these trials another important coalition was formed. We brought reporters and journalists into the courtrooms. This resulted in local and national publicity.

Fear and Loathing in America's Courts

We always knew the judicial system and media would not protect women. We would have to do it ourselves. In addition to arms training and media outreach, we produced ten thousand leaflets targeting in particular a brutal rapist who had walked free while the survivor suffered. We included his address, place of employment, facts of the trial, side and frontal photographs of him that we had secretly taken outside the courtroom, and educational statements about rape and our society. The leaflet was headed, *"This leaflet is not an accusation of guilt. It is a warning to all women of a possible threat to their safety."*

We worked diligently to make the leaflets accurate. We felt it our personal responsibility for legal as well as moral reasons. We leafleted his neighborhood and place of employment. We discovered that his employer knew nothing of the charges or the trial. Within the week he was fired from the job he had held for over ten years.[3]

Burning Old Newspapers

This was WASP's last action, then we disbanded. We were badly in need of rest. We isolated ourselves due to a long combination of factors; emotional hurt, police infiltration, fear of retaliation from rapists, all combined with burnout, had made us painfully rigid to ourselves and others. Inflexibility was making us unable to see new, more creative approaches.

Our goal had never been to build an institution. When WASP ceased to meet our needs, we dissolved the group as fast as we had created it.

We moved into a period of inactivity—a time for reflection. We took with us the experiences that will last for lifetimes and skills that would be invaluable in future work. We took with us feelings of power, accomplishment, and pride that made us each stronger. We have even given other women a bit of that strength and excitement. I see it glimmering in their eyes, as we sit, years later, talking of those times over coffee, burning wood and old newspapers.

Notes

This is edited from a longer essay originally written circa 1979 about Women Armed for Self-Protection (WASP), cofounded and organized by Nikki Craft and other women in the early 1970s in Dallas, Texas. Nikki Craft, "Drifting from the Mainstream: A Chronicle of Early Anti-Rape Organizing," http://www.nostatusquo.com/ACLU/Porn/WASP1.html, accessed June 28, 2017.

1   Consciousness-raising is a form of activism popularized by U.S. feminists in the late 1960s and early '70s. A group of people focus attention on some cause or condition and personally discuss it from different perspectives.
2   WASP was infiltrated and under intense surveillance by the Dallas Police Dept. Their most provocative poster was put together by one of the informants.

3   The success of this action eventually led to the Kitty Genovese Women's Project, a group of women who posed as sociology students under the pretense of doing "statistical study on violent crimes" and compiled, precomputer, the names of every indicted sex offender in Dallas County from 1960 to 1976. A year later the Kitty Genovese Women's Project distributed throughout Dallas over twenty thousand copies of a newspaper that contained news articles, personal accounts of rape, and the list of over 2,100 men indicted for sex-related offenses over the sixteen-year period. "Exposing the Rapist Next Door," *Seven Days*, April 25, 1977, http://www.nostatusquo.com/ACLU/Porn/KGWP1.html, accessed June 28, 2017.

Oka Crisis of 1990: Indigenous Armed Self-Defense and Organization in Canada

Gord Hill

> The people are convinced that they're right. They have a certain patriotism. Unfortunately, they are tossing aside the rules of our white governments. They're in a vicious circle. As long as we don't recognize them as a nation with their own protective force, we can't accept that they can bear military arms. But as long as they don't possess military arms, they will not be able to affirm their rights as a nation.
> —Canadian Forces soldier, quoted in *People of the Pines*[1]

Oka 1990

One of the most significant acts of armed self-defence in Canada by Indigenous peoples occurred during 1990 in the Mohawk territories of Kanehsatake and Kahnawake in the province of Québec. It became known as the "Oka Crisis." Oka had a significant impact on Indigenous social movements across the country, and set the tone for Indigenous resistance throughout the 1990s and to this day.

Oka is a small town located 53 km west of Montréal, Québec. It is next to Kanehsatake, a Mohawk reserve territory with a population of around 1,400. In 1989, the mayor of Oka announced plans to expand a nine-hole golf course and build a condominium project on land claimed by the Mohawks, threatening the last pine trees in the area.

For nearly a year, Mohawks and non-Native people from Oka protested, rallied and signed petitions. Runners were sent from Kanehsatake to other Mohawk communities requesting assistance, but in the end only the Warrior Societies responded by sending clothing, equipment, and personnel.

In the early spring of 1990, a small cabin was built on a hardly used dirt road running through the pines. After one attempt to raid the blockade was called off, the Québec provincial police (Sûreté du Québec, the SQ) organized a large, military-style raid involving over one hundred riot cops, as well as heavily armed tactical units.

The raid was carried out on July 11, 1990, beginning at just after 5:00 a.m. The police approached the blockade and demanded that it be dismantled. Later in the morning they fired tear gas and a short firefight erupted. One police officer was shot and killed (Cpl. Marcel Lemay, a thirty-one-year-old), and the police retreated, abandoning several of their vehicles. These were then used to build barricades as the Mohawks began reinforcing their defensive positions.

Shortly after the failed police raid at Kanehsatake, armed Mohawks in Kahnawake, another reserve territory located near Montréal, blocked the Mercier Bridge, a vital commuter link to the city from the surrounding suburbs.

That night, more warriors clandestinely entered the Pines despite SQ checkpoints that sealed off the area. Most warriors spent the night on patrol or positioned at bunkers and barricades. In the following days and weeks as many as two thousand police from the SQ and the Royal Canadian Mounted Police (RCMP, Canada's national police force) were deployed to both Kanehsatake and Kahnawake. The state's primary role was to contain the armed warriors and to control racist white settlers rioting in a suburb of Montréal called Châteauguay due to the blockade of the Mercier Bridge.

The next day, soldiers from the Royal 22e Regiment were secretly dispatched to Oka and Kahnawake. Police and political officials had been clearly caught off guard by the Mohawk armed resistance. A top-level aide to Premier Bourassa explained their problem: "It was an armed insurrection.... We didn't know what was next. Our police had been defeated and all we heard about was roaming Mohawks with guns. We thought this could be our version of hell—the city shut down, the police in retreat, and the Mohawks standing on top of police cars with their AK-47s held high above their heads."[2]

The Mohawks had a list of demands, including title to the disputed land, withdrawal of police from all Mohawk territories, a forty-eight-hour period of free movement in and out of Kahnawake and Kanehsatake, and the referral of all disputes arising from the conflict to the World Court at The Hague.

The Mohawks also had three preconditions for any further negotiations: free access to food, unhindered access to clan mothers and spiritual advisors, and the posting of international human rights observers. Both the federal and provincial governments rejected these demands. Despite condemning the warriors as thugs and terrorists, government officials continued to meet with senior Mohawk warriors at a Montréal hotel.

Kahnawake: Organized Community Resistance

In Kahnawake, the crisis brought all community factions together in a unified defence. Self-organization within the community included communications, distribution of food, medical supplies, and gasoline. The community radio station, CKRK, became a key communications center and source of info. Even the warriors on barricade duty were fed and informed. According to one firsthand account, "The media task force also sent runners out in shifts to all the barricades and distributed copies of press releases to the *Rotiskenrahkete* (warriors). These reports contained daily news ... [so] people on the barricades did not feel left out and isolated from the rest of the community."[3]

At first, there was little organization of barricades at Kahnawake. Once shifts and schedules were made, the situation improved. Kahnawake military veterans were requested to help, as many young warriors did not know how to build bunkers or conduct patrols.

Squads of five men with squad leaders were organized. At the peak of organizing, warriors had two squad leaders and as many as forty warriors per shift at each highway checkpoint. As support for the barricades grew, up to six hundred people took turns on duty. Many Mohawks serving in the U.S. or Canadian military requested leave and returned home to assist in defensive operations on the territory.

Kahnawake served as a main rally point for warriors. In mid-July, a request for assistance wampum was sent to Oneidas in Ontario (the closest allies to the Mohawks). About a hundred Oneida warriors from Ontario, New York, and Wisconsin arrived. Most stayed at Kahnawake, while some joined Kanehsatake.

Altogether, there were fourteen bunkers and barricades at Kahnawake. Bunkers were placed on either side of road barricades to better defend them. Around bunkers and in areas where enemy forces could flank them, booby traps including punji sticks and fish-hooks were placed. Other bunkers were used as decoys. Later in the summer, a series of tank trap trenches were dug near barricades to deter armoured personnel carriers. Another tactic used by warriors was placing fake explosive charges and wiring on the Mercier Bridge, making it appear as if it was rigged to explode should police (or later the military) attempt to retake it by force.

There were an estimated six hundred guns in Mohawk hands at Kahnawake (this number is the same given for how many armed war-riors were involved), including AK-47s, hunting rifles, shotguns, pistols, and a .50 calibre semiautomatic. Throughout the summer, warriors also continued to buy weapons, ammo, and equipment. In the third or fourth week of the crisis, for example, a shipment of eighty AK-47s was smuggled into Kahnawake. Although they had only pretended to wire the Mercier Bridge with explosives, the Mohawks could easily have done so using explosives from local construction companies in Kahnawake.

Indigenous Solidarity and Military Deployment

While the sieges at Kanehsatake and Kahnawake were ongoing, and as negotiations continued, the "Oka Crisis" was headline news across the country. The standoff had also generated widespread solidarity actions from Indigenous people across the country, including protests, occu-pations of government buildings, blockades of highways and railroads, and the sabotage of railway bridges and electrical power lines.

Canada faced an Indigenous uprising, and there is little doubt that this widespread solidarity, along with the great potential of Indigenous people to inflict significant disruption of infrastructure (such as highways, railways, and electrical lines), served to limit the use of lethal force by state security forces. On August 20, after a month of ongoing, armed standoff, military personnel formally replaced the police at both Kanehsatake and Kahnawake.

The deployment of troops at Kanehsatake and Kahnawake was labeled Operation Salon, the largest internal military operation in Canadian history. In all, 4,500 soldiers with more than a thousand vehicles, Leopard tanks, Grizzly and M113 APCs, trucks, artillery pieces, and other equipment were deployed (the Fifth Mechanized Infantry Brigade). In addition, there were also helicopters, Aurora surveillance planes, and naval ships on the St. Lawrence Seaway. The military cordoned off and contained the area, conducted patrols, and prepared for a final assault. They also applied slow but constant pressure, including troop advances backed up by Grizzly APCs.

On August 27, after days of frustrated negotiations, Québec Premier Robert Bourassa declared negotiations over and asked the army to dismantle the Mohawk barricades. In Kanehsatake, warriors went to red alert. The next day, civil protection authorities went door-to-door at Oka advising all remaining citizens to evacuate. The Red Cross brought in stretchers and body bags. Two Canadian Forces fighter planes flew over Kahnawake and Kanehsatake in a show of force.

Mohawk Withdrawal

In the afternoon of August 28, some residents of Kahnawake began to evacuate in a convoy of some seventy vehicles, mostly women, children, and elders. They used the north exit near the Mercier Bridge, but were detained by the SQ, who searched every vehicle, and delayed them for over two hours. In the meantime, local radio stations (including Montréal's CJMS) broadcast the location of the convoy. By the time the convoy was underway, a mob of over five hundred white people had gathered. They began throwing rocks at the Mohawk vehicles, smashing windows and injuring persons inside. Although there were approximately thirty to forty police on hand, they made no effort to stop the rock-throwing.[4] One elder, Joe Armstrong (seventy-one years old) was hit in the chest with a large boulder and died one week later of a heart attack.

The next day, Mohawks and soldiers began dismantling the barricades around Kahnawake. Based on agreements with the military, masked and camouflaged warriors who did not carry weapons were not to be arrested. Altogether, it would take a further eight days to dismantle the barricades and reopen the Mercier Bridge.

In early September, the military began advancing on and dismantling barricades in Kanehsatake, using hundreds of troops and armoured vehicles. Along with the warriors were over a dozen media personnel. By September 3, the warriors had retreated to a treatment centre located in Kanehsatake, well stocked with food and resources. The treatment center would be the final defensive position of the warriors until their disengagement at the end of the month, after the military had cut electricity and water.

Raid on Tekakwitha Island

On September 18, soldiers and police raided Tekakwitha Island, a deserted island on the edge of the Kahnawake territory connected by a short bridge. Dozens of troops and SQ landed on the western side of the island by boat and helicopter. As they advanced toward the bridge, hundreds of Mohawks rushed to confront them.

Some thirty soldiers moved to block the bridge by setting up razor wire. Mohawks dismantled the blockade and physically confronted soldiers. The soldiers used rifle butts and fired volleys of tear gas. The Mohawks dispersed and then regrouped. In a second attack, one soldier was beaten semiconscious and others were wounded. Soldiers fired warning shots into the air and pulled back into a defensive position. Reinforcements arrived, and Mohawks were faced with 140 soldiers.

After a seven-hour standoff, eight military Chinook helicopters airlifted the soldiers out. Twenty had been injured. For the Mohawks, there were seventy-five injured, including cuts, bruises, fractures, and tear gas. These included children as young as five, and one elder seventy-two years old. The military claimed to have seized forty-seven weapons from the island, most of them hunting rifles and shotguns.

Following the events of September 18, the military did not attempt another raid into Kahnawake. Lt. Col. Greg Mitchell, a commander of the operation, later stated, "The strong resistance surprised us.... It was amazing the way they reacted.... Next time my men will be equipped with plexiglass shields and face masks."[5]

Warrior Withdrawal

At Kanehsatake, the warriors eventually decided that the time to disengage had come, and on September 26, after lighting a ceremonial fire and burning their weapons, they attempted to walk out. Caught off-guard, the military scrambled to intercept and detain the warriors. Scuffles and fights broke out as armed soldiers attempted to apprehend unarmed warriors. Several warriors escaped, and made it into the town of Oka.

In the months following the siege, scores of Mohawks went to trial on charges ranging from mischief to rioting, obstruction of justice, and weapons charges. In one mass trial, thirty-four defendants were acquitted. The most targeted of the warriors was Lasagna (Ronald Cross), who eventually received four years and four months in jail after being convicted of assault, vandalism, weapons offences, and uttering threats. Most of the others who were convicted of charges received prison sentences of under a year.

New Counterinsurgency Plans

In the aftermath of the armed resistance at Kanehsatake and Kahnawake, internal debates occurred over the use of firearms, which affirmed their use as limited but ultimately necessary.[6]

After the events at Oka/Kanehsatake, military and political researchers made several recommendations. One report, titled *The Legacy of Oka* and published by the right-wing Mackenzie Institute for the Study of Terrorism in 1991, stated that the use of the military had given the warriors a moral victory in the minds of the public. The images of warriors versus soldiers, along with prolonged negotiations, only served to reinforce the view of the Mohawks as sovereign people with the warriors as their defensive force.

The report recommended that in future conflicts, heavily armed police be used quickly with no time for lengthy negotiations. One effect of such a strategy would be to portray the conflict as a criminal matter, as opposed to an insurgency or civil war, thereby "depoliticizing" the resistance. This strategy closely resembles that adopted by the British in Northern Ireland against the Irish Republican Army during the 1970s, during which the guerrillas were portrayed as drug smugglers and petty criminals.

Another recommendation from the Mackenzie Institute was that the government and security forces needed to gain greater control over the media. The media is a primary means of public communication with immense power to frame and shape public perception. At Oka, the media became imbedded among the defenders; on the final day of the siege, there were still ten reporters inside the barricades. Many continued to give reports right up to the final days. Their presence undermined the overall counterinsurgency effort.

Five years later, in the summer of 1995, this new counterinsurgency strategy was used in two separate conflicts with Indigenous peoples. The first occurred in the south-central interior region of BC, in Secwepemc territory. This was another armed standoff that began after an American rancher demanded that a Sun Dance camp be removed from government land that his cattle grazed on. After cowboys from the ranch threatened an elder and his family in the camp, armed warriors arrived to defend the camp, setting into motion a month-long armed standoff near 100 Mile House, BC (known as Ts'Peten, or Big Lake, in Secwepemc, and also referred to as Gustafsen Lake).

Instead of deploying military forces, the BC government deployed some 450 heavily armed cops from the RCMP Emergency Response Teams (ERT). They were provided with military assistance and gear, including nine Bison APCs (along with their crews). In addition, the media were not permitted to enter a restricted zone established by the police, which made it almost impossible for the defenders to publicly communicate their position. Instead, the media simply repeated police information as fact, which was later revealed to be disinformation provided by the RCMP. In the largest paramilitary police operation in Canadian history, the RCMP used explosives to destroy a truck being driven by defenders in an agreed-upon no-shoot zone, initiating an hours-long gun battle, which ended with one of the Bisons being disabled. The next day, RCMP snipers opened fire on an unarmed individual, again moving in a no-shoot zone. The standoff ended in late September when the defenders laid down their arms and were arrested.

In the second confrontation of that summer, heavily armed police with military assistance were deployed to Ipperwash Provincial Park to remove a group of Natives reoccupying their reserve land from which they had been forcibly removed prior to World War II. Their reserve of Stony Point was made into a military base and provincial park. In 1993, they had begun reoccupying a part of the base and, in 1995, expanded it into the park. The Ontario government responded with a large police deployment, which eventually resulted in a tactical police unit opening fire on unarmed defenders, shooting a fifteen-year-old youth, Dudley George, in the back and killing him. Following this conflict, the people of Stony Point remained on the former military base (as they do to this day).

Conclusion

The Oka Crisis of 1990 had a profound effect on Indigenous peoples in Canada and served to revitalize their fighting spirit and warrior traditions. The standoffs that occurred five years later were, in part, a result of the armed resistance at Oka. The resistance influenced and shaped Indigenous struggles from the 1990s to the present. Although the vast majority of confrontations between Indigenous peoples and state security forces are not armed, the armed resistance at Oka served as an inspiring example of Indigenous sovereignty and the necessity of maintaining a warrior force capable of defending and asserting that sovereignty. The image of the masked and camouflaged warrior, along with the iconic Mohawk Warrior flag, continues to be seen, including the recent anti-fracking resistance carried out by Mi'kmaq warriors in New Brunswick, during which six RCMP vehicles were set on fire and destroyed after police raided a blockade. What was especially inspiring about the Oka Crisis was not only that armed warriors confronted police and military forces, but that they also won. To this day, neither the golf course expansion or condominium project has been built.

Notes

1   Geoffrey York and Loreen Pindera, *People of the Pines: The Warriors and the Legacy of Oka* (Toronto: Little, Brown and Company, 1991 [paperback edition, 1992]), 315.

2   Rick Hornung, *One Nation Under the Gun: Inside the Mohawk Civil War* (New York: Pantheon Books, 1992), 205.

3   Donna Goodleaf, *Entering the War Zone: A Mohawk Perspective on Resisting Invasions* (Penticton: Theytus Books, 1995), 125.

4   See the video *Rocks at Whiskey Trench*, Alanis Obamsawin (National Film Board of Canada, 2000).

5   Goodleaf, *Entering the War Zone*, 105.

6   York and Pindera, *People of the Pines*, 420–21.

We Refuse to Die: An Interview with Dennis Banks

scott crow

Ed. note: Dennis Banks, born in 1937, is one of the cofounders of the American Indian Movement (AIM), which grew out of the U.S. social and political struggles for rights and liberation of the 1960s and 1970s. AIM, in addition to its protests and occupations of government buildings for native autonomy, fought for the U.S. government to honor its treaties. AIM chapters across many reservations, inspired by the Black Panther Party, also engaged in creating "survival programs" that included free schools and access to health care, as well as participating in collective armed defense across their communities. This interview, conducted in July 2015, focuses on some of those aspects and histories rather than AIM histories overall.

sc: Were guns common within your family and community when you were growing up as a kid?

DB: Very common. Young kids looked forward to hunting, because there was so much emphasis by the elders about hunting and getting your own meat. You know, getting your first. My grandfather, my father, they all had weapons for hunting; rifles like a .30–06, shotguns, and .22s, which were at that time considered all-around North American game rifles. There's actually ceremonies on the first hunt, and I

American Indian Movement members patrolling during the Wounded Knee standoff with the FBI, 1973. Credit: Wikimedia Commons.

looked forward to that when I was a young kid. Unfortunately I was taken away when I was five to a federal military boarding school, and I lost out on the early ceremonies which proved that you can help provide for the family. I didn't realize what I was going through in the transition of being sent to these boarding schools. But I did miss out on that very important ceremony of becoming part of the family, community rather, and that you'll be called upon to use your rifle for subsistence, for food. Young kids looked to the day when they would own a rifle or a shotgun with great pride.

sc: Do you think the events in your life of growing up largely rural, and hunting and fishing, shaped your interpretation and advocacy of armed self-defense within AIM later?

DB: No, I didn't, because I was raised in this boarding school, and it was a pro–U.S. military, pro-U.S. school, so it never taught us how to hunt. It taught us how to march!

sc/DB: [Laughter]

DB: I think about how ironic they wouldn't teach us how to hunt, and here they were teaching us how to march. And they gave us wooden replicas of rifles to carry them on our shoulders like real weapons.

sc: Of course as part of the larger U.S. machine! Do you think past histories of fighting colonization helped shape AIM's decision to continue to practice when AIM took up arms, as an idea?

DB: Well, we took up arms the moment it happened. We went to the town of Wounded Knee, South Dakota, on February 22, 1973, and we went there only to blockade the traffic and to keep the town of Wounded Knee in our perimeter. There were four roads leading in and out. Most of the people who were in on the blockading were from Wounded Knee itself. Of the two hundred people gathered maybe about twenty of us were not from there. They wanted to barricade so that no federal police official or any kind of official could come to the town. So that's how it started. During the first meeting that evening we heard gunshots. It surprised and startled us that somebody was shooting. All of a sudden AIM security guys come through the door and say, "Somebody's shooting at us out there! What should we do?" And both Russell Means, another AIM leader, and I just turned around and we said, "Shoot back, shoot back!" You know, meaning, don't start the fight but if they shoot at us, then shoot back.

sc: That was the first time that AIM had really thought about taking up arms at all for community defense?

DB: Yes. That was our very first time.

sc: Was AIM influenced by other groups that had taken up arms during that time, like the Black Panther Party or other groups like that?

DB: We were friends with the Black Panthers. We had met Fred Hampton before he was gunned down in Chicago. And we found friendship there in our meetings. The Panthers of course had initiated the police patrols out in Oakland, California. We went over to Oakland to meet with the Panthers because we wanted to see how they were doing the street patrols. So we copied it.[1]

sc: Were there many women in AIM who took up arms also?

DB: Oh, absolutely! I would say about 30 percent of the two hundred warriors that we had out there at Wounded Knee.

sc: When AIM finally had a stance to take up guns was it controversial among the native/indigenous communities for you all to do that?

DB: Oh, no! No, it wasn't. As a matter of fact, some people didn't think we were armed enough!

sc/DB: [Laughter]

DB: I mean, every day at Wounded Knee was gunfighting. The FBI estimated that over five hundred thousand rounds were expended on a gunfight that lasted for seventy-one days! That's from their side, that's how much they used. We couldn't afford to, but we returned fire occasionally. We were not taking this lying down. We were serious about the gunfight. If they come in shooting, then somebody was going to get hurt.

Our guns actually strengthened our positions whenever we went to negotiate at Wounded Knee. The U.S. Marshals said that the U.S. government would never negotiate with a gun pointed at their head, and I responded: "Neither will we!" But the negotiations went on. We finally arrived at a conclusion. They said that they would investigate the wrongdoing of the Bureau of Indian Affairs (BIA) administration.

They would investigate the 1868 treaty to see whether the government has been wrong all these years. And they would look into the illegal practices of the Dickie Wilson regime's nepotism and violence.

You know, we laid down our weapons. The government wanted us to put all our rifles in piles. They were monitoring from a long ways off with binoculars. We started piling up all the rifles standing up in a little, like a teepee shape. But they were mad they got duped on that one. We had about six of those all in a circle like that. So the government thought we were laying down our rifles. That was the plan. We agreed to do that. We would lay down our weapons. During all that day of negotiations, when we knew that we were going to be making the agreements, we came back and got a big bunch of hollow lumber and some black paint. We took two-by-fours and cut 'em into four-foot lengths and painted them all black. We had about six of those all in a circle like that. So the government thought we were putting rifles, you know, laying them down. That was the plan. We agreed to do that. We would lay down our weapons. I left because I didn't have a million dollars for my bond. I was in a small ranch home near Rapid City watching the news media going into Wounded Knee. And here are those marshals and FBI, saw those wooden sticks piled up like that, and they were knocking and kicking them down.

sc/DB: [Laughter]

sc: How was it perceived for AIM to take the position of armed defense by other radical communities?

DB: Well, there was by Gallup Poll, and two questions were asked, "Do you believe in the American Indian Movement's tactics of occupying Wounded Knee as a means of bringing about political change?" And the second question: "Arms have been taken up by members of the American Indian Movement. Do you believe arms are needed to bring about this change?" And in both polls, 71 percent answered "yes"!

sc: That's amazing! You wouldn't get that result now unless it was the right-wing Tea Party taking up arms. You survived the Wounded Knee occupation, then the trials started and things unraveled for AIM in many ways. Did it change AIM's position as seeing community armed self-defense as part of its larger goals of liberation at all?

DB: Oh, no! It was a historic time, 1973, when the battle was taking place. People including fighter Muhammad Ali, actor Marlon Brando, and singer Tony Bennett were on our side coming out of Wounded

Knee and then into the political year that followed. Tony himself is not an advocate for armed insurrection or anything like that, but he said, "I know you guys have to do what you have to do."

sc: After Wounded Knee did AIM ever continue to take up arms as a strategy or as a thought in any of the communities or autonomous AIM chapters?

DB: No. In fact, Russell Means and I realized that politically, at that moment, up against the wall, we had to take that position. But we never encouraged our chapters to try to use armed self-defense as a strategy for getting what you want. It can never work out because it's the U.S. military, they could wipe us out very quickly.

sc: In what years would AIM have said, "We definitely don't want to take up arms"?

DB: Well, it was kind of crafted during the Wounded Knee trial of Russell Means and myself in the mid-1970s. Both Russ and I said we can't be using Wounded Knee tactics to get the U.S. government to the table, because it should never be a point. If it was reversed and if the government used their weapons to push us to the communication table, then we wouldn't want to go. That was our strategy at that time. We told the chapters, "Don't lay your weapons down," and we still have the Second Amendment to the United States Constitution. Don't be throwing away your weapons. You still have to provide for your community; you still have to go hunting. You have subsistence living way up in the northern parts of the United States and into Canada.

sc: Would you, as an indigenous person and as somebody who wants to fight against your people being killed or erased, advocate that communities have a right to defend themselves—not armed takeover of the government—whether there's a U.S. Constitution or not?

DB: Oh yes, we would! Definitely. As a matter of fact, the Eighth Circuit Court of Appeals in Des Moines, Iowa, sided with AIM in a case. In 1975, the FBI had circled one of our encampments in South Dakota and they came in shooting at AIM's camp. All of our people that were there just took a defensive position and began firing back. There were two FBI agents that were killed during that exchange of fire. The jury in the federal court in Cedar Rapids, Iowa, agreed that the native people had a right to defend themselves with arms and allowed the self-defense theory to be used in the first murder trial, when they charged Dino Butler and Bob Robideau of the killing of those two FBI agents.

sc: Interesting. I find that today's gun advocates of the Second Amendment are often whites and their "rights" not necessarily for community defense—especially marginalized people. Most are white men who are afraid that the government is going to take their guns, while they're stockpiling arsenals. To me, they're not our allies necessarily in struggles for liberation, which I would fight for whether there's a U.S. Constitution or not.

DB: There are people who are supporters of ours that are strong believers in the Second Amendment but also strong defenders of self-defense of your home. There's a lot of people I'm sure that would not think of community armed defense, but they believe in the protection of our homes.

sc: There's First Nation communities in Canada that are still practicing community armed self-defense today along with blockades and uprisings. Could you see anything like that reemerging in the United States?

DB: I think it will happen. You go to protection of your home and you go to the next level, then it's protection of your community. I'd say yes, of course, it will go to the next level.

sc: Would you have any advice for younger generations that may take up these ideas from any of the lessons that you've learned and the reflections over your years?

DB: I think they should take it up with the very clear thought of what's the reality of the outcome; what's the reality of even just discussing it. I'm sure that pretty soon we're going to have laws where you may not be able to discuss taking up arms for the community. That's going to be a very bad time. When and if that ever happens, then I think insurrection against those kinds of restrictive policies will happen.

sc: Do you believe that taking up armed self-defense at Wounded Knee kept AIM and its supporters in the communities from being slaughtered? Would you do it differently now?

DB: Yes, it did. You know, when push comes to shove I want our people to be ready. I'm sure it will happen again.

Notes

1   Brianna Wilson, "AIM Patrol, Minneapolis," *MNOpedia*, December 28, 2016, http://www.mnopedia.org/group/aim-patrol-minneapolis, accessed June 28, 2017.

Ampo Camp and the American Indian Movement: Native Resistance in the U.S. Pacific Northwest

Michele Rene Weston

Being involved with AIM put me under fire from hostile forces including being targeted by the U.S. government and other white supremacist organizations. We were on the defensive from weapons aimed at us or shot around us, helicopters overhead, and constant raids. All of our stories and perspectives should be told, and this one is just my little experience of armed self-defense when under that kind of aggression in the 1990s.

The American Indian Movement is a civil rights organization formed to protect indigenous sovereignty on Turtle Island (North America). The group formed only decades ago, but is one arm of five hundred years of native resistance to colonial oppression. This and other indigenous rights organizations continue to be under fire, not because AIM is armed, but because colonialism depends on the control of other peoples and the exploitation of their resources.

Colonialism continues as long as there are still native resources to exploit, the war will continue. It now looks more like a war of attrition,[1] not just gunfights. The native culture is under attack as part of the colonial strategy, so any single practice of culture is a successful defense against that attack. Being armed is, of itself, a cultural practice in indigenous culture, so staying armed is sustaining the culture.

Therefore, I advocate that armed self-defense helps to achieve one of AIM's goals of cultural self-determination. We've always been armed. We should stay armed. We should stay dancing the dances, singing the songs, eating the food, speaking the language, and we should stay on the land and continue the culture in the way that we decide for ourselves.

From the time that Indian civil rights started getting national attention in the early 1970s members of our family have been supportive of AIM. My Granny Dean has been a staunch supporter of Indian rights and AIM from the beginning. Do *not* say the name Andrew Jackson in her home! My Uncle Rusty fought on the front lines for the right to practice religion in federal prison. I fell into AIM quite naturally, really, or some say that I was captured. Here's my story.

Captured by Indians

After a tribal law class one evening in the mid-1990s, I was talking to my professor about a paper I was presenting to a colloquium on the recent Supreme Court decision denying the First Amendment freedom of religious rights of native elder Al Smith to use peyote in ceremony.[2] That's when I was approached (or maybe captured) by some AIMsters from South Dakota and Oregon.[3]

Two guys with braids and bandanas asked me a few questions about my paper, then asked if I'd like to go meet Al Smith to discuss the case with him before I published it. I got into their car the next day. We went to interview Al Smith and many other elders for various legal cases, documenting their testimony about use of sacred sites, artifacts, ceremonies, burial sites, and other things of cultural significance.

The day after I met the AIMsters, two men in suits knocked on my door and introduced themselves as the FBI. From then on, it sounded as if the house phone was tapped from clicks on the old landline that we never had before.

Almost daily there were cases and battles to be fought. Most of them in boardrooms, courthouses, private offices, and public rallies. We met with hospital administration when native youths were mistreated, sought injunction against clear-cutting a sacred site, talked to university leaders about renaming buildings that were named for Indian killers. We were very active with the Willamette Valley Sacred Sites Preservation Committee about native bones found in road and dam excavations. We supported the Kalapooia Sacred Circle Alliance, for the return of their bones from the University of Oregon. Everything that AIM and other activists went to Washington in 1972 to try to protect, the fights continued to practice cultural sovereignty, which was vehemently under attack in certain areas. Rights to religion were being denied, rights to keep foster and adoptive children within the family or tribe, rights in criminal law, rights to our own bodies against sexual assault. Fights on every level. We showed up in solidarity with all these local battles.

We took elders to the sacred places, drove them to court, to meetings, all over. I never went anywhere alone. I had a bodyguard. They always joked that they captured me. I'm not sure now whether that wasn't true. I was certainly captivated. Although everywhere I went with different people of different tribes and organizations and movements almost all were AIM supporters or members, I was never involved in a campaign that was organized officially by AIM. The Sun Dance camp was held by Warm Springs tribes (Wasco and Paiute). By then there were second-generation kids of the blend of the Plains refugees and the local tribes. AIM was fluid and autonomous by then through all regions. There are local official chapters of AIM and autonomous chapters of AIM, but many individual AIM members also live and work with independent campaigns. Just keeping cultural traditions going within the family takes active resistance.

During those days most campaigns were not officially sanctioned by AIM but tended to bow to local sovereignty and locals. This is how I see AIM existing beyond the organization from the northern plains where we grew up.[4] AIMsters were on constant move to support local battles to save their sacred things. I would be at some obscure powwow in some small northwestern town in and then hear the "AIM song" start on the drum.[5] I teared up witnessing people coming out of the woodwork to stand behind the drum and proudly sing that song. Most of the tactics used by the movement don't involve arms; they involve maintaining cultural norms. Attending ceremony, singing the songs, eating the food, dressing the dress, and speaking the language were the most important things that they talked about, not the use of weapons.

It was a hard fight to maintain cultural norms, as I will explain, when even ancestors' bones are under attack. The sacred areas are being destroyed, ceremonies are illegal, there are high rates of poverty and human trafficking into nonnative sex industries. For some of them, keeping their families together, or even just getting up and being themselves was revolutionary.

Ampo Camp

We did carry arms when we were up in the mountains, at Ampo Camp, up on Wy'East (Mount Hood). Ampo Camp, named from Lakota traditions, was a religious camp on land that belongs to the Warm Springs Tribes where the local tribes have been having sacred religious ceremonies for literally thousands of years. The ceremonial area on Wy'East is tribal land but considered federal land.

Up past Government Camp a ways, without meeting any more cars, there's a couple of dirt roads to get to Ampo Camp.[6] Every single time we got to that part of the mountain, we would be followed. They'd almost always come out of the same side road. I felt intimidated. No wonder the Indian community members would never let anyone go anywhere alone.

The men who followed us were part of a white separatist paramilitary training camp just down the hill from Ampo Camp. They conducted training exercises even after dark, when it was illegal to shoot guns, even in hunting season. Regardless, they were allowed to operate their automatic weapons throughout the night almost every night. We would hear the cracks of bullets hitting the trees above our heads and around us, and see the red laser dots of their riflescopes reflect on the trees in the dark. It was too close for comfort.

Conversely, if a native from Ampo Camp did anything illegal, they were arrested immediately. Vehicles were often pulled over and the whole load taken to jail for minor violations. We often traveled separately but never alone. I remember one of the times when federal law enforcement blocked our food supply, some of our hunters killed an elk, but it was one day early for hunting season, so they were hauled off to jail for poaching.[7] Elk is the spirit food to the Warm Springs tribes. Ampo Camp, being a religious healing center, often housed elders who were on special diets and medicinal treatment; blocking the food supply and hauling off caretakers was especially risky to their health.

We always slept with our rifles under the sleeping bags, our keys in our jean pockets, and our shoes by the door; ready to leap out at any minute. Between the military, law enforcement, and the white militias around us, we never knew whether they were going to storm up the hill some night. We were under constant gunfire at night. Sitting by the campfire we'd hear the occasional close bullet whizzing over our heads or crack against the trees above us. Once the bullets did get close enough that our AIM security team returned fire, thinking they were getting shot at. Several volleys were fired back and forth, but they stopped and no one was hurt.

Several times our security teams found empty federal ATVs parked outside of our perimeters. Where were the agents if their vehicles were empty, and what were they doing? Another time when we were raided by federal law enforcement, I threw a new car battery into a vehicle loaded with women and children to get out of there.

There was local hostility all over the Pacific Northwest region. Nonnative fishers were very hostile toward tribal sovereignty, in part because some fishing rights had been returned to the natives, and the fights against federal timber sales on sacred land also angered loggers. We knew that some of these white paramilitary guys had it in them to kill an Indian. The environment was undeniably one of fear and intimidation within our peaceful religious camp, a place of sacred beauty and reverence.

Our security team kept a checkpoint by the gate down below taking turns watching and doing other duties largely unnoticed. There weren't armed people around the ceremonial area. In my times there I wasn't aware of any women on the security team, but I was handed a weapon at times and given instructions for how to protect myself and those around me. Everyone, it seemed, was responsible for security, and one of the best was a wife of a chief and a respected grandma who brought the Sun Dance to Wy'East.[8] She could hear a suspicious radio through the trees and jumped right on top of it. Security teams reported to the chief, but the chief of security and chief of the Sun Dance and all the chiefs were accountable to the elders.

Part of the security strategy included allowing a camp of nonnative environmental activists, mostly from Earth First![9] The media attention they attracted to forestry issues and their commitment to nonviolence made it hard for the local white militants to justify a direct violent attack on the Indian compound. The "hippies" weren't allowed to camp in the ceremonial area with us, but their support and solidarity with our camps was felt and appreciated.

Sun Dance

The Sun Dance practice has been under attack due to colonialism. Its religious practice is still an act of resistance. It began on the Northern Plains but spread across Turtle Island in the past 150 years. The ceremony was suppressed and made illegal by U.S. and Canadian governments as part of the overall strategy of cultural genocide in the early twentieth century. This religion, a cornerstone of Indian culture, went underground and continues to this day. It has come to provide spiritual support for the warriors and nations of people in daily life.

Many AIM members were Sun Dancers and spread the religion further in the 1970s after the siege at Wounded Knee in South Dakota.[10] After the siege, dozens of AIM members and supporters were brutally murdered back in South Dakota. The threat of jail or murder loomed, and many activists fled the violence to the Pacific Northwest and to support other local causes on a more widespread level. My grandparents, who were at Wounded Knee immediately after the siege in '73, told me that the trauma was so great in people's faces that there were no words to express that pain, and they felt powerless to help the local survivors.

So added to the hostile environment toward native rights locally during the 1990s was this black cloud of pain and anguish from what happened twenty years earlier. We were extremely careful. That trauma was still palpable and informed their current actions. When native people raised arms at Wounded Knee, that was also in self-defense knowing that doing anything for Indian rights could be risky.

There was always an air of hope around the Sun Dance, because at least you could hold onto your religion, even if you've lost everything else. It was something positive that the young native warriors, who have a higher chance of getting shot by police than black men, could do to keep them out of trouble in the cities. They would help take care of the elders, help prepare food in the traditional way, wake up with the sun in song, sweat in the sweat lodge, hunt, chop wood, and provide security.

Sun Dance camp was also a place where young native women could be protected from predators. Tribal courts at that time couldn't even prosecute domestic violence charges against nonnatives, who are the perpetrators in eight or nine out of ten assaults. Holding ceremony at these safe places is even more important to the culture.

Self-Defense

Natives have always been armed. Nations of hunter-gatherers, warriors, even farming tribes have traditionally carried weapons for hunting and self-defense. You can't imagine a line of braves on horseback at the top of the hill without any weapons. Hunting especially is part of our culture. It's a connection to animals and ecosystems that's a sustainable way of life. To put down our weapons is submission of culture and to carry them validates our autonomy, even to our way of economics.

Rural lifestyle, in general, utilizes weapons as tools, along with any other tool in the shed. Women in my family have also been encouraged to bear arms. My grandmothers always had rifles in their country homes, and Granny Dean carried her .38 pistol until her stroke late in life.

We were armed way before Columbus arrived. The tactic to discuss in resistance strategy meetings wasn't whether to take up arms against the colonizers, but whether to lay them down and give up our culture. A lot of people tried that already, and you could argue that it hasn't always worked, especially for women. Our "resources," women, and children just get stolen faster and easier by settlers, governments, and later corporations. When the "discoverers" arrived, that's when resistance began, and the need for self-defense grew.

Indigenous women face 2.5 times the rate of assault of any other group and up to ten times the murder rate. Tribal courts still can't prosecute felony rape or murder. These assaults go largely unpenalized. Federal charges have to be filed in cities, sometimes hours away. Who's going to protect native women if we don't do it ourselves? Our native men are mostly bound. They try to be escorts and to teach their daughters and nieces self-defense. There's no congressional representation for reservations; federal court precedent doesn't uphold the Bill of Rights for individual tribal members; the UN won't interfere with Canada and U.S. policy toward domestic nations, but they do criticize Canada and the U.S. for the inequality of justice for indigenous women, especially for the disappeared and murdered.[11]

The inhumane treatment of indigenous women is part of the practice of colonialism. The theft of natural resources and the rape and pollution of the land go hand in hand with the rape and trafficking of the women of that land. That is very clearly seen in the oilfields and operations of mineral extraction where some of that land hasn't been ceded. They clear the forests and stick their drills in without consent.

"Man camps" of workers at these sites pop up and become hubs of human trafficking, violence, and crime. There are huge problems now surrounding the Bakken oilfields.

We have to defend ourselves, with arms if necessary, and it seems necessary. For all those stories of survival, there are also many stories of successful self-defense. One more thing about the colonization of indigenous women is that most of our tribes are matriarchal—culturally and economically. In the Southeast, where my grandparents are from, women owned the homes and the property. Children lived with the women's family and identified with their mother's clan. Patriarchy is new here. The need for feminism is new also. No longer could the women give away their farm goods to the community. The application of capitalism on a communal economy is part of the colonization of native women and of the whole of their nations. The uprooting of our economies through forcing private property and commodifying our natural resources may be the biggest force of destruction of native cultures. Cracking women's culture is how the colonists were able to attack the economic culture of matriarchal systems.

For my grandmother, having to be a feminist is part of being Indian and maintaining our cultural tradition. You could call her, and me, an intersectional anti-capitalist ecofeminist, but she would just give you that eye. She would tell you she's just Indian. There's no intersection, it's who we are, and we must be free to choose that. Individual Indian woman's sovereignty is tribal sovereignty. Feminism isn't new or radical here on Turtle Island. It's traditional.

Up and down the Willamette Valley, activists within these groups were both women and men, but mostly women, like Kalapooia activist Carol Logan. There were grandmothers behind everyone who people went to for consent and guidance, though. As a young college woman, it impressed me that every time anyone organized a demonstration or took any action, they always met with the grandmas; even some of these veteran braves who have counted coup had to go ask grandma before doing anything of relevance.[12] Even I had to run the gauntlet of grandmas to get accepted into the community in the Pacific Northwest.

Reflections on Survival and Liberation

There's been an outright war to destroy native cultures here that continues to serve modern colonialism today. It's easier to steal resources if one can pretend that there's no culture there and the people don't exist. Ongoing systematic destruction of native sacred areas and attacks on native ceremonies, federal unrecognition of tribes, limits on tribal legal jurisdiction, and the extraordinary high rate of violence against native women by nonnative perpetrators prove that these methods of colonialism are still working today. It's been an ongoing war of attrition over sovereignty. There's legal warfare, cultural warfare, and physical warfare.

I would argue that personal self-defense and defense of small groups are the main reason that AIMsters carried firearms. When they did go on the offensive, they were armed with lawyers and cameras, bullhorns and petitions, some tobacco, sage, and maybe some sacred eagle feathers. I could comment on the warrior culture of the Northern Plains tribes where AIM sprouted up and how important arms are especially to that specific culture. My grandparents are from southern tribes who feared the Lakota and northern tribes. I might be biased to say that they brandished their weapons in warrior pride. We have this old image of the Pawnees and Wichita and other tribal members, especially young women, being captured by them. I guess it still happens in the '90s. Our family was not a part of that warrior culture, but all of us were armed. That may have played a part of their armed strategy in the '70s, but, by the '90s, the warriors were waging battles from the back of the lines and on different battlefields.

I would also argue that their tactic of armed self-defense has been successful on many levels, if you measure success by survival. The movement has yet to be successful at ending colonialism, but cultures survive. Cultural practices, like carrying weapons, continue in native communities. Whether its joining the round dance, or sweat lodge, using the peyote stitch in bead work, smudging yourself in the mornings, or carrying your weapon, every cultural practice that we can continue is important when the ultimate goal is cultural autonomy.

That's what works for us, works for the native population, because that's the way it is. Groups should be armed if that's their culture. I appreciated the coordination of other groups that did not bear arms. The fact is that our tactics are different, yet we benefit from each other's use of tactics. Having different tactics, according to each culture, but working in coordination has been the best strategy for both groups. We exist in a multicultural society. Respecting diversity and sovereignty is paramount to exist together peacefully in this world.

Notes

1   There are many tribes, including the Inde (Apache), Yavapai, Winnemem Wintu, Blackfeet Nation, Sicangu of the Rosebud Sioux, Dineh (Navaho), Hopi, Western Shoshone, and an alliance of indigenous of the Puget Sound region, for example, that are in continuing battles within Indian Country in what is now called the U.S. to maintain sovereignty over colonial interests that include resource extractions, disputed claims over stolen land and fishing waters, and destruction of sacred burial grounds.

2   Supreme Court Case *Employment Division, Department of Human Resources of Oregon v. Smith, 494 U.S. 872*

3   "AIMster" is a nickname among people involved with the American Indian Movement organization.

4   I'm not going to name many names because I don't know who is being hunted. I don't know if some people didn't act in official AIM capacity out of fear, or because they wanted to act in solidarity with the local tribes for the most success.

5   The AIM song was a pan-tribal song used by members of AIM who belonged to various tribes and spoke different languages. As such, the song is used to unite people with a common cause and to develop a feeling of morale or spirituality.

6   Government Camp is an unincorporated community south of Mount Hood. It was given its name by white settlers who discovered abandoned wagons of the Mounted Riflemen Regiment in the 1800s.

7   We didn't know who all the federal agencies were; many branches of federal agents were keeping an eye on us in the woods. The U.S. Forest Service was hostile toward Indians, appearing often with their weapons out over protests in forested areas over timber sales. The head of the Forest Service was overheard by several people reviving that racist adage about the "only good Indians." It was hard to work with them or get permits.

8   Their names have been intentionally left out. See note 4.

9   Earth First! is a radical environmental advocacy movement of autonomous chapters across the world that uses campaigns, direct action, and civil disobedience to stop destruction of ecosystems.

10 Alysa Landry, "Native History: AIM Occupation of Wounded Knee Begins," *Indian Country Today*, February 27, 2017, http://indiancountrytodaymedianetwork. com/2014/02/27/native-history-aim-occupation-wounded-knee-begins-153765, accessed June 28, 2017.

11 Please visit the National Indigenous Women's Center at www.niwc.org and https://themonumentquilt.org/, both accessed June 28, 2017.

12 "Counting coup" refers to warriors winning prestige by acts of bravery in the face of the enemy, which could be recorded in various ways and retold as stories by the Plains Indians of North America.

Mujeres en Acción: Indigenous Women's Activism within the EZLN

Laura Gallery

The EZLN and Women

The Zapatistas became known to the public with the passing of the North American Free Trade Agreement, on January 1, 1994. The EZLN (Ejército Zapatista de Liberación Nacional or Zapatista Army of National Liberation) is a guerrilla army of indigenous men and women who rose up against the neoliberal economic model and the obliteration of their culture in this process. Their purpose and views are most concisely articulated through their various "communiqués" or written messages, speeches, and musings presented to the public through independent media and also public appearances made by the EZLN command. As they say in their First Declaration of the Lacandón Jungle:

> We are the product of 500 years of struggle: first against slavery ... and later the dictatorship of Porfirio Díaz denied us the just application of the Reform Laws, and the people rebelled and leaders like Villa and Zapata emerged, poor people just like us. We have been denied the most elemental preparation so that they can use us as cannon fodder and pillage the wealth of our country. They don't care that we have nothing, absolutely

nothing, not even a roof over our heads: no land, no work, no health care, no food, no education....

But today, we say *enough is enough*. We are the inheritors of the true builders of our nation. The dispossessed, we are millions, and we thereby call upon our brothers and sisters to join this struggle as the only path, so that we will not die...." (EZLN Command, 1994).[1]

The Zapatistas base their entire existence on their belief of equality for all people of Mexico. They believe that the indigenous people of Mexico have been exploited, ignored, and abused for long enough; now is the time to be recognized as citizens of Mexico, just as the mestizo population have been. Over time, their movement has evolved to become a movement for worldwide justice, striving to achieve an end to the oppression of all the invisible people of the world. As of 2006, the Zapatistas have expressed solidarity with "the millions who are not indigenous: workers, peasants, employees, small business people, street vendors, sex workers, unemployed, migrants, underemployed, street workers, homosexuals, lesbians, transgendered people, women, young people, children, and the elderly."[2] This solidarity with all oppressed peoples, and the commitment to equality, has given women within the movement a unique platform from which to engage in activism.

Since the EZLN's inception in 1983, the activist organization has been a decentralized, horizontally organized movement. There is no specific leader, and no one person has ultimate power. Further, unlike many (if not all) other resistance movements in Latin America, the Zapatistas have done more than just give lip service to gender equity. Women have always been significant actors in the rebellion.

In 1994, when the Zapatistas seized several cities in Chiapas, women were among the most visible actors. Insurgent Infantry Captain Irma, Insurgent Infantry Captain Elisa, Insurgent Infantry Captain Silvia, Infantry Insurgent Isidora, First Lieutenant Amalia, Lieutenant Elena—these are just a few of the women present on January 1. Later Comandanta Ramona would emerge as a spokesperson for the EZLN. She observed: "Women have been the most exploited.... We get up at three in the morning to prepare corn for our husband's breakfast and we don't rest until late at night. If there is not enough food we give it to our children and our husbands first. So the women now have decided to take up arms and become Zapatistas."[3]

EZLN (Zapatista National Liberation Army) insurgents and community members in Chiapas, Mexico, 1995. Credit: Ángeles Torrejón.

According to the Irish Mexico Group, women make up one third of the military command of the EZLN and 55 percent of the support communities.[4] Most of the women who join the EZLN are in their late teens. Age is important to note because it shows that gender roles create an impossible barrier for married or childbearing women to join. Joining the EZLN requires a woman to leave her community and live deep in the Lacandón Jungle, where the Zapatista command has its headquarters, and where training occurs. The incentive for women to join the EZLN (rather than remain in a support community) is highly rewarding. Upon arrival, women are taught to read, write, and speak Spanish. They are taught their own history as indigenous people and how to fight for their existence. Within the ranks of the EZLN, women and men share all duties and traditional gender roles are not enforced. In fact, they are consciously broken down. Women and men share duties on a rotating schedule. On certain days, women have the job of cooking the meals and cleaning the living area. On other days, the responsibility for the domestic chores falls to the men. Both sexes are trained in military strategy and the use of arms. Both sexes hold equal ranks in the organization; there are male and female majors, lieuten- ants, soldiers, commandants, and subcommandants. Both men and women work together to produce and deliver the many speeches and declarations of the EZLN. The EZLN has made many journeys to Mexico City to address the Mexican Congress on the issue of indigenous rights. At all of these addresses, women have spoken to the Congress equally with the men.

The Zapatistas' aim is to incorporate women fully and equally into their organization; they have cemented this commitment in the *Revolutionary Law of Women*.[5] Finalized in 1996, the Revolutionary Law of Women was a project of many of the female commanders of the EZLN. They set out to speak with other women soldiers of the EZLN and also women in the support communities. They came up with a list of thirty-one demands including the right to rest, stopping prostitution and polygamy, the right not to marry or have children, and the right to be respected as human beings by their male counterparts. These laws were presented to the EZLN command and added to the official EZLN documents in 1996. Within the ranks of the EZLN, these laws are accepted and enforced. Although they are also accepted in the base communities, enforcement is not as strong (Mujeres Zapatistas). Often women in support communities are working toward social justice for the community as a whole, rather than their specific concerns as women. Further, traditional gender roles have not been eradicated in the base communities as they have been in the EZLN command. As we saw with the cooperative Mujeres Marginadas, which is part of a Zapatista base community, women had been able to engage in activism and include men in their activism specifically because they worked within their assigned gender roles. Being that Mujeres Marginadas is in a Zapatista base community, and they are able to engage in activism that other indigenous women cannot, this proves that steps are in fact being taken toward the alteration of gender roles beyond the EZLN. Although this is true, complete progress is far from being achieved at this point.

Women who remain in the support communities by choice or obligation also have a place in the Zapatista struggle. These women are the people who implement the Zapatista program on the ground. Currently, the Zapatistas are working to enact the future they wish to see for Mexico in their base communities. They have officially declared autonomy from the Mexican government in their Sixth Declaration of the Lacandón Jungle (2005) and are effectively setting up an autonomous Zapatista zone in Chiapas. They have organized their base communities into five *caracoles* headed by "Good Government Juntas" made up of individuals elected by their communities.[6] These juntas work together to provide Zapatista communities with the infrastructure, education, and health care that the government has so long denied them.

Analysis of Women's Role in the EZLN

Unlike many revolutionary movements in the world, the Zapatistas have made a specific effort to include women. Beyond inclusion, they are making strides toward breaking down gender roles and stereotypes in indigenous communities. The women of the Zapatista movement have actively spoken up for the rights of all indigenous peoples, and have also spoken up for their specific rights as women. The EZLN has provided women with a platform to speak out against their oppression in ways that the cooperatives women have set up are as of yet unable to do. Within the EZLN support communities, women experience a level of equality, which women in nonsupport bases are not able to receive. Although women in the support communities still remain relatively bound by gender roles when it comes to activism, they remain key actors in the success of the Zapatista movement through their contribution to the material needs of the revolution and also in the contribution of their minds through their education.

Within the communities, women are the ones actively working toward the Zapatista goal of autonomy. Women organize cooperatives (as we saw with Mujeres Marginadas) to help the communities generate income, as they can no longer survive on subsistence alone. Besides the informal, consciousness-raising education that they engage in through handicraft cooperatives, they formally learn from Zapatista representatives in classes set up by the Good Government Juntas. Through these classes, they are able to learn basic math and literacy, as well as the Spanish language and revolutionary strategy. Most indigenous women in communities are monolingual in their indigenous languages and learning Spanish is a way to understand the oppressor, and consequently a way to fight back. The knowledge of Spanish in Mexico, just like the knowledge of English in the United States, allows a person to better understand the society and participate more fully. For the women of Chiapas, knowledge of Spanish allows them to communicate with nongovernmental organizations, state agencies, and anyone else who may be able to help them promote their cause. Further, they learn about Mexican politics and how and why they affect everyday life in the communities. Again, this knowledge better equips the women to know what they are resisting and ways of resistance. Through their roles in the domestic sphere, women can contribute to the EZLN by supplying food, clothing, and even money from their handicraft cooperatives. As Subcomandante Marcos noted, "The women are the spiritual and material support of this army; if we can survive in large numbers, it is thanks to them."

Notes

This is excerpted from Laura Gallery's larger paper *"Mujeres en Acción*: Indigenous Women's Activism in Chiapas, Mexico," which originally appeared in Albany University's *Transcending Silence* Spring 2008 issue (http://www.albany.edu/womensstudies/journal/2008/gallery_text.html#s8, accessed June 28, 2017). The Zapatistas, who have orchestrated a postmodern revolution for over thirty years, have often claimed they are "armed, so future generations do not have to be."

1   Latin American Network Information Center, *Zapatistas! Documents of the New Mexican Revolution* (Brooklyn: Autonomedia, 1994, http://lanic.utexas.edu/project/Zapatistas/anticopy.html, accessed July 8, 2017.

2   Subcomandante Marcos, "The Zapatistas and the Other: The Pedestrians of History," http://www.elkilombo.org/documents/peatonesI.html, accessed July 8, 2017. Subcomandante Marcos is the spokesperson of the EZLN. Although he is often mistaken for the leader, he specifically denies this identity. He is called the Subcomandante because he takes his direction from all members of the EZLN, and serves as a mouthpiece for their words. His counterpart was Comandanta Ramona, who also served as a mouthpiece, although she often spoke on behalf of women specifically. She passed away in 2006.

3   Cited in "Women's Work, Women's Struggle in Chiapas," July 1998, http://schoolsforchiapas.org/wp-content/uploads/2014/03/Womens-work-womens-struggle.pdf, accessed July 8, 2017.

4   The EZLN has control over more than forty communities in Chiapas. These are called "support communities," as they have expressed solidarity with the EZLN but are not actively engaged in the EZLN military component. These support communities provide the Zapatistas with financial, material, and moral support.

5   "Zapatista Women's Revolutionary Laws," *Mexican Awakener*, January 1, 1994, http://schoolsforchiapas.org/wp-content/uploads/2014/03/Zapatista-Womens-Revolutionary-Laws.pdf, accessed June 28, 2017.

6   In Spanish, *caracol* is translated literally as "snail shell." The EZLN likens their municipalities to snail shells because they represent "a spiral path, inward to the heart of the communities and back out into the world abroad."

Twelve Women in the Twelfth Year: January 1994

Subcomandante Marcos

Ed. note: This is a communiqué from the EZLN/Zapatistas originally issued in March 1996. It is a rare document that was written to give both the indigenous and mestizo women within the Zapatistas their deserved credit for leading and taking part in the 1994 armed rebellion, as well as for their roles as leaders in running the organizations and within the villages of Zapatista communities since that time.[1]

Yesterday...

A face wreathed in black still leaves the eyes free and a few hairs dangling from the head. In that gaze is the glitter of one who searches. An M-1 carbine held in front, in that position called "assault," and a pistol strapped to the waist. Over the left side of the chest, that place where hopes and convictions reside, she carries the rank of Infantry Major of an insurgent army which has called itself, this cold dawn of January 1, 1994, the Zapatista Army of National Liberation. Under her command is a rebel column which takes the former capital of that southeastern Mexican state Chiapas, San Cristóbal de Las Casas. The central park of San Cristóbal is deserted. Only the indigenous men and women under her command are witness to the moment in which the Major, a rebel indigenous Tzotzil woman, takes the national flag and gives it to the commanders of the rebellion, those called "The Indigenous Clandestine Revolutionary Committee." Over the radio, the Major says: "We have recovered the Flag. 10–23 over."

She came to the mountains of the Lacandón Jungle in December 1984, not yet twenty years of age, yet carrying the marks of a whole history of indigenous humiliation on her body. In December 1984, this brown woman says, "Enough is Enough!," but she says it so softly that only she hears herself. In January 1994, this woman and several thousand indigenous people not only say but yell "Enough is Enough!" so loudly that all the world hears them....

Outside of San Cristóbal another rebel column commanded by a man, the only one with light skin and a large nose who belongs to the indigenous who attack the city, has just finished taking police headquarters. Freed from these clandestine jails are the indigenous who were spending the New Year in jail for the most terrible crime in the Chiapanecan southeast—that of being poor. Eugenio Asparuk is the name of the insurgent Captain, an indigenous rebel Tzeltal, who together with the enormous nose is now overseeing the search and seizure at the headquarters. When the Major's message arrives, Insurgent Captain Pedro, an indigenous rebel Chol, has finished taking the headquarters of the Federal Highway Police and has secured the road which connects San Cristóbal with Tuxtla Gutiérrez; Insurgent Captain Ubilio, an indigenous rebel Tzeltal, has taken the entryways to the north of the city and with it the symbol of the government handouts to the indigenous people, the National Indigenous Institute. Insurgent Captain Guillermo, an indigenous rebel Chol, has taken the highest point of the city. From there he commands with his sight the surprised silence that peers out the windows of the houses and the buildings. Insurgent Captains Gilberto and Noe, indigenous Tzotzil and Tzeltal respectively, and equally rebellious, end their takeover of the state judicial police headquarters and set it on fire before marching on to secure the other side of the city, which leads to the barracks of the 31st Military Zone in Rancho Nuevo.

At the municipal palace, the Major organizes the defense of the positions that will protect the men and women who now govern the city, a city now under the rule of indigenous rebels. A woman who is armed protects them.

Among the indigenous commanders there is a tiny woman, even tinier than those around her. A face wreathed in black still leaves the eyes free and a few hairs dangling from the head. In that gaze is the glitter of one who searches. A twelve-gauge sawed-off shotgun hangs from her back. With the traditional dress of the women from San Andres, Ramona walks down from the mountains with a hundred more women toward the city of San Cristóbal on that last night of 1993. Together with Susana and other indigenous men she is part of that Indian command of the war which birthed 1994, the Clandestine Indigenous Revolutionary Committee–General Command of the EZLN. Comandanta Ramona will, with her size and her brilliance, surprise the international press when she appears during the first Dialogues for Peace held in the Cathedral and pulls from her backpack the national flag retaken by the Major on January 1. Ramona does not know then, nor do we, but she already carries in her body an illness which eats her life away in huge bites and dims her voice and her gaze. Ramona and the Major, the only women in the Zapatista delegation who show themselves to the world for the first time declare: "For all intents and purposes we were already dead, we meant absolutely nothing," and with this they almost count the humiliation and abandonment. Ramona laughs when she does not know she is dying. And when she knows, she still laughs. Before she did not exist for anyone, now she exists as a woman, as an indigenous woman, as a rebel woman. Now Ramona lives, a woman belonging to that race which must die in order to live....

The Major watches the light take the streets of San Cristóbal. Her soldiers organize the defense of the old city of Jovel and the protection of the men and women who in those moments sleep, indigenous and mestizos, all equally surprised. The Major, this indigenous rebel woman, has taken their city. Hundreds of armed indigenous people surround the old City. A woman who is armed commands them....

Minutes later the rebels will take the city of Las Margaritas; hours later the government forces that defend Ocosingo, Altamirano, and Chanal will surrender. Huixtan and Oxchuc are taken by a column that is heading towards the principal jail of San Cristóbal. Seven cities are now in insurgent hands following the seven words of the Major.

The war for the world has begun ...

In other places, other women, indigenous and rebellious, have remade that piece of history that they have been given, and which until that day of January 1, had been carried in silence. They also have no name or face.

IRMA, *Insurgent Infantry Captain*

The Chol woman Irma leads one of the guerrilla columns that takes the plaza at Ocosingo that January 1, 1994. From one of the edges of the central park, together with the soldiers under her command, she attacks the garrison inside the municipal palace until they surrender. Then Irma undoes her braid and her hair falls to her waist as though to say, "Here I am, free and new." Captain Irma's hair shines, and continues to shine even as the night falls over an Ocosingo in rebel hands....

LAURA, *Insurgent Infantry Captain*

Tzotzil woman, fierce in battle and fiercely committed to learning and teaching, Laura becomes the captain of a unit composed completely of men. Not only that, but they are all novices as well. With patience, in the way of the mountain that has watched her grow, Laura teaches and gives orders. When the men under her command have doubts, she shows them by doing. No one carries as much or walks as much as she does. After the attack on Ocosingo, she orders the retreat of her unit. It is an orderly and complete one. This woman with light skin says little or nothing, but she carries in her hands a carbine that she took from a policeman who only saw someone to humiliate or rape when he gazed upon an indigenous woman. After surrendering, the policeman ran away in his shorts, the same one who until that day believed that women were only useful when pregnant or in the kitchen....

ELISA, *Insurgent Infantry Captain*

As a trophy of war, she still carries in her body some mortar fragments planted forever on her body. She takes command of her column when the rebel line is broken and a circle of fire fills the Ocosingo market with blood. Captain Benito has been injured and has lost his eye. Before losing consciousness, he explains and orders: "I've had it, Captain Elisa is in command." Captain Elisa is already wounded when she manages to take a handful of soldiers out of the market. When Captain Elisa, an indigenous Tzeltal, gives orders it is a soft murmur ... but everyone obeys....

SILVIA, Insurgent Infantry Captain

She was trapped for ten days in the rathole that Ocosingo became after January 2nd. Dressed as a civilian, she scuttled along the streets of a city filled with federal soldiers, tanks, and cannons. At a military checkpoint she was stopped. They let her through almost immediately. "It isn't possible that such a young and fragile woman could possibly be a rebel," say the soldiers as they watch her depart. When she rejoins her unit in the mountain, the indigenous Chol rebel woman appears sad. Carefully, I ask her the reason that her laughter is less. "Over there in Ocosingo," she answers me, lowering her eyes, "in Ocosingo I left my backpack and with it all the cassettes of music I had collected, and now we have nothing." Silence and her loss lies in her hands. I say nothing, I add my own regrets to hers, and I see that in war each loses what he or she most loves. . . .

ISIDORA, Infantry Insurgent

Isidora goes into Ocosingo as a buck private on the first day of January. And as a buck private, Isidora leaves Ocosingo in flames, after spending hours rescuing her unit, made up entirely of men, forty of whom were wounded. She also has mortar fragments in her arms and legs. When Isidora arrives at the nursing unit and hands over the wounded, she asks for a bit of water and gets up again. "Where are you going?" they ask her as they try to treat her wounds, which bleed and paint her face, as well as redden her uniform. "To get the others," answers Isidora as she reloads. They try to stop her and cannot. The buck private Isidora has said she must return to Ocosingo to rescue other *compañeros* from the music of death that the mortars and the grenades play. They have to take her prisoner in order to stop her. "The only good thing is that when I'm punished at least I can't be demoted," says Isidora, as she waits in the room that, to her, appears to be a jail. Months later, when they give her a star which promotes her to an infantry official, Isidora, Tzeltal and Zapatista, looks first at the star and then at her commander and asks, as though she were being scolded, "Why?" . . . But she does not wait for the answer. . . . .

AMALIA, First Lieutenant in the hospital unit

Amalia has the quickest laughter in the Mexican southeast, and when she finds Captain Benito lying in a pool of blood unconscious, she drags him to a more secure place. She carries him on her back and takes him out of the circle of death that surrounds the market. When someone mentions surrender, Amalia, honoring the Chol blood that runs in her veins, gets angry and begins to argue. Everyone listens, even above the ruthless explosions and the flying bullets. No one surrenders....

ELENA, Lieutenant in the hospital unit
When she joined the EZLN she was illiterate. There she learned to read, write, and that which is called medicine. From caring for diarrhea and giving vaccines, she went on to care for the wounded in a small hospital that is also a house, warehouse, and pharmacy. With difficulty she extracts the pieces of mortar carried by the Zapatistas in their bodies. "Some I can take out, some I can't," says Elenita, insurgent Chol, as though she were speaking of memories and not of pieces of lead....

In San Cristóbal, that morning of January 1, 1994, she communicates with the great white nose: "Someone just came here asking questions, but I don't understand the language. I think it's English. I don't know if he's a photographer, but he has a camera."

"I'll be there soon," answers the nose as it rearranges the ski mask.

Into a vehicle go the weapons that have been taken from the police station, and he travels to the center of the city. They take the weapons out and distribute them among the indigenous who are guarding the municipal palace. The foreigner was a tourist who asked if he could leave the city. "No," answered the ski mask with the oversized nose, "it's better that you return to your hotel. We don't know what will happen." The tourist leaves after asking permission to film with his video camera. Meanwhile the morning advances, the curious arrive, journalists and questions. The nose responds and explains to the locals, tourists, and journalists. The Major is behind him. The ski mask talks and makes jokes. A woman who is armed watches his back.

A journalist, from behind a television camera, asks, "And who are you?"

"Who am I," says the ski mask hesitantly as it fights off the sleepiness after the long night.

"Yes," insists the journalist, "are you 'Commander Tiger' or 'Commander Lion'?"

"No," responds the ski mask, rubbing the eyes that are now filled with boredom.

"So, what's your name?" says the journalist as he thrusts his camera and microphone forward.

The big-nosed ski mask answers, "Marcos. Subcomandante Marcos"... Overhead, the Pilatus planes begin to circle.

From that time on, the impeccable military takeover of San Cristóbal is blurred, and with it is erased the fact that it was a woman, a rebel indigenous woman, who commanded the entire operation. The participation of other women rebels in other actions of January 1 and during the long road of ten years since the birth of the EZLN becomes secondary. The faces covered with ski masks become even more anonymous when the lights center on Marcos. The Major says nothing. She continues to watch the back of that enormous nose that for the rest of the world now has a name. No one asks her for her name....

At dawn on January 2, 1994, the same woman directs the retreat from San Cristóbal and the return to the mountains. She returns to San Cristóbal fifty days later as part of the escort that guards the security of the delegates of the CCRI-CG of the EZLN to the Dialogue at the Cathedral. Some women journalists interview her and ask her for her name. "Ana Maria, Major Insurgente Ana Maria," she answers with her dark gaze. She leaves the Cathedral and disappears for the rest of the year of 1994. Like her other *compañeras*, she must wait, she must be silent....

Come December 1994, ten years after becoming a soldier, Ana Maria receives the order to prepare to break out of the military blockade established by government forces around the Lacandón Jungle. At dawn on December 19, the EZLN takes position in thirty-eight municipalities. Ana Maria commanded the action in the municipalities of the Altos of Chiapas. Twelve women officers were with her in the action: Monica, Isabela, Yuri, Patricia, Juana, Ofelia, Celina, Maria, Gabriela, Alicia, Zenaida, and Maria Luisa. Ana Maria herself takes the municipality of Bochil.

After the Zapatista deployment, the high command of the federal army orders silence around the rupture of the blockade, and it is represented by the mass media as a purely "propagandistic" action of the EZLN. The pride of the *federales* is deeply wounded; the Zapatistas escaped the blockade, and to add insult to injury, a woman commands a unit that takes various municipalities. It is of course impossible to accept, so a great deal of money must be piled onto the event to keep it unknown.

Due to the involuntary actions of her armed *compañeros* and the deliberate actions of the government, Ana Maria and the Zapatista women at her side are dismissed and made invisible....

Today...

Meanwhile on the other side of the blockade, appears—She. She has no military rank, uniform, nor weapon. She is a Zapatista, but only she knows. She has no face or name, much like the Zapatistas. She struggles for democracy, liberty, and justice, the same as the Zapatistas. She is part of what the EZLN calls "civil society," of a people without a party, of a people who do not belong to "political society" made up of rulers and leaders of political parties. She is a part of that diffuse but real part of society that says, day after day, its own "Enough is Enough!"

She smiles, because she once admired the Zapatistas, but no longer. She ended the admiration the moment she learned that they were only a mirror of her rebellion, of her hope. She discovers that she is born on January 1, 1994. From then on she feels that her life, and what was always said to be a dream and a utopia, might actually be a truth.

She begins to knit in silence and without pay, side by side with other men and women, that complex dream which some call hope: everything for everyone, nothing for ourselves.

She meets this day (March 8) with her face erased and her name hidden. With her come thousands of women. More and more arrive. Dozens, hundreds, thousands, millions of women who remember all over the world that there is much to be done, and remember that there is still much to fight for. It appears that the thing called dignity is contagious, and it is women who are more likely to become infected with this uncomfortable illness....

This March 8 is a good time to remember and to give to the insurgent Zapatistas, to the Zapatistas, to the women who are armed and unarmed, their rightful place.

To the rebels and uncomfortable Mexican women who are now bent over under that history which, without them, is nothing more than a badly made fable....

Tomorrow

If there is to be one, it will be made with the women and, above all, by them....

Notes

1   The Zapatistas have issued thousands of communiqués from the jungles of
    Chiapas since 1994. They have been collected in numerous books internationally.
    It is their main form of communication with civil society worldwide. In them
    they have addressed many topics related to the continued growth and experi-
    mentations of the autonomous regions, answered critiques, talked about world
    affairs, and challenged civil society's engagements for a better world.

    This translation of "Twelve Women in the Twelfth Year," like that of many
    other EZLN communiqués, was freely shared by those who followed the
    Zapatistas' activities in the 1990s and was posted in various versions across the
    web. See for example, http://www.csuchico.edu/zapatist/HTML/Archive/Marcos/
    marcos_12_women_march.html and http://struggle.ws/mexico/ezln/1996/
    marcos_12_women_march.html. It was also published in a different transla-
    tion in a book collecting texts by Marcos culled from the internet: *Our Word Is
    Our Weapon: Selected Writings* (New York: Seven Stories Press, 2001), 5–12. Here
    it has been lightly edited for inclusion in this collection.

On Violence, Disasters, Defense, and Transformation: Setting Sights for the Future

scott crow

Rearview Mirror

> Within the war we are all waging with the forces of death, subtle and otherwise, conscious or not—I am not only a casualty, I am also a warrior.

> —Audre Lorde

Violence, drug addiction, alcoholism, and imprisonment were common in my extended family. I watched their combination ruin so many lives, it seemed normal. In the 1960s and '70s, the bastard who called himself my father was a drummer for country music legends George Jones and Tammy Wynette. A lot of his time was spent on the road developing a major drug habit. I grew up watching him on TV. That was exciting, but when he was home it could be either great or awful. I often looked forward to his coming home, then regretted when he was there. Too many times there was verbal and physical violence—mostly against my mom. I learned to watch out and be afraid.

I remember the last time I tried to stop him from beating my mom. I was around thirteen years old. He towered over her, hitting her as she lay on the bed hiding her face. I clumsily stepped between them, fists clenched. For a moment he and I grappled each other. He always kept a loaded revolver in the top of his bedroom drawer; at the same moment, we both remembered it and looked at the drawer. I thought of reaching for the gun, though I had only shot it once in my life and it scared me tremendously. The standoff passed. Neither of us reached for the gun. He finally pushed me out of the way and left the room. My mom and I grabbed a few things, left with no money, and never went back.[1]

I always felt small and powerless against my dad, even though my mother told me decades later that my actions had made him stop. That feeling of powerlessness haunted me for years as a teenager. The early violence in my life shaped the way I have almost always sided with the most vulnerable. I always knew I had to intervene, though I didn't always know how. Seeing nothing good come from the violence in our house, I grew up to be a pacifist, rejecting anger and avoiding violence completely. I thought that reason, negotiation, and nonviolent methods could overcome in any confrontation. I learned to use words to negotiate and deescalate conflicts. But I became too passive about stopping violence. I gave the power of violence to others without question and thought I was above it all.

Later, as an adult during the political tumult of the '90s, exposure to three disparate political tendencies—the examples of the Black Panthers in the U.S., the Spanish anarchists during that country's civil war, and the Zapatistas in Chiapas—shifted my thinking about community armed self-defense and its role in collective liberation. These tendencies, although very different, share some common themes. None of the tendencies made arms the central focus of their organizing, but took them up among other strategies to realize freedom on their own terms. They were offering underserved communities tools for creating dignity and self-determination in the face of overwhelming oppression. My thinking on violence was evolving while I was still trying to reconcile revolutionary politics with my own experiences and fear. Defense and violence in those contexts were something that still seemed to have happened long ago, or in other places, or in traditionally oppressed communities.

Then an incident in Dallas brought home for me the complex nature of violence, both in theory and practice. My neighbor, a woman living across the street, was being beaten in her front yard—again—by her large, drunken boyfriend. I had seen it before and offered little real support. It always triggered old fears. Sometimes another neighbor would call the cops, they would both be arrested, and once they were out of jail the cycle would begin again. It always bothered me deeply. I wondered who should take responsibility. The woman? The neighbors? The police? Me? All of us?

That day, I assumed personal responsibility with a baseball bat in hand. I walked across the street and in a calm voice I told the hulking figure now looking down on me to stop. I kept my stance and voice firm while shaking inside, mostly with anger. He stopped hitting her and she left. He then threatened and cussed at me, but, after a few minutes, he looked me over and said, in a quieter voice, that he would never do it again. Stunned, I walked back to my house. The next day, he moved out; I didn't see him around for years. The woman and my neighbors thanked me for doing something; even those who disagreed with my approach were grateful.

When I stood there, facing him, I saw multiple realities playing out. Socially, I was defending women, many of whom are subjected to daily violence. Politically, I was defending our neighborhood from being emotionally held hostage by the violence of a bully and the guilt of not doing anything about it. Personally, it was the unfinished business of a child once again defending my mom from my dad. But then, the disconnects dissipated; the political became personal. At that moment it was clear he had to be stopped, to defend her and our neighborhood. That event moved me from thinking abstractly about community self-defense as a far-off concept that happened a long time ago to practicing it. I couldn't ignore the contradictions between the hypocrisy of the state's "legitimate" violence and the Left's aversion to self-defense in any form.

That small step, taken with great thought, only moderate care, and a little righteousness, allowed me to grasp that if I could do something, then we all could. In my house and on our block, we had conversations with neighbors about the police, learning in the course of discussion that people only called them because it was easy and they would use force. The police have guns and the backing of the state. That does not mean they are good at dealing with conflict, reducing violence, or solving problems. Community self-defense was relevant.

Eventually, I recognized that in our larger struggles, our strengths and weaknesses are intertwined. Both marginalized and privileged communities are connected as if in a web that can create security, safety, and nurturing. Violence affects all of us, directly and indirectly, in our homes and in our communities. We need to work to reduce it, as well as defend ourselves from it. We have the power to do this ourselves without letting politicians and bureaucrats set the terms.

Community armed self-defense opens up the possibility of changing the rules of engagement. It doesn't always make situations less violent, but it can help to balance the inequity of power among individuals and diverse communities. I am not calling for us all to rise up in arms but to rethink how we defend ourselves. We can dream, we can build new worlds, but to do so we must not forget to resist on our own terms.

We Go Where They Go

I had been participating in anti-fascist organizing since the mid-1980s. Dallas, the spawning place of the Confederate Hammerskins, was ground zero for the rising white supremacist movement. Many of us tried to keep them out of the punk music scene and away from political rallies, using everything from posters to street clashes. I avoided violence then but had friends beaten and stabbed during those early years.[2]

In 2002, I joined the Austin chapter of Anti-Racist Action (ARA), a decentralized network of anti-fascist groups across North America that have confronted white supremacists with direct action since the Reagan years. I was drawn to the militancy of the ARA network. Their willingness to use direct action to physically confront fascists of all stripes without appealing to Power was striking. Our ARA chapter, which fluctuated between twenty to fifty members at any time, incorporated community self-defense as a practice within its framework. This including arming ourselves through a tactical defense caucus that trained together for three years. It only took a little anti-fascist history and some altercations to understand why this was important. White supremacists from Greensboro to Nevada had killed anti-fascist organizers over the years, and our lives were being seriously threatened almost weekly.

As a chapter we developed our armed tactical analysis and capacity. I had come a long way from the fear of violence in my household, having purchased my first semiauto rifle, which I learned to trust and use well over the coming years. Armed self-defense was necessary for us as a group and for communities who were being targeted around us, including people of color, immigrants, queer and trans people, Muslims, and abortion providers. We defended abortion clinics, confronted white supremacists in many places, and organized street mobilizations against right-wingers. In all those years, we never had to pull our weapons out but always had them nearby.[3]

Those rudimentary anti-fascist armed trainings and exercises, combined with furious seasons of political activity in the previous decades, would inform my decisions to go New Orleans in the days after Hurricane Katrina and prepare me theoretically—but not psychologically—for what would come.

A Battle in Algiers

And our heroes all died crazy
Broken, poor or shot
Let's celebrate their tragedy
And sanctify the loss
And manifest the daydream
Like those who fell before
And glorify our small attempts
And hate ourselves no more
—A Silver Mt. Zion, "Horses in the Sky"

On Sunday, September 4, 2005, I received a call from Malik Rahim, a former Black Panther member in New Orleans and lifelong community organizer I knew. He had remained in his home in the Algiers neighborhood of New Orleans during and after the devastation of Hurricane Katrina. He told me racist white vigilantes were driving around in pickup trucks terrorizing black people on the street and he needed support. I knew he meant, bring guns and people willing to use them.

I had just spent several unfruitful days in New Orleans looking for our mutual friend Robert King, another former Panther who we thought was missing. I had returned home to Austin exhausted and empty-handed. Malik hoped I would come back to New Orleans to give them support and use it as another opportunity to search for King.

I stopped at a meeting called by local activists who were doing some aid organizing for evacuees, including people I had trained with for years in Anti-Racist Action. I tearfully shared the stories of the

scott crow, Austin, Texas, 2014. Credit: Ann Harkness.

frightening realities I had encountered. Then I asked if anyone in the crowd of sixty would go back with me, knowing the potential danger. There were no takers. The prospect of potentially using arms provoked serious discussions. Some said it was crazy. Others who had advocated and trained for armed self-defense made excuses. My heart sank. Only two people chose to return immediately, myself and a man named Brandon Darby. I left Austin disappointed, exhausted, and anxious.[4]

I understood why people were not going. They could not grasp the immediate need or the absolute destruction that had occurred. I couldn't either, until I had seen it myself.

Our truck sped along the highway, my thoughts in a tumult. Fear crawled under my skin. I knew the situation was getting more

221

desperate. Was a race war going to erupt? How many people had already died needlessly? Few cars moved our way, apart from the occasional military vehicle. In the other direction, the roadway was overflowing with desperate people piled into and on top of vehicles, carrying with them the remnants of their lives; others walked alongside the road. All looked displaced—left and forgotten. On the radio, a voice repeated: "Order will be restored." But what people wanted to hear was that help was on its way.

There were military checkpoints at every turn. The soldiers only understood badges and uniforms; they wouldn't let civilians in. So we had made doctored passes to get us past the bureaucracy. Half-truths and skin color got us through. After the last checkpoint, we entered the empty city streets, ignored the few useless stoplights, and headed to Malik's.

We were back at Malik's on Monday the 5th for the second time in a week. Everyone pitched in to unload the supplies of rifles, ammunition, food, water, candles, and first aid kits. His home was on its way to becoming a makeshift distribution center.

Malik took us down the street by the Arthur Monday Community Center to cover up a bullet-riddled corpse with a piece of sheet metal we found. It was all we could do for him. We later found another body a few blocks away. Both were black men with no signs of struggle or robbery. These bloated, putrid bodies had been rotting for days. We could smell them as we approached; it's a gagging odor I will never forget. Who killed these men? Was it the vigilantes or was it the police? The image of that first man haunted me for a decade afterward—the first of many deaths I encountered during my time in New Orleans. They had met unnecessary and ignoble deaths, left to decay on the sunbaked streets.

Tableaus of Violence

Malik reported that in the time since our first arrival two white militias had formed, in Algiers Point and in the French Quarter. These vigilantes were barely more than organized lynch mobs made up of drunken fools and racists from Algiers Point, a small, very wealthy, white enclave, surrounded by a scattering of poor whites on the edges. The abandoned Algiers Point houses were decorated with hateful and fearful signs. The thin veneer of civil society that kept them from acting out their most racist tendencies had broken enough to allow their hatred to emerge.

They rode around armed in low-income black communities and meted out intimidation from the backs of their trucks. What they called defense amounted to harassment and potential death of any black person on the street.

In the days just after the storm, the Algiers Point Militia openly threatened and killed desperate unarmed civilians, foolishly bragging about their exploits to anyone who would listen—including media.[5]

According to the neighbors, the vigilantes regularly drew their guns on, and shot at, innocent people who were unarmed, poor, and black. Malik said the Algiers Point assholes mockingly called him "the mayor of Algiers," pointing guns at him as they drove by, threatening to "get 'im." Because he was a high-profile organizer in the neighborhood, the police did nothing but close their eyes to this, while continuing their own harassment. The lines between authorities and thugs blurred, leaving everyone else with nowhere to turn.

We began meeting with neighborhood people who were fed up with being terrorized by the militia and the police. They were mostly men, young and old, with little or no resources. They told us the stories of their lives and why they had stayed. Some were forgotten veterans; others had seen prison time for trivial offenses; some were quiet and deeply religious men, and others had been written off by society as nothing more than so-called gangsters. They had all stayed because they cared what happened to their neighbors. There were no other options. They had long family histories within their city blocks; many houses were intergenerational. These were people who had been reduced to statistics, characterized only as poor, black, and unemployed, branded as hoodlums or drug addicts. And now they were being called looters.

Our small group discussed how armed defense would look if it became necessary. There were conflicting opinions about how the police might react, but we felt we had no other choice. We inventoried the arms between us. Who was in? Who would have nothing to do with carrying guns? That day we set up our own rudimentary armed security teams, both guarding Malik's home and on patrol in the surrounding areas. We moved on foot with a handful of the closest neighbors—Reggie B., Clarence, two white men from Texas (me and Brandon), and another black man from Washington, DC, Suncere Shakur. The last three of us had been invited, with arms, into this community to help defend it.

We began the first watches, standing or sitting on Malik's porch and waiting, fully sober and fully armed. There was no machismo about this. I was anxious but honored to be among some of these people. To me this was an expression of solidarity. I had been asked for support and did not make my decision to come blindly but based on principle. I was ready to defend friends and strangers. It looked as if these people had been left to die. I had to at least help give them a fighting chance for survival.

I was resolute. I was also terrified. Before I arrived, my practice of self-defense had been tested on a much smaller scale: resisting neo-Nazis, confronting police brutality during protests, and facing threats from private security. This was unlike anything I knew. I was taking a conceptual framework of armed self-defense into a reality with many unknowns and far more danger. Self-defense of our communities, by any means, is our right whether the U.S. Constitution says so or not. People will fight for liberation when the boot is on their neck, not when governments give permission.

The Air Hung Heavy: An Armed Standoff

The midday humidity hung heavy; helicopters continued their constant noise overhead. A few neighbors were with us at Malik's. His was a narrow shotgun-style house built in the 1930s. It sits high off the ground, with a tall concrete porch behind a rusting chain-link fence. The Algiers Point vigilantes came around the corner in their truck and, as before, slowed in front of the house, talking their racist trash and making threats. We could see they all had guns, but they didn't raise them at us. This time it was different. They met an armed group that, however nervously, held our ground. There were five of us, three black and two white men. We held the higher ground, more firepower, a better firing position, and we were sober. Finally, one of our people told them to move on down the road, and another added that they would not be able to intimidate or threaten any more residents around there. Everything froze for a long, tense moment. My finger rested on the trigger of my rifle, ready to fire. At last, the truck drove on.

My heart pounded in my chest and head. By opposing them, we had made our presence known—to the racists and to the police. My head swirled with unanswerable questions. How were the authorities going to react? Was this the right thing to do? What if they came back? Would any political movement support us? What if I had shot someone or, worse, killed him? Would it have been worth it?

Their withdrawal showed us that the militia had no real power once they were challenged. As they left, there was guarded joy and relief among us. But we feared that they might continue their attacks on the neighborhood. Over the days to come, a handful of volunteers would sit on Malik's porch and keep watch. We also increased our neighborhood patrols.

I had come to help, not to end up on a porch with guns facing down a truck full of armed men. But, like the others standing there, I was ready to die defending ourselves and the people in this community. It meant something to often-ignored communities that white people would come to their aid and put their lives on the line. More would do so in the days to come. We had all taken the first step to rebel against losing hope in the face of the ongoing disaster around us. Under siege, we stayed. Our protection was what we were willing to organize ourselves. The presence of whites and blacks working together would later be cited by locals as one of the factors that helped ease tensions in that difficult time.

Later, as the military and media presence increased, the Algiers Point vigilantes receded back into the swampy waters of their lives. *Their* patrols were withering away while *our* armed patrols and larger projects of solidarity flourished. We still saw a few of them, individually armed, on foot within their own neighborhood of Algiers Point, but they did not leave those few blocks anymore.[6]

It was strange to see these men who had terrorized the community now walking down the street by themselves, drinking at a bar or talking to their neighbors, white, black, or Latino, as if nothing had ever happened. Anger would well up when I came near them. My emotional wounds were still fresh. I could not forget, and neither could the people who had been terrorized by them. Is this how Klansmen acted in the not-so-distant past? Night riders under the cover of darkness, good citizens by daylight? I channeled my anger into the larger rebuilding efforts.

Can You Relate? We're Livin' in a Police State

> Do they protect those who don't have the wealth
> Think about that and then ask yourself
> What protects a rich man's property and status
> Answer, the repressive police apparatus
> —Truth Universal, "Serve and Protect"

As our outreach expanded into more communities, the police became increasingly volatile. They continued their harassment of our distribution center at Malik's house and the clinic at the mosque, and of our volunteers delivering supplies. They pulled us over—especially the local black volunteers—and accused us of all sorts of things from stealing and selling supplies to running guns. It seemed as if the whole community was under siege. The police instituted a curfew at dusk and threateningly drew guns on volunteers and residents. Who was going to police the police?

On four occasions in the month following the standoff with the white militia I was almost killed by police, from varying agencies, and Immigration and Customs Enforcement agents—situations similar to those that too many communities have to endure every day. Their aggression culminated in an armed raid on our distribution center complete with a helicopter overhead. One out-of-control racist cop waved his gun around, shouting the N-word. What they didn't know was that had they attacked us, we would have defended ourselves with arms. Two people from our security teams were at the ready for the moment the cops broke through the gate. The police were confident they had the upper hand, but they would have met escalated resistance—we would not go quietly. The military personnel, who were also heavily armed and not necessarily on our side, stepped in and put themselves between police and us. The atmosphere was tense.

It was another night in Algiers, coming after days of crisis after crisis. Was there going to be a deadly confrontation with the police? The fact that it might happen was left unsaid, but it frightened all of us—especially those of us on the security teams who were taking turns with late-night watches. I wondered whether I would be shot. Or was it going to be some random volunteer who didn't know better?

Events like these were part of an ongoing plan to shut us down. Despite the good we were doing, the state treated us as the enemy.

Although the police continued to be a problem, we used other strategies to deal with any engagements with them as the months, then years, progressed. Within two months, we put the guns out of public sight—as soon as we had enough people for protection. In this, we followed the example of the Zapatistas, who came out with weapons to defend their communities against oblivion, then put them away as soon as civil society stepped in to keep them from being killed wholesale. They put away the guns when they were no longer necessary for their immediate survival.

We still kept a few locked away until early 2007, just in case.

Ending Reflections and Repercussions

Why do they fear us? Why so much hate for so few and so small a group? Because we have defied them, and the worst part about defiance is that it establishes a precedent.

—Subcomandante Insurgente Marcos

Our use of guns did save some lives after Katrina. As much heartache and post-traumatic stress as we all had in the aftermath, I know it was worth it. Our efforts in community armed self-defense, as minimal as they were, kept more people in the neighborhoods from being killed by the white militia or police. I believe we would have faced repercussions from the police whether we had guns or not, but I know they would have killed some of us if there had been no armed resistance.

Relating these stories has been troubling and difficult. It has taken time to sort it all and to learn to listen my own healing voice. Many actions I have engaged in, with arms specifically, were some of my proudest moments and simultaneously some of the most painful events in my life. From all the violence before and after Katrina I carried posttraumatic stress for almost a decade. (I don't call it a disorder, because I see my emotions and reflections as natural responses to extreme violence.) Acts of violence haunted my psyche. I slept with a loaded .45 pistol under my pillow the first year I was back. It wasn't rational, but it helped me to feel safe while the FBI threatened to raid my house for political activities. Sleepless nights became the norm, I avoided crowds, and for years felt like the world was collapsing while no one seemed to notice. With therapy, lots of writing, and storytelling,

I have been able to shake off the trauma and be a functioning human being. But I know I am a different person than I once was.

Disasters come in many forms—ecological, economic, political, and military. Having a varied toolbox beyond activist doctrine will be needed as our worlds are rapidly and unstably are changing. Guns will never transform our worlds, but they are powerful tools, like others that have a use and a place, that can give us the chance to rely on each other and fight on our terms. I hope to never again be in a situation like New Orleans or worry about alt-right fascists killing me, but that doesn't mean there aren't some distinct possibilities. So how do we want to face them? With moral superiority or obtuse theories? Community armed self-defense is something we should revisit as we head toward our unknown futures.

Can a tactical and finite use of community armed self-defense lead to worlds of my anarchist ideals that can transcend violence? Our futures are unknown, and I am as unsure as anyone, but I can say in my thirty years of political engagement examples of armed struggle have by far been the smallest examples of resistance. I am still a gun owner who fucking hates the National Rifle Association and its conservative corporate fearmongering. I don't train regularly and don't place higher values on guns and that kind of power over others, but if we are not relying on the state, then we must at points engage in some levels of conflict, even violence—whether we like it or not; that is part of the real world. Of course we must prioritize de-escalation tactics, along with conflict resolution, restorative justice, etc., but community armed self-defense has a legitimate place alongside these other tactics. I see guns as part of community armed self-defense to be used at appropriate times and places, just like other tools and tactics. I want a world that transcends violence, but I recognize that, at least in the shorter term, that still includes conflict—violent and otherwise. We should stay prepared on all fronts.[7]

Notes

Parts of this essay originally appeared in vastly different versions in the book *Black Flags and Windmills: Hope, Anarchy, and the Common Ground Collective*. Oakland: PM Press, 2014.

1   After ten years she left him. He ended up doing fifteen years in prison for numerous arrests for dealing and making controlled substances and for DWIs. I've

only seen him once in almost thirty years, and it wasn't a Hallmark moment. That early violence still occasionally haunts my memories. He couldn't break the cycles of drugs and violence, and the world had no support or use for him. Sometimes his specter is still over my shoulder.

2   Hammerskin Nation overview on Wikipedia, https://en.wikipedia.org/wiki/Hammerskins, accessed July 8, 2017.

3   In 2002, I attempted to buy my first gun through legal means—four times! Each time the vendor, at gun shows or shops, would delay then back out of the sale without reason. I passed the background checks. Surreptitiously it turns out that FBI agents showed up after my attempt every time to scare the vendor into cancelling the sale due to unfounded and unproven accusations around my politics. By accident an employee who didn't know went through with a sale and mentioned the FBI had visited. That was how I first learned and became concerned about why the FBI was so obsessed with me and how it was going to impact my life.

4   Kristian Williams, *Witness to Betrayal: scott crow on the Exploits and Misadventures of FBI informant Brandon Darby* (Oakland: Emergency Hearts/AK Press, 2014), 11

5   Rasmus Holm, *Welcome to New Orleans* (Fridthjof Film, 2006) https://www.youtube.com/watch?v=V__lSdR1KZg, accessed July 8, 2017.

6   Weeks later, one of the men even sought medical attention for his mother at our Teche Street Common Ground Collective clinic as if nothing had happened.

7   Despite our best efforts, Anti-Racist Action and many other U.S. antifa groups that may take up arms often do so with a rudimentary anti-fascist analysis and reactionary actions that don't leave a lot of doors open for sustained militant resistance, much less converting it into building counterpower. It was easier to get people to the gun range than to confront our organizing, analysis, or actions, which was glaringly revealed after Hurricane Katrina, when no antifa came to the Gulf immediately following the storm to take up community armed defense or rebuilding efforts. I believe the antifa framework still has some of the most potentially militant direct action possibilities to combat the alt-right by any means necessary, even if we recognize the scope is limited.

Gut Check Time: Violence and Resistance after Hurricane Katrina

Suncere Shakur

The Fight Begins

Ever since I was a little boy around three years old I knew I had, for the lack of a better word, a hero complex. I used to take up for my siblings when they did something that warranted a whopping from my grandmother. I lied to her for weeks and took the punishment for them, until my grandmother called me into the kitchen and said to me, "I know what you've been doing. I should tear your little ass up, but I'm gonna let you slide. You did it for your family." I never got another whopping from my grandmother.

In elementary school in Washington, DC, I was always under attack. I got jumped and fought daily. It felt like a damn Mad Max movie! I had homemade chucks,[1] a machete, a bat, and a knife in my locker to defend myself. When I was in the streets I was far from being a *real hood* boy like some cats I knew. So much so that my father got my aunt to take me out of DC. I survived, though.

There were a few who taught me how to handle myself in the mean and unforgiving streets of DC. But I did enough to have some people take me serious—I had a rep. When I was older, dudes used to say, "He'll fight you, but he won't shoot another black person." Don't get me wrong. If there's a situation where someone is shooting at me, no matter what color they are, I will bust back.

Revolutionary Consciousness Rising

All of these experiences molded me into what I wanted to be all of my life, a revolutionary activist. For years I listened and learned from my elders, who were black political revolutionary legends from back in the day. People from revolutionary black movements and some white radicals. I used to hear about all the brave and risky things they did. But they also told me about their comrades who gave their lives for the people. I very much have always wanted to and tried to embody the essence of the stories and lives as best as I could.

When Hurricane Katrina and the aftermath happened in 2005, I was ready. George Bush and the racist response motivated me to go to New Orleans for my people. Bush was on CNN telling the world how he was going to take troops out of Iraq and send them to New Orleans to speak to those people in the only language those people seem to understand and that was the language of violence. For me, it was time to put up or shut up. I love my black people, problems and all. I went down to New Orleans to take a life if necessary and give my life if need be. I packed up my truck and left immediately. I just knew I was needed. Something told me it was going to be more dangerous than the news was even saying. I just felt in my bones I was going to need to be armed once there. And I don't mean from "black looters," as the media was calling desperate people fighting for survival. When I hit Hattiesburg, Mississippi, I was met with Klansmen who I am pretty sure were killing black people after dark, although the killings weren't making the news. After a stressful overnight stay, the next day I left with a convoy of anarchist housing rights and street medics to meet with our contact in New Orleans, former Black Panther member Malik Rahim.[2] When I touched down in Algiers, a New Orleans neighborhood south of the city center, Malik welcomed me but quickly informed me of the dangers of being a black man there.

The mostly black Algiers community there was under attack by a group of white vigilantes calling themselves the Algiers Point Militia.[3] When I arrived there were unconfirmed reports that there were over thirty of them, well-armed, who had killed at least nineteen black males within Algiers.[4] They were threatening to kill Malik and his neighbors. The average person would probably have run from all of this. Fuck that! With my revolutionary consciousness I was staying to defend this Black Panther and the black community from racist attacks from cops or the vigilantes. History would not close on me as a coward when my people needed me the most. I jumped back into my truck, which I named in honor of Harriet Tubman, who risked her life running the Underground Railroad that freed U.S. slaves. I followed Malik back to his house on Atlantic, which in the coming days would be the birthplace of the Common Ground Collective, an organization I helped cofound.[5]

As soon as I got out of the truck at Malik's, I met a white anarchist from Austin, Texas, named scott crow. Right away he asked me if I knew how to handle a gun. I smirked and said, Dude, I am from DC. I followed him into the house next door to Malik's, where some computer techs were setting up a command center that included satellite communication and internet, without steady electricity or internet access. He led me down a short hallway into a bedroom with a sliding-door closet. He slid the door back and there was a gang of guns. He said to pick one. I asked which one held the most bullets, and he pointed to a black carbine rifle with a clip. I grabbed a blanket to wrap it up in and carried it over to Malik's house to set up our first official round-the-clock security watches.

In those first few weeks we also put into motion a large-scale radical grassroots relief effort under the Common Ground Collective banner—setting up clinics, feeding people, doing search and rescue, and more. Our revolutionary commitments took after the Black Panther "survival programs" and anarchists' mutual aid. A handful of us set up armed security patrols in and around Malik's house when volunteers were going out to deliver supplies, to protect them from being targeted. I, with a couple of others, mostly held down the defense of the Common Ground's headquarters. Carrying guns in the open after Katrina was not unusual, but for a black person it was more dangerous. Anytime I was driving around in Harriet I always had a two-way radio and my rifle for protection. When scott had to make trips back to Austin I was left in charge of security for all the volunteers and of course Malik. At night I would sleep on the floor right outside his bedroom door.

In those early days, when we didn't hardly have any volunteers, at the close of another tiring day the New Orleans police (NOPD) raided our distribution center with guns drawn and a helicopter. We had put most of the supplies away already behind a fence under tarps when they showed up. Malik, scott, and another volunteer, David A., met them at the gate, and the other volunteers stood far back, scared. I and another security person stood in two doorways, hidden, with our rifles ready on the police, who was making racist comments and wild accusations. Had they fired on us, we would have busted back, because scott and Malik weren't unarmed at that time. Finally they just left and left us alone.

The Algiers Point Militia and the police were afraid of us: revolutionaries with guns and political ideals. The police turned a blind eye while the militia continued to kill black men. Us being armed stopped the militia from more harassment and dropping people in the street. Weeks after our run-ins with the vigilantes I would see these murderous *crackers* out on my supply runs, and they would look the other way cause they knew I was there with Common Ground. They looked like they knew I was ready to shoot at a drop of a hat.

At one point we finally put the guns away. We didn't need them anymore. It was a difficult decision. The killings had stopped and there were more people around watching. Common Ground started using cameras to monitor the police, and the militia slid back under their rocks.

Reflections: It's All of Us or None of Us

I went to New Orleans to defend myself, my comrades, and community members who were providing a much-needed service and rebuilding in the midst of the most fucked-up situation in U.S. history since black people hit the shores during the mid-Atlantic slave trade.

Years later when I came back to New Orleans to live for the second time I would run into these same vigilantes at the corner stores, at the Algiers Ferry, or the local coffee shop. They would see me get up and move from one room to the other or just leave, looking back at me. It had nothing to do with being a badass black man, but being armed and them knowing I was willing to use it to keep me safe for the time and those I protected safe.

The lesson I learned from those experiences is you need to be armed in America, especially if you black or poor. I also learned that there *are* white people who will risk their lives to save your own. I read about it but had lost faith that I would ever be in situation where I could count on any of them to help me out, especially giving me a weapon to shoot back at other white people. My pops used to tell me you should be cool with everyone, you never know where you might get help from. I just wish that our youth that are killing each other could have been there with me to experience the whole scene. I will tell you the racist white cowards murdered young black men with the nod of the NOPD and the military. When I had to make supply runs I would run into the crackers on patrol and, hell yeah, I was nervous, but I knew I could not blink. Just like the hard streets of DC, arming yourself or killing is not something the average person wants to do. But it becomes common sense to survive or just make a statement. Sundiata Acoli, a former Black Panther, former member of the Black Liberation Army, and U.S. political prisoner, in his article called "A Brief History of the Black Panther Party" states that it's simply common sense to protect yourself against people who are willing to take your life.[6]

> Self-Defense: This is one of the fundamental areas in which the BPP contributed to the [Black Liberation Movement]. It's also one of the fundamental things that set the BPP apart from most previous Black organizations and which attracted members (particularly the youth), mass support, and a mass following. The concept is not only sound, it's also common sense. But it must be implemented correctly, otherwise it can prove more detrimental than beneficial. The self-defense policies of the BPP need to be analyzed in this light by present day Afrikan organizations. All history has shown that this government will bring its police and military powers to bear on any group which truly seeks to free Afrikan people. Any Black "freedom" organization which ignores self-defense does so at its own peril.[7]

I ask you to look at black history in this country. First, they kidnap us from the loving arms of mother Africa. Then four hundred years of slavery and Jim Crow. Murdering black leaders, locking them up forever, or chasing them into political asylum from Cuba back to Africa. What do we get? Minimum wage, drugs, poison in our water, air, and food, and gang warfare from coast to coast. The ghettos are hopeless; it's repulsive to think that shit will never get any better. Not to mention it's legal for the police to murder us at will. "Overall in 2015, black people were killed at twice the rate of white, Hispanic and native Americans. About 25% of the African Americans killed were unarmed, compared with 17% of white people. This disparity has narrowed since the database was first published on 1 June, at which point black people killed were found to be twice as likely to not have a weapon."[8]

Poor housing, poor education and health care, jobs with ceilings—that is war—and it's never stopped. I am tired of these motherfuckers making bullshit excuses when they gun us or our children down in the street. Black people are still slaves and it's not safe on the plantation. We have longer chains but we're not free. Don't think for one moment that the civil rights movement would have happened without armed self-defense by groups like Revolutionary Action Movement that existed in the early 1960s.[9] It's more than hating whitey or hating the police. Community armed self-defense has a role in getting our enemies to take us seriously so our babies don't have to live on their knees like their parents. This goes out to those black youth murdered by police in recent years: Tamir Rice, Mike Brown, Sandra Bland, and Kindra Chapman.

Notes

1   Nunchakus are ancient Japanese fighting weapons, https://en.wikipedia.org/wiki/Nunchaku, accessed June 29, 2017.

2   Malik Rahim was the defense minister of the New Orleans chapter of the Black Panther Party in the early 1970s. See https://en.wikipedia.org/wiki/Malik_Rahim, accessed June 29, 2017.

3   Josh Horwitz, "The Lessons of Algiers Point," *Huffington Post*, May 25, 2011, http://www.huffingtonpost.com/josh-horwitz/the-lessons-of-algiers-po_b_166083.html, accessed June 29, 2017.

4   To this day, even after all the investigations, both public and private, it is still unknown how many black men were killed by the militias or the New Orleans police after Katrina. Only a handful were ever prosecuted.

5   scott crow, *Black Flags and Windmills: Hope, Anarchy, and the Common Ground Collective* (Oakland: PM Press, 2014, [2nd edition]).

6   For more information on Sundiata Acoli and his case, see http://www.abcf.net/abc/pdfs/acoli.pdf, accessed June 30, 2017.

7   Sundiata Acoli, "A Brief History of the Black Panther Party: Its Place in the Black Liberation Movement," Sundiata Acoli Freedom Campaign, 1985, http://www.hartford-hwp.com/archives/45a/004.html, accessed June 30, 2017.

8   Jon Swaine, Oliver Laughland, Jamiles Lartey, and Ciara McCarthy, "Young Black Men Killed by US Police at Highest Rate in Year of 1,134 Deaths," *Guardian*,

December 31, 2015, http://www.theguardian.com/us-news/2015/dec/31/the-counted-police-killings-2015-young-black-men, accessed June 30, 2017.

9   Maxwell C. Stanford, "Revolutionary Action Movement (RAM): A Case Study of an Urban Revolutionary Movement in Western Capitalist Society" (master's thesis, Atlanta University, 1986), http://www.ulib.csuohio.edu/research/portals/blackpower/stanford.pdf, accessed June 30, 2017.

Breaking the Curse of Forgotten Places in Mexico

Simón Sedillo

The first successful strategy for community-based self-defense against the Knights Templar cartel in Michoacán came about on April 15, 2011, in the indigenous Purépecha community of Cherán, Michoacán. The implications of the success of this original uprising against the Knights Templar and the narco-government are immeasurable; however, what is evident today is that the strategy has spread contagiously throughout the state and has now even inspired nonindigenous mestizo communities to replicate it. Since February 2013, a variety of communities, both indigenous and mestizo, have risen up in arms, evicted municipal police from their municipalities, evicted the Knights Templar cartel from their territories, and have begun to engage in self-governing strategies founded upon a consensus-based general assembly model. Most nonindigenous mestizo communities in the state of Michoacán have been known to be racist toward indigenous peoples and communities of the state. To now see these mestizo communities exercise indigenous strategies for community liberation is truly historic and groundbreaking.

The Inescapable Imposition of Public Perception
One of the biggest obstacles faced by the *comunitarios* (self-defense movement) in Michoacán has been the general public's perception on

Community members take up arms to protect themselves from the drug cartels and corrupt police in Michoacán, Mexico. Credit: Simón Sedillo.

a national and international level. To the misfortune of the comunitarios, public perception is primarily manufactured by the mainstream media, which attempts to standardize and simplify social movements into little palatable boxes labeled good or bad, black or white, and right or wrong. The standards used to determine the social and political validity of social movements are clearly set by very specific financial and political interests. The problem is that as a global society we have continued to allow such media to be our primary source of collective communication despite all of the obvious hypocritical contradictions. Allowing social movements to be standardized and simplified by the mainstream media suffocates the diversity found in movements for community-based liberation around the world.

There is yet another external imposition on the public perception of the comunitarios, in that most academics, intellectuals, and even many solidarity activists seek "purity" in social movements. There is a tendency to demand a strict political line from the social movements with which they choose to stand and work in solidarity. This selective solidarity has generated a power dynamic of exclusion about who receives attention and who does not, who receives solidarity and who does not, and what is considered a social movement and what is not. Social movements deemed impure are discarded and discredited almost instantly.

Historically, entire sectors of Mexican society have been consistently excluded from consideration as social movements until these communities make themselves heard. The state of Michoacán is one is of those places. Mexico and the world have excluded the people of Michoacán from attention, solidarity, support, acceptance, understanding, and from a chance at a dignified life for well over a decade. Even radical leftists have always held the so-called "narco-states" like Michoacán at arm's length like a pair of dirty underwear and simply concluded, "These places are doomed. These people are doomed. There is nothing to be done here. There is too much corruption. It is too violent. There is no hope." This dismissive attitude toward communities that have been surviving a very dirty war for the last eight years is partially responsible for the 100,000+ deaths and 10,000+ disappearances celebrated by a variety of cartels throughout Mexico with overwhelming collusion by all levels of the Mexican government.

Both indigenous and nonindigenous mestizo communities in Michoacán have been confronted by the same monster. Despite a generalized shunning in public perception, Michoacán has now risen and is clearly prevailing. The ever-growing community-based armed self-defense movement has forced the world to finally look at Michoacán in a very different way. This comunitario movement has forced the Mexican federal government to mount a highly publicized charade of finally taking the people of Michoacán into consideration. Today it has become painfully clear that Michoacán's problems are not just about drugs, corruption, and organized crime, but are much more related to the very same problems faced by the rest of Mexico: they are the consequence of an imposed military, political, and economic system that, for over twenty years, has treated entire sectors of society as disposable in order to secure territory, cheap labor, natural resources, and profits.

The Military, Political, and Economic Imposition

Through the North American Free Trade Agreement, politicians, banks, and corporations have been imposing a military, economic, and political strategy in Mexico since 1994, which has included the privatization of telecommunications, transportation, education, health care, energy, and, of course, land and natural resources. Indigenous communities throughout Mexico have organized and resisted the privatization of their communally owned lands. In response to a largely unsuccessful land privatization strategy, the Mexican government, with the help of the U.S. government, has increasingly employed a military strategy of internal defense and paramilitarism. Today, a culture of paramilitarism permeates all walks of Mexican society, not just indigenous communities. For every social group that attempts to resist and organize against the military, political, and economic impositions of neoliberalism, there is a paramilitary counterpart ready to act as a provocateur, a shock troop, or even a death squad in order to derail efforts for social change through the threat of violence and brute force.

Paramilitarism entails several specific criteria:

1. That the paramilitary organization be formed of civilians with an opposing point of view to a given civilian social movement, be it social, cultural, labor, religious, geographic, economic, or political.
2. That the paramilitary organization be financed and trained by an official entity such as the military, police, or other official government entities, corporations, banks, or local land barons.
3. That the paramilitary organization carry out acts of violence and brutality as a primary strategy in order to take control of territory and natural resources.
4. That the paramilitary organization functions with complete impunity from prosecution by official government entities.
5. That the acts of violence carried out by the paramilitary organization function as "deniable atrocities" from which state, corporate, banking, or government officials can deny involvement or responsibility, claim internal civilian disputes, and therefore justify further military or police intervention in a given region.

The whole purpose of paramilitarism is to divide and conquer without appearing to do so on an official level, to then justify official militarism and accomplish the ultimate goal of controlling territories and natural resources. The most prevalent cases of paramilitarism in Mexico can be found in land dispute issues within indigenous communities, in particular in the states of Chiapas, Oaxaca, and Guerrero. Extensive analysis, research, and investigations have unveiled the extent to which the strategy of paramilitarism has been used to undermine indigenous struggles for land autonomy and self-determination in these states. There is no longer a single doubt about the existence of this low-intensity warfare strategy in these regions.

The Deafening Silence of Narco-Paramilitarism

When it comes to states such as Michoacán, however, somehow the mainstream media, academia, and many solidarity activists have ignored the paramilitary tendencies of organized crime cartels. The people of Michoacán have struggled to survive and persevere in the face of a violent onslaught by three different cartels: the Familia Michoacana, the Zetas, and now the Knights Templar. Michoacán is known worldwide for marijuana cultivation and trafficking, but with a growing U.S. trend toward marijuana decriminalization and legalization, the Knights Templar cartel has now diversified into the production and trafficking of methamphetamine. In a globalized marketplace for cheap labor, land, and natural resources, cartels throughout Mexico have also diversified into a much more profitable industry, which is the use of coercion through violence in order to gain territorial control. Today the Knights Templar cartel continues to harvest terror with the precision of a military death squad and engages in an international drug smuggling operation. The cartel, however, has also quietly been engaging in private security roles in the interest of illegal natural resource extraction strategies employed by corporations, banks, and political oligarchies.

If we apply the five aforementioned criteria that constitute a paramilitary organization to the cartels, what we see is a level of professional paramilitarism that has now surpassed classic forms of paramilitarism, in that the territorial control exercised is absolute. In addition to trafficking narcotics, kidnappings, torture, coercion, the charging of protection money, rapes, assassinations, organ trafficking, cannibalism, and public displays of mutilations, in Michoacán, the Knights Templar cartel has taken control of entire legitimate industries, such as avocado and lime agribusinesses and mining operations. In other cases, such as in Cherán and Ostula, the cartel has provided armed security for illegal logging endeavors. This is the true face of narco-paramilitarism in Mexico today.

From Smear Campaign to "Legalization"

Despite all the evidence showing that the Knights Templar cartel is the real problem in Michoacán, the mainstream media have continued to vilify the comunitarios by trying to attribute their support networks to other organized crime cartels, in particular to the Cartel de Jalisco Nueva Generación. A serious concern of intellectuals and activists alike is that the federal government is co-opting the comunitarios. Several activists and academics have discredited them as opportunists, mercenaries, and even as state-sponsored paramilitaries modeled after the U.S. military intervention in Colombia. The claim is that they are functioning without community support or involvement and that they do not answer to the communities they liberate.

There may very well be instances of opportunism behind part of the comunitario movement. There may even be evidence of some of their supposed groups receiving financial support from other cartels in isolated cases, or even cartel members fronting as comunitarios. There is even some evidence of the isolated presence of mercenaries on the front line of some of their advances. There is also clear evidence of the federal government attempting to co-opt the comunitario movement by registering them and their weapons through the Secretariat of National Defense. Yet there is much more evidence of growing community support for the diverse expressions of the self-defense movement on a local level. The movement on the ground is beginning to foment community-based forms of alternative self-governance and self-determination, which are not only directly challenging the cartel but also the government itself and the military, political, economic system that has led to this situation.

As the community liberation strategy spread through Michoacán over the course of several months this last year into the communities of Tepalcatepec, La Ruana, Buenavista, Coalcomán, Aguililla, Nueva Italia, and Antúnez, among many others, the federal and state governments began to convulse. As comunitarios began to surround the Knights Templar urban stronghold in Apatzingán, the federal government responded with a strategy to discredit, criminalize, and disarm the self-defense groups. On January 13, 2014, shortly after liberating the town of Antúnez, the Mexican Army rolled into town and began to aggressively disarm the comunitarios. This was not the first or the last attempt at disarmament of self-defense groups by the military, but on this day things went terribly wrong. Community members from Antúnez came out in support of the comunitarios who were being disarmed, and members of the Mexican Army opened fired into a crowd of unarmed civilians, killing four people, including an eleven-year-old girl.

After months of a mainstream media campaign to criminalize the comunitarios, the federal government suddenly began to speak about the legalization of the self-defense groups by registering them into a little-known public security force known as rural police. The state and federal government asked that the comunitarios cease their advance into new territory while they hashed out the details of the legalization agreement. On January 27, 2014, several representatives of self-defense groups from throughout the state of Michoacán signed an accord with the federal and state government to proceed with a legalization process for the comunitarios, which would include the official registration of members and their weapons with the Mexican Army through the Secretariat of National Defense.

As of the beginning of February 2014, only five hundred of the comunitarios had actually registered with the Secretariat of Defense, while there is evidence of the presence of upward of fifteen thousand of them throughout the state of Michoacán. Despite a now-transparent government attempt to co-opt their movement, the strategy has been largely unsuccessful due to a general distrust of the government and in particular of the army, which has been commissioned to supervise the registration process. Many of the comunitarios I spoke to fear they will be criminalized by the state and federal government. In response to the arrest of a comunitario leader by the name of Hipólito Mora from the community of La Ruana and ongoing conflicts with government officials, on Sunday March 16, the official spokesperson of the comunitario movement, Dr. José Manuel Mireles, announced an official break in relations with the government.

Breaking the Curse of Forgotten Places

Though a ceasefire was technically in effect, the comunitarios on the front line did not stop their advance into new territories and on January 27, 2014, the same day as the signing of the peace accord with the government, they advanced into the community of Peribán, Michoacán. The liberation of Peribán on that day was peaceful and even seemed festive. Peribán was liberated by self-defense groups from the communities of Buenavista, Tepalcatepec, Nueva Italia, Los Reyes, among others, as well as community members from Peribán who had previously left the community in exile from narco-violence and joined self-defense groups in their advance throughout the Tierra Caliente region of Michoacán. Several comunitarios from Peribán told me that they joined up in the hopes of one day liberating their own community, and on Monday, January 27, 2014, that day came.

After Peribán was liberated, the majority of self-defense groups from other communities continued their advance into Los Reyes, yet some members from outside Peribán remained in the community with members from Peribán to assist in the follow-up strategies of liberating property, identifying lookouts and enforcers still in the community, and engaging in a long-term self-defense strategy for the community. This is the face of the local community base that is the actual backbone of the comunitario movement.

In addition to setting up sandbag barricades as checkpoints throughout the city of Peribán, the comunitarios carried out several guerrilla-style operations to liberate homes, businesses, and property under Templar territory. Any pieces of property with an original owner were returned to the rightful owner. Any property under Templar control without a rightful owner was expropriated by the self-defense groups and is entering a process of collective redistribution. Several vehicles and the vast majority of the weapons used by the comunitarios have been expropriated from the Templars. The final "cleaning" strategy employed by comunitarios was to liberate the avocado orchards surrounding Peribán from Templar control. The day-to-day trips into the surrounding mountains and orchards to hunt down any leftover Templar lookouts and enforcers that I witnessed were very thorough, intense, and also very effective. The people of Peribán agree that their community is safer today than it has been in a very long time.

Peribán's primary natural resource is the avocado orchards. The "green gold," as Michoacános refer to the avocados, is a multimillion-dollar industry, which primarily entails exportation to the rest of Mexico and to the United States, Canada, and Europe. Unbeknown to most guacamole and avocado smoothie consumers in the USA, for the last several years the primary exporter of avocados to the U.S. has basically been the Knights Templar, who, in a process of territorial domination, took control of virtually every aspect of the avocado industry. Landowners, avocado pickers, transporters, resellers, and packagers were all forced to pay protection money directly to the Templars. Not paying meant you would be tortured. Not paying again meant your family would be murdered in front of you, and not paying yet again would result in your assassination. In this way the Templars absolutely dominated profits from the avocado growers and exporters and, over time, completely appropriated several facets of the entire industry. Today comunitarios have liberated Peribán's avocado orchards and have liberated the avocado industry itself. The citizens of Peribán who depend on the avocado industry for their basic survival show their appreciation through direct solidarity and financial support for the comunitario movement.

The comunitarios in Peribán have an intergenerational element to them that has all but been lost in most Mexican mestizo communities. Elders and young men have collaborated with one another to create a self-defense team that is respected by community members. I also met three young men from an outside community who had embedded themselves in Peribán for the long haul. These three young men were no younger than eighteen and no older than twenty-five years old. They have been on the front lines of the battle for self-defense for just over a year now and have become experts in security and in hunting down and assassinating Templars. These three young men left a lasting impression on me. Despite having lost friends and family and then growing into respected and trained killers, they have not lost their humanity. How does anyone live through what they have and not lose their sense of humanity? This is a quality I expect to rarely find among young men with assault rifles anywhere in the world.

The youth and elders from Peribán took informal field leadership from these three young men who were extremely humble, respectful, and dignified. Together with these young men, the elders and young men from Peribán employed a security strategy that on the early morning of February 4 proved to be extremely effective. At around 3:00 a.m., a group of well-trained enforcers from the Knights Templar came into Peribán through the avocado orchards on the edge of town and they opened fire on three out of four different barricades in town. The comunitarios returned fire and held their ground. No one on their side was injured but two *Templario* enforcers were killed in the firefight. The Templarios retreated and to this day have not returned to Peribán. The next day comunitarios combed the orchards on the edge of town and found evidence of the presence of a large group of well-trained Templar enforcers. Several tracks with military-style footwear were visible to the naked eye, as well as resting spots that included knocked over banana trees as well as makeshift beds. Between 2:00 and 2:20 a.m. on March 27, 2014, a second shoot-out took place in the community of Peribán. Someone in a pickup truck shot at a barricade near the city's center. When the truck tried to make its getaway it was chased by self-defense patrol vehicles from all the other barricades. At that time an additional firefight began at two other barricades closer to the edges of town. Once again the comunitarios reported no injuries. On both occasions the comunitarios were able to defend themselves and their community from this narco-paramilitary advance. The Templar enforcers were clearly employing guerrilla warfare tactics in these two incursions into the community. The fact that the elders, grown men, and young men from the comunitarios were able to fend off these professional attacks and protect their community from what very well could have been a massacre is also historic and incredible. These particular attacks were never mentioned in any of the mainstream media, anywhere.

On February 27, 2014, one month after the uprising in Peribán, comunitarios organized a general assembly in the town center and have now elected a citizens self-defense council as an alternative security force recognized and supported by the community. This is a first step in looking after not only the self-defense and security of the community but also the future of Peribán so that it never falls into the hands of another cartel or organized crime group. One comunitario elder tells me:

> We need to figure out how to take community control over the avocado industry. We need to be able to develop small businesses in order to process and market avocado products on a national and international level. We can't go back to foreign corporations taking all the profits from the avocado industry and cutting us out from receiving the fruits of our labor. We don't need government assistance programs, we don't need political parties, and

we don't need cartels. What we need is to be free and to be able to make a living and provide dignified employment for our youth so that they will never be tempted to engage in organized crime.

Peribán can now be added to the list of communities in Michoacán who are beginning to practice alternative forms of self-governance.

I think about the young and elder warriors from Peribán, and I realize that Peribán is teaching the rest of us a life lesson. They are teaching us that even though the world of mainstream media, academics, and activists may not be ready to understand and empathize with their situation, the people of Peribán are willing and able to turn to themselves in order do whatever it takes to make a necessary change in their reality. There are too many forgotten places in this world that are discredited and stigmatized as hopeless, but the people of Peribán are on the front line of communities all over the world who are actively breaking the curse of forgotten places.

Feminism, Guns, and Anarchy in the Twenty-First Century: A Southern U.S. Story

Mo Karnage

The Personal

In the rural, mostly white area in Hanover County, Virginia, where I was raised, guns are a normal part of everyday life. I was a tomboy my whole life—a rural predecessor to genderqueer, I think—but even that did not grant me the same privileges respective to guns as boys received. As a kid I grew up knowing about gun safety but personally didn't use guns a whole lot. I always had issues with guns because of how I felt about animals and hunting, which was much of my context for their use. Those uses were of zero interest to me. There also wasn't much in the way of gun violence growing up, which places me in a privileged position in relation to guns statistically. People who have had friends, family, and neighbors become victims of gun violence often feel differently about guns than I do.

As I grew up and became more radical in my perspectives, identifying as an anarchist by the age of fifteen or sixteen, my interest in guns also rose. I didn't own a gun at that point, but I began learning about times when guns were used by radicals and anarchists. Guns began to make sense to me as a useful tool for something other than hunting nonhuman animals. I read about John Brown and the raid on Harpers Ferry, Gabriel's rebellion (a suppressed slave revolt in nearby

Richmond), Nat Turner's rebellion, and other slave uprisings, how the Black Panthers used guns in self-defense of their communities, and how Zapatistas used guns to fight for autonomy and claim space as their own. It seems obvious that any revolutionary or liberatory movement might end up in a time and place where they will need to have, and possibly even use, their guns.

I bought my first gun after a traumatic experience with a shitty Craigslist-found roommate. Long and the short of it, he pulled a gun on my best friend at our house and threatened to kill them and our dogs. The police wouldn't do anything about it, as they knew my friend and me as anarchists who had squatted an empty building. We had histories of antagonism toward each other, and they weren't willing to do anything to keep this dude out of our house.

We threw his things outside, and he ended up moving out of town that day. But I didn't feel safe, and I didn't know if and when he might come back. So I bought a gun to protect myself, my friend, and our dogs if he came back after us.

Not everyone has the same reaction to a traumatic gun experience. I know of friends who were held up at gunpoint and never want to see a gun again but also friends who feel empowered after being mugged by owning a gun themselves. There is no right answer—no right way to respond to those feelings of helplessness, fear, and trauma.

Some basic tenets of anarchist ideology are concepts like empowerment and autonomy. Having a gun, and knowing how to use one safely, is an empowering thing for me. It gives me more autonomy in my ability to deal with my own problems. The police are not a resource that I want to engage whenever I can avoid it and not a resource I find to be very effective either. Calling the police often brings more danger into a situation than there was before. While this one incident was my push into gun ownership, knowing that I have guns and can carry one with me (I have a concealed carry permit) gives me a greater sense of freedom of movement and freedom from fear than I might otherwise have.

The Political

The North American anarchist movement does not have the numbers or strength to overthrow the government or even to effectively initiate armed struggle at this time. But we do have the ability to start working to build the world we want to see as best we can within the capitalist context. And in doing so, we will show people what an anarchist world can look like, and they will be much more likely to join us. Part of building this world we want to see is being prepared to step in where the government cannot or will not. Acts of solidarity and community go a long way toward showing people why anarchist politics make sense.

Guns are one of the many tools that help anarchists stay prepared and keep people safe. For example, when a hurricane came to our neighborhood and knocked down a lot of trees, blocking roads, I felt unprepared because I did not own a chainsaw. I have since gotten one and now feel more prepared to help my community and neighbors.

The police are our enemy. They are a well-organized, well-funded gang that exists to protect the powers that be. We must develop alternatives to the police, as well as resistance to and protection from the police. Some alternatives to the police we can and should develop include mediation teams, crisis hotlines, therapists, and community building.

Thousands of people die each day, directly or indirectly, because of capitalism and the state. From victims of police brutality to victims of wars over resources through victims of hunger and poverty to victims of neglect or stress, there is constantly harm being done. Pacifism has not yet and, in my opinion, will never defeat these mechanisms of suffering. I think any act against capitalism or the state can be viewed as an act of self-defense—at least theoretically.

If our movement proceeds and truly becomes a threat, we are likely going to need to practice self-defense. As my friend Ben Turk of Insurgent Theatre has pointed out, the fabled "Rev" would more likely look like a collapse than a coup. Political instability due to economic or environmental collapse seems likely. If only heteronormative, conservative, white males own guns, that unstable situation would be incredibly dangerous for people of color, queers, immigrants, and women. Allies and directly affected parties who can safely access and maintain guns and gun skills ought to, in order to be available to act in solidarity with oppressed groups who do not have access to or desire for guns within the current system.

The Personal Is the Political

I identify as genderqueer, although much of our society persists in perceiving me as female. Being viewed as a female puts me at risk for a variety of types of attacks and assaults. Taking up arms is one thing I am able to do to protect myself from a patriarchal society, which far too often views women and nonbinary people as targets. Often either viewed as a sex object to be propositioned, or a "dyke" or "thing," the feeling of fear on the street is something with which I am familiar. Trans women of color (TWOC) in particular face disproportionately high amounts of violence and murder each year. An anarchist movement might decide to support TWOC and other nonbinary and queer folks by offering gun training and financial help for purchasing guns. The personal identities of individuals are connected to larger political issues, which can in turn affect the risks and privileges each person might face when choosing to have or carry or use a gun. Some risks (like a person of color being shot by a cop) might be increased by the presence of weapons.

I own four guns—a .38 revolver, a 9 mm handgun, a .22 rifle, and a twenty-gauge shotgun—all pretty standard types. All legal, and I even have a state-sanctioned concealed carry permit. My approach around guns (and most things) has always been to be very frank and honest about them. I'd rather have it be well-known that I own legal guns than to later have the police try to act surprised and potentially escalate a situation. The state has made attempts to demonize my owning guns, due to my politics.

In 2012, the Virginia legislature was voting on some really patriarchal, restrictive, invasive abortion laws. There were a series of protests on the issue, which culminated on Saturday March 3, 2012, where thirty protesters were arrested by heavily armed riot cops. The visual of these heavily armed riot cops garnered media attention and public critique. The reason behind the armed cops turned out to be myself and the other members of the Wingnut Anarchist Collective—even though we hadn't participated in that particular protest. The Wingnut Anarchist Collective has been involved in a wide variety of organizations and protests since 2009, and by 2012, we had had numerous interactions with the Richmond Police Department, gaining a good deal of media attention. The RPD knew who we were and that members of the collective legally owned guns.

The local paper, the *Richmond Times Dispatch*, reported on March 8: "Senate Majority Leader Thomas K. Norment Jr., R–James City, said the law enforcement presence, which included police in riot gear, was justified. Norment noted that several of the participants were members of the Occupy Richmond movement and The Wingnut, a local anarchist collective. 'That is what raised the level of concern,' Norment said, calling The Wingnut 'an identified anarchist, armed terrorist group.'" We all found this both confusing and funny. None of the Wingnuts, as we called ourselves, were even at that protest, and yet, somehow our possession of legal guns was enough to set the state on edge. Riot cops are used in all kinds of situations where no one is suspected to have guns, so it is most likely that we served as a convenient excuse for the state to justify their overreaction. Most folks realize that activists of all stripes are routinely referred to as terrorists, regardless of their gun ownership. Very likely, white privilege had a lot to do with why the situation did not escalate further.

The members of the Wingnut Anarchist Collective at the time wrote this response, titled "Norment Tries to Blame Anarchists for Government Bad Behavior":

> It's easy to feel upset about being called a terrorist. It's pretty widely known how the government treats people after it starts calling them terrorists, so having a fairly important politician call you a terrorist is a lot like a threat. Rather than getting all bent out of shape about it, we're probably going to go ahead and make terrorist glitter paint T-shirts or something. We're not going to let this stuff get to us because getting all outraged about Senator Tommy's (ignorant, irresponsible) name-calling is giving him what he wants, which is to distract from the bad behavior of his side.[1]

The take-home for me from this whole incident is that, guns or no guns, the state and police understand that we are enemies. When you add guns to the picture, the state has more leeway and desire to push against you and respond aggressively. This is not because the state engages in repression based on militancy, but because the state attacks groups that are effective. Militancy just happens to correlate with success or effectiveness in many circumstances.

Accessibility and Privilege

Realistically speaking, I don't want to shoot anyone. Rationally speaking, the harm to my own psyche that would occur from shooting someone is enough motivation to avoid doing so unless absolutely necessary.

On a larger scale, this question of when shooting someone would be necessary or morally acceptable is a major undertone for much of the gun debate. Throwing race, class, gender, and sexuality into the mix, we can get into some scary waters. For some white folks, black people, and specifically black men, seem scary. This heightened, although irrational and racist, fear justifies to these people their "self-defense" responses to real or perceived threats by people of color. That is why "stand your ground" laws have blurred the discussion, perpetuated institutional racism, and created false conceptions of justifiable shootings.

Historically, people of color in the South were not allowed to own guns, as fear of slave uprisings and slaves murdering white people dominated white society. Now that people of color have equal gun rights, centuries of racism mean they are still not viewed the same by larger society. A white person with a gun might be a hunter or a good ol' boy, but a black person with a gun is a thug. This racism is perpetuated in the media and taints every reaction to guns.

White folks with guns have a history of being racist and oppressive. For many people of color, the sight of a white person with a gun can evoke historical trauma, such as recollections of the Klan and extraordinarily hateful movements. Also, the privileges of being white means that for a white person the open carrying of guns is less a risk of police violence than for a person of color. I would also be remiss in not acknowledging the history of racism with the NRA, their failure to support the rights of the Black Panthers to open carry, and the overall failures of all national gun-lobbying groups to advocate against oppression.

There is a certain amount of privilege that is needed in many circumstances to own a gun—gender, class, race, and immigrant status. U.S. gun culture tends to be dominated by white men with privilege. It is also incredibly government-, cop-, and military-loving. It is more difficult for people outside of the white male dynamic to deal with gun culture. Sitting through a concealed carry gun course at a local gun show, for example, isn't exactly fun if you aren't a supporter of the white patriarchy. We're talking a room full of mostly white dudes, very coded racism and sexism, and being instructed by a retired cop.

Not to mention that gun stores and gun shows and gun ranges are chock full of racist, America-loving, sexist crap. This social character can manifest varying levels of intensity depending on the place, and it will affect everyone differently depending on their privileges and mental and emotional states. Money, documentation, and personal safety are all factors that can make access to guns more difficult for some people. Anarchist movements that embrace guns as a tactic might want to examine access and find concrete methods to broaden access to guns and gun training.

Other areas where access to guns is an issue are for folks with felony convictions (who are disproportionately people of color) and for folks who have been incarcerated in psychiatric hospitals for mental health reasons. My friend Megan Osborn with Richmond's Mind(ful) Liberation Project, a branch of the Icarus Project, which promotes radical mental health helped me realize many of the mental health issues surrounding guns in the anarchist scene. There are people who will choose for their own mental health reasons to not be around guns or not want themselves to have access to guns. Examples of this might be people with posttraumatic stress disorder or anxiety attacks who realize that they might overreact to trauma or startling events and noises and do not wish to risk inappropriately shooting someone. People with suicidal or self-harm tendencies and depression may also choose to not have access to guns. As an anarchist community, we need to be supportive of people with mental health issues and not try to guilt or pressure anyone into participating with guns who does not want to. There is room for everyone, regardless of ability and preference, in our movement.

Radical Critiques

Reactions within radical circles to radicals with guns really run the gamut. Many radicals or anarchists maintain a liberal politic informed by the Democratic Party's perspective on guns—guns are scary, the state ought to protect people from themselves by restricting access to guns, and only inbred rednecks like guns really anyways. Appearances of guns and those toting them seem to upset the delicate sensibilities of those who enjoy their capitalism from a more middle-class seat. As my friend Dave says, the violence that happens at Target is all in the products on the shelves (sweatshop labor, animal cruelty, and environmental destruction). The more middle-class and liberal point of view finds violence and guns to be distasteful unless used by the state. This perspective comes from not typically having to engage in hunting, fishing, and gathering for survival or being around police, institutional, and personal violence as much. There is an antagonistic psychology to it as well—the right wing likes guns, so the left wing rejects them without thought as a reaction. Politics in the U.S. has been curated in such a binary manner that it can be difficult to break free of one or the other mind-set.

There is a feeling that guns are an arena in which anarchists cannot compete with the government and ought not try. But we can do, and have done, guns differently, and that is where our strengths really are. Not in competition, but in changing the rules of the game, breaking the rules, and seeking a path outside of the boundaries. This might be the boundaries of conventional warfare or just the boundaries of social expectations. There is a lot of creativity and intelligence within anarchist movements and freedom from the bureaucratic institutions that command our enemies.

On the other hand, some radicals might fetishize armed struggle. Fetishization is the act of being obsessively or irrationally devoted to an object or activity. When this happens with *any* tactic or idea its problematic because focus tends to be so much in one arena that it does not engage fully with intersectional issues which surround that arena.

White anarchists fetishizing armed struggle by people of color is also problematic. More accurately, it is racist. White folks who do so are idealizing the violence dealt with and risks taken by people with less privilege than themselves. White anarchists acting like they have ownership over a tactic that has been used around the world by many different radical groups of people of color isn't okay either. Understanding and acknowledging that white folks weren't the inventors or the first ones to use various tactics is really important. Just like guns aren't the exclusive realm of oppressive regimes, they are also not exclusive to white anarchists. There is a necessary balance of giving credit and homage to the people of color and organizations of color who have historically taken up arms for liberation without tokenizing or fetishizing those people and organizations or appropriating aspects of their movements that are not okay for white people to take.

Moving Forward

In creating a culture of resistance, those who don't want own or use guns can still support their comrades who do. If folks in anarchist communities stay on top of building a culture that is educated around security culture, knowing your rights, and copwatching, we can help keep everyone more safe. *Security Culture* is the concept of making sure people do not discuss illegal activities, speculate about who might be cops, or other sorts of rumor-spreading and potentially dangerous activities that can harm movements and lead to arrests. *Knowing Your Rights* can help prevent police from holding more power in a situation than they already do and can prevent arrests. *Copwatching*, or the filming and recording of the police when they are interacting with people, can act as a deterrent to the police violating someone's rights or causing them physical harm, as well as create physical evidence if any objectionable activity does occur. This is especially helpful for people with guns, who are likely to receive a little bit more government attention than others. In Virginia, my concealed carry permit status shows up when a cop runs my driver's license.

I have had a cop who pulled me over for copwatching come back to ask me about my gun. Educated comrades can be wonderful backup in situations like these. In my situation, my friend was able to help remind me of my rights and how to assert them and was also able to video record the situation. Beyond guns there are many different tools and methods of self-defense and community defense that radicals can learn, train in, and share. We can support each other in finding what is comfortable and within each of our abilities to do.

Notes

1   Michael Paul Williams, "Lawmaker's 'Terrorist' Claim Reckless," *Richmond Times-Dispatch*, March 9, 2012, http://www.richmond.com/archive/michael-paul-williams-lawmaker-s-terrorist-claim-reckless/article_0618ee04-e3aa-585c-aaf0-6bc73de8efd8.html, accessed June 30, 2017.

Defending Communities, Demanding Autonomy: Self-Defense Militias in Venezuela's Barrios

George Ciccariello-Maher

From Ñángaras to Tupamaros to Bolivarians

Latin America saw a sustained debate over the virtues and vices of armed self-defense over the latter half of the twentieth century, with political events playing an occasionally decisive role in reinforcing theories. The violent liquidation of peasant self-defense zones in Marquetalia, Colombia, in 1964, and workers' self-defense in Bolivia led the radical French intellectual Régis Debray to declare "the death of a certain ideology" in which self-defense as a strategy had been "liquidated by the march of events."[1] These events, alongside the rapid and unexpected success of the Cuban Revolution, led Debray to reject a strategy of territorial control in favor of the hypermobility of small guerrilla units that strike and retreat almost without leaving a trace. This doctrine, known as *foquismo*, was quickly imported into the Venezuelan guerrilla struggle of the 1960s, but it proved disastrous.

Foquismo made it difficult, if not impossible, to develop sustained *political* relationships with the masses, and since those masses themselves were increasingly moving to the exploding semi-urban *barrios* ringing the cities, the rural armed struggle was a nonstarter and the Venezuelan guerrillas were quickly doomed to a losing fight. This

failure did not mean that the armed struggle of the 1960s was irrelevant, however. With its very limitations it would plant the seeds for
much that has come since. Specifically, those radicalized by the guerrillas would seek to develop new strategies in an urban setting, and in
particular in those barrio communities ravaged by both the violence
of the drug trade and the related violence of the police. Much like in
the United States, many believe that drugs were introduced into the
barrios in a conscious attempt to destroy movements, and while this
is contested, what is undeniable is that the police played a major role
in controlling the supply of the drugs and weapons that quickly began
to tear neighborhoods apart.

The response of many young radicals in the 1980s—denounced by
police at the time as "ñángaras"—was a spontaneous return to grassroots self-defense. Small groups emerged, fed up with the destruction
of communities, first with sticks and knives, then with whatever guns
they could get their hands on, issuing cryptic threats to those dealing
drugs: stop dealing or leave. If the warnings were not heeded, a beating
would ensue, and if that didn't work, possibly even an execution. Once
such spontaneous tactics began to spread, local residents and police
alike began to call such shadowy groups "Tupamaros," in reference to
the Uruguayan revolutionary group.

As such tactics spread organically across the most radical barrios,
the groups that coalesced around them consolidated their control
over larger territories. As the old Venezuelan political system entered
into crisis—a crisis marked more than anything by the massive 1989
anti-neoliberal riot known as the *Caracazo*—some of these groups
even pushed police out of their communities, establishing de facto
self-governed autonomous zones. This was especially the case in the
revolutionary stronghold of 23 de Enero, just to the west of the historic
city center of Caracas, and La Vega to the south.

In 23 de Enero, the revolutionary collective La Piedrita ("The
Pebble") is emblematic of this long-term struggle for autonomous
self-defense. It began nearly three decades ago in the same spontaneous resistance to the scourge of drug trafficking and violence. "This
place was a dump, a drug zone," the leader of La Piedrita, Valentín
Santana, explained to me: "Here in 23 de Enero, if you wanted to occupy
a space it was necessary to use revolutionary violence. *I* had to use
revolutionary violence." Self-defense for La Piedrita, as for many other

revolutionary collectives with long histories and longer memories, is not a merely local or nonideological commitment; they consider themselves communists and Guevaraists and supplement political organizing with revolutionary education.

While historical collectives like La Piedrita are an exception dotting the Venezuelan landscape, the practice of self-defense in the present also far exceeds these most organized and ideologically developed elements. Just down the street, a tall apartment block with a history of revolutionary influences is governed by a more informal collective of neighbors who draw upon the repertoires of armed self-defense to protect their zone. "If we catch someone dealing drugs in our neighborhood," one neighbor tells me, "first they get a warning. If they show up again, they get a beating. And if they show up a third time…" He trails off, indicating with a hand gesture that the outcome will not be pleasant.

Self-Defense and the State

Many of these revolutionary communities also threw themselves into the national movement to topple a decades-old system of corrupt and exclusionary representative democracy that had turned murderous, killing hundreds, if not thousands, in the aftermath of the Caracazo. The ensuing alliance of revolutionary guerrillas and soldiers catapulted Hugo Chávez to the status of a national hero, leading to his release from prison and eventual election in 1998. From being against the government, most if not all of Venezuela's revolutionary self-defense militias were now for it—in a complex situation of supporting Chávez while hostile to the bloated and corrupt monstrosity that is the petro-state.

Today, La Piedrita stands like a sort of fortress—a relatively small and self-enclosed tangle of short apartment blocks surrounded by revolutionary graffiti, including most famously a mural of Jesus with an AK-47 that once read, "Christ supports the armed struggle." The zone is ringed with security cameras and loudspeakers, and no one enters unnoticed. Once inside the inner sanctum, a mural greets all guests: "Here La Piedrita gives the orders and the government obeys." This is not an exaggeration, either; one time, the Chávez government sent a military captain into the zone to scout possible escape routes for the president in the event of another coup attempt. He was quickly seized by collective members to send a stern message: the government does not tell us anything; it must ask.

While most if not all in La Piedrita support the current government, some relate to it more closely—accepting more funding, engaging in more government-sponsored events and activities—while some defend their autonomy at all costs. The importance of this relationship became especially apparent in April 2002, when the Venezuelan opposition and private media, with support from the U.S. government, provoked a coup that removed Chávez from power for less than two days and nearly saw him killed. It was only the massive and spontaneous mobilization of hundreds of thousands in the streets that led to the unprecedented reversal of that coup, and amid that undeniable spontaneity, revolutionary collectives, militias, and other organized and armed elements played a central role.

Not only did such groupings participate in the mass mobilizations in the streets, spreading word throughout the barrios of Caracas that a coup was underway, but they also made active plans to seize Miraflores Palace themselves if necessary. More than anything, they defended their territory as they had done in some cases for decades—especially in 23 de Enero, which peeks out over the hills toward the palace and became a military target for the coup plotters, because of both its strategic location and its history of militancy. Opposition-led police attempted to storm the zone but were stopped short by the militias themselves. Several Chavista ministers escaped the coup into the safe haven provided by these revolutionary autonomous communities, and the Chávez government only returned to power through the efforts of these revolutionary organizers in the streets.

Despite this, La Piedrita has often entered into conflict with the state, with Chávez even declaring them terrorists and CIA-infiltrated spies for their overly provocative actions, which included attacking an opposition television station with teargas and threatening the lives of opposition leaders. But this was more rhetoric than anything else; Chávez once ordered the arrest of Valentín Santana, but no one ever followed through. The provocative action of such undisciplined and autonomous groups, while occasionally giving the government a headache, has also represented a catalyst and motor for radicalizing the political process as a whole, heightening tensions with the opposition while sharpening social contradictions in a way that reinforces the revolutionary commitment of the grassroots. This is why Santana and other radical elements, despite claiming revolutionary self-defense above all else, despite emphasizing local and autonomous self-government, nevertheless pledged their loyalty to Chávez as they do to Maduro today, not as presidents but as important elements in a revolutionary process that includes local self-defense as a key element.

Armed Ambiguities

In the past year, however, the debate surrounding armed self-defense has leapt to the forefront of public debate in worrying ways. Shortly after Chávez's death in 2013, the Maduro government, with the support of many grassroots activists, pressed for a disarmament law in an attempt to confront spiraling levels of violent crime. Given the historic importance of armed struggle and later armed self-defense, however, many militants were skeptical of a law that seemed more geared toward assuaging the middle class than truly confronting the drug cartels behind the violence. This concern seemed validated when the first public display of decommissioned weapons occurred, of all places, in 23 de Enero, hotbed of armed self-defense militias. When a Chavista television personality named Alberto Nolia used his evening program on state-run Channel 8 to criticize the law as replete with petty-bourgeois prejudices—even launching the hashtag "Chávez wanted the people armed"—his show was quickly pulled.

Opposition youth took to the streets in early 2014, moreover, in a wave of protests that—despite claiming the banner of nonviolence—generated forty-three deaths on both sides of the political divide. When grassroots Chavistas resisted these street blockades, however, they were smeared with the panicked denunciation of *"colectivos"*—simultaneously as blind followers of demagogic leaders and as dangerously autonomous of the state. The truth is much more the latter; many such groups are fervent supporters of their government, precisely because they see it as an institutional beachhead for a broader revolutionary process.

In the past year, fearful opposition rhetoric about armed *colectivos* has coincided with some indications that elements of the repressive state apparatus are reasserting themselves against more radical sectors. On October 7, 2014, a highly specialized police force known as the CICPC entered a building and killed some members of two previously unknown revolutionary collectives before later returning. In the interim, the leader of one collective, José Miguel Odreman, told the press that the attack was political and that his death would fall on the head of the interior minister. When the CICPC returned, Odreman and others wound up dead as well, with five deaths in total.

The official line on the massacre was that Odreman and others were operating under the guise of a revolutionary collective but were in reality a violent criminal gang—and many Chavistas believed this (it didn't help that Odreman was a former Metropolitan Police sergeant). Others that knew Odreman better told a different story: that he was a true revolutionary whose collective was stepping on the toes of either the corrupt economic interests of the CICPC or its demand for a monopoly on violence. According to the radical intellectual Roland Denis, this was the revolution's "first massacre"—the first time since Chávez's election that the brutal force of the state had been turned against its own.

At a secret meeting of collectives later that month that Denis himself chaired, a document was hammered out that reiterated continued support for the Bolivarian process and proposed a nuanced dialogue with the national government around the question of armed self-defense. While the document recognizes the national Bolivarian Armed Forces as the "highest expression of the 'people in arms,'" reserving for it a monopoly of *military* weaponry, it nevertheless quotes Chávez's own repeated insistence that the Bolivarian Revolution is "peaceful, but not unarmed." The revolutionary collectives, for their part, would agree to support the disarmament of criminal gangs and to purify their own ranks of violent activity, while insisting nevertheless on the right to maintain arms "for the purpose of effective community and popular self-defense."[2]

Notes

1   Régis Debray, *Revolution in the Revolution?* (New York: Grove Press, 1967), 27.
2   "Propuesta inicial de una Mesa de Diálogo Por la Paz, La Justicia, y la Revolución— Documento-Acuerdo entre los Colectivos de Trabajo Revolucionario, Movimiento de Defensa Popular Juan Montoya y el Gobierno Nacional" (November 2014).

Toward a Redneck Revolt

Dave Strano

Our relationship to violence is deeply personal and often goes back to our childhoods. I grew up working class in a military family and was raised in firearm culture in Georgia and Kansas. As I became politicized, like so many other working-class and poor folks who court social justice politics, I became ashamed of my past steeped in gun culture. I was taught to feel guilty about having come from communities that celebrated hunting and gun ownership. By the time I hit my twenties, I believed fully that individual firearms ownership was antithetical to the world of love, harmony, and equality I was now fighting for. So many of us have experienced violence personally by the time we reach adulthood that it makes sense on some level for us to push for nonviolence in our politics.

I didn't reconsider gun ownership for myself until the 2003 Miami protests against the Free Trade Area of the Americas (FTAA). Thousands of people had come together to mobilize against a neoliberal trade agreement expansion that directly endangered workers, the environment, and communities in the U.S. and Central America. For several days, protesters attempted to disrupt the FTAA summit and were attacked in the street by one of the most intense crowd suppression campaigns enacted by American law enforcement, now known

263

as the "Miami Model." Preemptive arrests, sunset curfews, targeting of media, and massive shows of militarized force shocked the country. For over an hour on one of those November nights in Miami, I was held at gunpoint by a scared young National Guard soldier and the experience forced me to finally rethink my position on armed resistance.

Nationally at that time state repression was intensifying and directly threatened many of the projects I was involved with back home in Kansas. By 2004, dozens of my friends in the Great Plains Anarchist Network were facing allegations that our organization planned on violently disrupting the Republican and Democratic Party conventions that summer. Fortunately, none of us ended up in prison as a result of those Grand Jury investigations, but it was made very clear to us that there were no safe ways to organize our community. All anarchist organizing at the time was regarded as a threat to the state, and we could either quit entirely or find ways to keep each other safe in a climate of fear and suspicion. As FBI agents were knocking on the doors of our friends, family, and coworkers, members of our local collective decided to send a clear message that we would not be intimidated. We bought high-powered rifles, and the John Brown Gun Club was born.[1]

Unlike most anarchist groups, most of us in the original John Brown Gun Club came from working-class backgrounds. Many of us had tried desperately to turn our backs on our families, and even the communities we grew up in—as though our internalized classism would allow us to walk away from their racism, sexism, and reactionary ideologies. Now, instead, we decided to embrace our backgrounds, even going so far as proudly calling ourselves Rednecks. We aimed to take back that classist word, which had been used to disparage poor people and isolate them. Within the gun club, we came to understand that the shared experiences of our class background set us apart from many of our comrades and friends but also gave us perspectives that are often missed in social justice organizing.

Working together with firearms, we learned how important it was to have real trust and commitment to each other. We made many mistakes in the beginning, some which could have gotten us arrested or killed, and we learned invaluable lessons about taking firearms seriously. Over time, those lessons evolved into a mind-set that we now try to incorporate into every project we work on, involving revolutionary discipline. Simply put, we feel that we must build relationships of

Phoenix Redneck Revolt/John Brown Gun Club 2016. Credit: Redneck Revolt.

trust by keeping our word, showing up on time, and following through with our commitments. We must build the types of strong, long-term relationships that allow us to trust each other with loaded firearms and make us less susceptible to state repression. Knowing that you can trust someone to stand beside you with a loaded weapon in a hostile situation takes a much deeper level of trust than most of us had built within previous social justice projects, where many of our peers felt more like coworkers than friends or family members. To build real resilience in the face of state repression and reactionary violence, we have to build the types of relationships where none of us are disposable and all of us are worth fighting for. We have to be honest about our flaws and open to growing together. We have to be committed to each other first and our projects second.

When the John Brown Gun Club first started offering public firearms trainings in late 2005, we found ourselves shunned by some who had been our closest allies. Our efforts were labeled dangerous and suicidal, and many of our former friends began predicting our capture or murder at the hands of police. They argued that our organizing represented an escalation that would provoke the state to respond. Instead of seeing our efforts as a defensive reaction to the overwhelming violence of the state, our former allies saw them as provoking violent reprisals. Others assumed that we must be police officers or paid provocateurs. There was very little willingness among our Left and liberal friends to understand the use of firearms as praxis for liberation.

That John Brown Gun Club focused on two main program points: to facilitate armed organizing and arms knowledge within radical movements and marginalized communities, and to use gun culture as an opening to reach white working folks who might otherwise be recruited into organizations like the Minutemen or local militias. To that end, that first John Brown Gun Club tabled at dozens of gun shows and distributed thousands of pieces of literature. We helped push the Minutemen and the Missouri Militia out of the local gun shows by holding space ourselves and building a culture that was not welcoming to such formations. We also built relationships with several local Minutemen, who then left the organization and helped us shut down their national conference.

Fast forward to 2016, when it seemed like the whole country finally started talking in one way or another about the "problem of the white working class." These conversations have ranged from vilifying and blaming white workers for the rise of Donald Trump to observations about the abandonment of the white working class by both liberals and radicals. All of a sudden, the political work we were advancing over a decade ago feels even more relevant.

In mid-2016, several former Kansas John Brown Gun Club members came together to build Redneck Revolt, a national project of armed organizing against white supremacy. Some of our branches are John Brown Gun Clubs, but all of our national work focuses on firearms and community defense as a two-part strategy: using firearms as a way to do anti-racist outreach and relate to other working-class people from all backgrounds, and as a way to build real, meaningful cross-racial solidarity among working-class folks. Redneck Revolt values projects that build infrastructure to make our communities safer and healthier. Within our national branches, we have local programs to grow food, teach livestock farming, do harm reduction, and offer free firearms training. We make ourselves accessible to our communities as a form of accountability: our faces are uncovered and many of our names are known because we have a responsibility to engage directly with our neighbors and speak to our words and actions.[2]

Redneck Revolt also engages in direct outreach in the places where white nationalists traditionally recruit, such as gun shows, state fairs, cattle sales, and flea markets, and our goal is to build long-term relationships with people, not just hand them a flier. We believe in engaging with people as neighbors, which means treating folks with respect and expecting to have more conversations with them in the future. It also means having the integrity to stand by our beliefs, while respecting the person we're talking to and trying to find our common ground. These are not skills easily acquired, and we are always working to improve on them, but meeting people where they are at used to be a central tenet of social justice organizing. Building firearms familiarity has helped immensely with opening those conversations at gun shows and other outreach events, largely because differentiating ourselves from academic anti-gun liberals has been a first step in building trust with the working folks who are our coworkers, family members, and next-door neighbors.

Any meaningful and widespread working-class movement will include firearms and armed self-defense, not only because that's an important aspect of working-class culture, but also because it is a logical response to rising reactionary and state violence. Within the safe prescriptions of liberal academic politics, many social justice advocates have failed to respond to the urgency of the conditions that poor and marginalized people in America now live in, and thus have lost credibility with the mainstream working class. Meanwhile, armed reactionary groups like the III% (a.k.a. Three Percenters) and Oath Keepers have seen their numbers and popularity increase. Instead of seeking common ground on anti-government sentiment and building real, sustainable, and inclusive community defense models, the Left increasingly sees our ranks filled with middle- and upper-class people who engage with the working class only as anthropologists and through academic studies and published essays. Misunderstanding firearms culture has heavily contributed to the disenfranchisement of the working class from Left and progressive politics, and, over-whelmingly, there is a lack of understanding of working-class values because they are not seen as meaningful or important. A movement that abandons the majority of the population as unreachable will only make itself marginal and irrelevant.

Notes

1   The tactics of the Miami Model were first used at the Republican National Convention in Philadelphia in 2000, then later became standard operating procedure for law enforcement's handling of protesters at mass demonstrations. See https://en.wikipedia.org/wiki/Miami_model, accessed June 30, 2017.

2   For more on Redneck Revolt, see https://www.redneckrevolt.org/about.

Defense in Dallas in the Twenty-First Century: An Interview with Members of the Huey P. Newton Gun Club

Interview by scott crow

Ed. note: This interview was conducted shortly after the creation of the Huey P. Newton Gun Club, a black revolutionary defense group in Dallas, Texas. We speak with Erick Khafre, cofounder, and Kilaika Anayejali Kwa Baruti, a member of the club, about its history, praxis, and aims.[1]

Q: *When did the club start and why?*
Erick Khafre: The Huey P. Newton Gun Club (HPN-GC), named after the cofounder of the original Black Panther Party, Huey P. Newton, was started in July of 2014 in Dallas, Texas. It grew from the black community's impatience with the continuing lack of accountability concerning police harassment, brutality, and the murder of black and brown people. A number of organizations and community members felt like a more aggressive approach was needed in the fight against police terrorism. So we, the HPN-GC, decided to do armed patrols as a symbol of resistance. We knew that it could draw a lot of national attention and could possibly encourage other communities to show resistance by doing armed patrols on a regular basis.

I envision that the HPN-GC will be a spark for armed resistance and self-defense throughout the country. It is my hope that we can pass our courage and skills on to the youth to prepare them to take

Members of the Huey P. Newton Gun Club marching in downtown Dallas, 2015. Credit: Huey P. Newton Gun Club.

community defense to a new level. As a member of a global African people I understand that armed self-defense has been a continual process for us since the domination of Western world politics. I expect that in the future more oppressed communities will realize the importance of institutionalizing community defense. At this point in time it is necessary to have as many self-defense units as possible. With that being said, the education of the masses is also very important. We must help raise the level of consciousness of the people in order to gain their total support. Otherwise defense will not be possible on a mass level.

Q: *What is the stated mission of the group?*
Khafre: As our website and literature state, inspired by the original Black Panther Party for Self-Defense in their 10-point program, "We want an immediate end to police brutality and murder of the Black community by the police state. Our position dictates that by organizing Black Self-Defense groups dedicated to defending our Black Community from police repression and brutality we can find some semblance of peace; the 2nd Amendment to the U.S. Constitution gives us a right to bear arms. We therefore believe that all Black People should arm themselves for Self-Defense."

Q: *Why is it important for people of color today to practice armed self-defense or self-reliance?*

Kilaika Anayejali Kwa Baruti: Armed self-defense is a necessity when it comes to self-determination. When we as African people create and build institutions, gain control of our own resources, and determine our own destinies in every aspect, we must be able to defend and secure what we create. If not, it can be destroyed at any time.

History has proven that power only respects power. Unfortunately, the people lack power. The biggest enforcer of the United States of America's power structure is the arms that it bears as tools used to intimidate the people and maintain control. The people, however, can only be intimidated when they are unable to contend with their enemy on equivalent ground. Police brutality and terrorism are prime examples of the people being victimized because they don't collectively practice armed self-defense.

Q: *What has the reaction been, both among other political groups and in the community?*

Khafre: Well, of course most working-class black and brown communities in this country support the idea self-defense in general, and armed patrols are something a lot of them see as necessary. So we have been received well by most community-based groups. In fact, many of them have reached out to us for membership or to show their support. However, there are a few peace groups who disagree with our tactics. But I must say that one thing all of these groups share with us is a consistent effort to organize against police terrorism.

Q: *How can armed groups keep from becoming vanguardist?*

Khafre: It is simple: we must organize around basic principles of unity and establish community standards that everyone will respect and honor. Any armed defense group claiming to be for the people must see themselves as part of the community. If they see themselves as better or as higher than the people, then that community will surely turn their backs on them. You have to be seen as members of the community and not some outsiders trying to force your way of thinking on them.

Q: *How can armed groups keep from becoming perpetuators of violence and control like the state?*

Baruti: By being sure to have a political line and objectives that are reflected in their actions and programs are communal. They should have an ideology that serves the people with a humbleness, humility, and consistency. This can in no way mimic the state.

Notes

1   For more info see the Huey P. Newton Gun Club website, https://www.hueypnewtongunclub.org.

Trial by Fire: Democracy and Self-Defense in Rojava

Alexander Reid Ross and Ian LaVallee

Revolutionary Self-Defense

The fight to maintain Kurdish identity and autonomy against both state repression and the new self-described Sunni Caliphate, better known as the Islamic State or Daesh, represents one of the most important struggles in the world. In a sense, the struggle against IS is a trial by fire for the international community. The stakes include whether or not we can protect direct democracy, the rights of women, and the earth.

The self-defense movement has emerged to both defend and to practice ecological, feminist, and democratic values rooted in a deep-seated sense of cultural and geographic identity. Its revolutionary nature has drawn comparisons from contemporary radicals to the Spanish Civil War, which saw sweeping land reform, unprecedented advances in feminist politics, and the empowerment of anarchist institutions in 1936.[1]

The front lines of the struggle for Kurdish self-determination and against the Islamic State (IS) have taken place principally in two different places: Rojava (also known as Northern Syria or Western Kurdistan) and Northern Iraq (also known as Iraqi Kurdistan).

These two fields of combat are different and complex with a diverse array of actors. This essay will explore the emergence of self-defense groups in Rojava, along with a movement for direct, ecological, and feminist democracy and its relationship with Iraqi Kurdistan's much more hierarchical and established regional government.

Rojava!

Before the Arab Spring, there was Damascus Spring in 2000, an uprising of Kurds in Rojava. Sparked by the death of Syria's dictator, the riots in the northeast canton of Cizîrê were described as "unprecedented," expressing a need for self-determination that has spanned centuries of fighting and organizing.

Starting with the Democratic Society Congress in 2005, the drive for self-determination among communities in Kurdistan began to take the shape of neighborhood and city councils, civil society organizations, and political groups like the Peace and Democracy Party organized through the Group of Communities in Northern Kurdistan (Turkish Kurdistan).[2] This motion toward community organizing represented part of a movement led by Abdulla Öcalan's Kurdish Workers Party (PKK) away from guerrilla struggle after the end of the Cold War.

Initially, the movement saw its leaders, advocates, and activists arrested in waves of state repression. Pushing back, the Kurdish campaign to establish local councils accelerated in both Turkey and Syria beginning around the time of the Arab Spring in 2011.[3] As the movement in Syria collapsed into civil war during 2012, the Syrian government became overwhelmed with rebel fighters and retreated from the northern region, leaving the area largely up for grabs among conflicting groups. Many Kurds withdrew to three main cantons in Rojava: Cizîrê, Kobanê, and Efrîn, where they have established a de facto autonomous region and held out against the onslaught of IS.[4]

Because Kurdistan spans a large area with contradictory political configurations, from ancient tribal relations to the modern international diplomacy of the Kurdistan Regional Government (KRG) to the autonomous movement of Democratic Confederalism, a collective sense of identity becomes hugely important. Such an identity, according to Öcalan, relies upon the need for self-defense against state repression by the governments of Turkey, Syria, Iraq, and Iran:

> Societies without any mechanism of self-defense lose their identities, their capability of democratic decision-making, and their

political nature. Therefore, the self-defense of a society is not limited to the military dimension alone. It also presupposes the preservation of its identity, its own political awareness, and a process of democratization.[5]

The establishment of Democratic Confederalism involves not simply a central party but a diverse array of "social and political groups, religious communities, or intellectual tendencies" that contribute to "local decision-making processes" in a precarious autonomous space that dismantles the nature of patriarchy through ecologically responsible relationships.[6]

Under democratic autonomy, Kurdish communities encourage greater political participation and a normalization of self-defense for the sake of survival as a diverse and integral culture not only on its own, but in relation to other cultures with whom the Kurds trade, communicate, and develop. The Kurds have emerged through complex relationships with exogenous and endogenous groups in an ethnically diverse area, including many Alevi, Arabs, Armenians, Assyrians, Christians, Êzîdîs, Jews, Turkomen, and Chechens among their own.

The relatively new turn to direct democracy opened the way for direct participation of other ethnicities, mandating, for instance, the representation of different ethnicities within deputies of elected officials in order to guard against undemocratic favoritism. Neighborhood, municipal, and regional councils that consist of at least 40 percent women make local decisions.[7] Women's councils also exist to bring concerns, needs, and demands to the attention of regional councils.[8] The emergence of this feminist Democratic Confederalism has also coincided with nascent ecological struggles against environmentally destructive projects like massive hydroelectric dams.[9]

Cizîrê as Hub

Today, Cizîrê is the portal through which many international volunteers enter Rojava to join forces against the Islamic State. Most notably, anthropologist David Graeber has written about his experiences in Cizîrê, commenting on the "dual power situation," wherein a governmental system is established alongside a civil society without coercive imposition of police or the enfranchisement of a nation-state. Graeber recounts his experiences visiting a police academy (Asayiş): "Everyone had to take courses in non-violent conflict resolution and feminist theory before they were allowed to touch a gun. The co-directors explained to us their ultimate aim was to give everyone in the country six weeks of police training, so that ultimately, they could eliminate police."[10]

The internal security apparatus of Cizîrê was voted in by the community, which retains oversight and sovereignty. Military officers are elected by their soldiers, and hierarchies institutionalized for the purpose of efficiency are open to reassessment by the communities in which they operate. The systems being set in place practice "social isolation" as an alternative to imprisonment or execution, and maintain egalitarian forms of participation in the economic, social, and political functions of a given community or grouping of communities.[11]

Influential anarchist thinker Janet Biehl returned from the same delegation to Cizîrê that Graeber was on with similar praise:

> Rojava's economic model "is the same as its political model," an economics adviser in Derik told us: to create a "community economy," building cooperatives in all sectors and educating the people in the idea. The adviser expressed satisfaction that even though 70 percent of Rojava's resources must go to the war effort, the economy still manages to meet everyone's basic needs.[12]

The canton trades with the Kurdistan Regional Government (KRG) and benefits from the wealth of Iraqi Kurdistan, which comes in no small part through the oil trade with Turkey, a country that has placed an embargo against Rojava and systematically oppressed Kurdish self-determination.[13] Most of Cizîrê's trade operates through the autonomous jurisdiction of the KRG in Iraqi Kurdistan and is protected by well-funded Peshmerga forces. This trade brings in the crucial money and resources necessary to push IS further out of Rojava and Iraqi Kurdistan.

Because Cizîrê is so close to Iraqi Kurdistan, where the provisional government of Barzani has collaborated with the U.S. for more than a decade, it has been a staging point for successful incursions against the IS-held positions. For instance, in December 2014, Kurdish forces retook Mount Şingal, making use of some weapons provided by the German military, such as Dingos, 40 MG3s, 8,000 G3s, 200 Panzerfausts, 40 heavy Panzerfausts, 30 Milan launchers, 8,000 Walther P1s, and 10,000 hand grenades.[14] These coordinated military assaults, which utilize standard military tactics, are particular to collaborations with the Iraqi Peshmerga, and are less possible in Rojava, where the formation of self-defense groups has less funding and organization.

Holding Kobanê

The weapons trade in the region is extremely diffuse, and there is no short supply of Chinese, Yugoslavian, and Egyptian AKs, and even anti-aircraft guns. While the KRG's Peshmerga can be seen with a diverse array of weaponry, as they are well funded and exist with the backing of the Iraqi government, the self-defense groups based in Rojava itself have less access to weapons and supplies. At the same time, IS is supplied with a vast amount of equipment, arms, and supplies by Gulf States that have syphoned U.S. arms deals to spread that Salafist movement of which IS is part.[15] One prince of Saudi Arabia, among the U.S.'s staunchest allies in the region, has insisted that the U.S. should prioritize fighting Syria over IS.[16] Since the Kurdish political party in Rojava, the PYD, is closely connected with Öcalan's PKK, Turkey, another strong U.S. ally, has refused to allow fighters and supporters to cross the border with Syria, leaving the PYD's armed self-defense groups, YPG and YPJ, painfully undersupplied.[17]

Female fighters have always been treated as a curiosity in the way that the West views the Kurdish struggle for autonomy, and this tradition is taken up today by the storied YPJ, which was created in 2013 as the civil war raged. With hundreds of battalions throughout Syria, the YPJ is an autonomous force independent from the YPG. The YPJ's female-only defense units have played crucial roles in holding back IS's assault, particularly in Kobanê (Ayn al-Arab).[18]

Kobanê lies at the middle of the Syrian border with Turkey, and is the hometown of the leader of the YPG. In October 2013, the Islamic State mounted an attack against Kobanê from Turkey, leading experts to assert that Turkey was giving succor to IS.[19] However, the Kurds have mounted an austere, stalwart combat against IS, repelling them from the border to the surprise of pundits who expected the city to fall like a domino.

Importantly, when the PYD called on Kurds to join the struggle in Kobanê, copresident Salih Muslim declared:

> In Urfa there are our tribes, the Shekhani, Berazi, Ketkani and
> Beski. These tribes are in Kobanê, too. Would a member of the

Berazi tribe in Suruç accept the selling of a Berazi woman or girl in another place? Would the other tribes? The border has divided families. These families are from the same tribes. I don't think any Kurd will accept this. In that case they should rise up and resist.[20]

This urgent plea to the tribes highlights the felt duty to fight to protect kin and community. While advancing a tradition of feminist power from the history of Kurdish cultural identity, Democratic Confederalism also seems pragmatic about the existence and importance of the existing tribal structure. The YPG has also made successful overtures to Arab tribes.[21]

The Kurdish self-defense groups operating in Kobanê are not only from Western Kurdistan and the KRG Peshmerga but from the easternmost part of Kurdistan in present-day Iran as well. They report from the front lines to the world with the help of websites and social media. Meanwhile, fighters move around the city with a cautious eye out for snipers, rockets, and mortars. They traverse buildings using holes in the walls and maneuver through the rubble that much of the city of Kobanê has become with a sense of camaraderie and cautious optimism.[22] While the city is not secure, with the help of U.S. air strikes, more than 80 percent of Kobanê remains in Kurdish hands.[23]

Defending Democratic Autonomy

On the westernmost border of Rojava, the city of Efrîn holds out against Syrian repression and IS. City officials describe the situation as a "revolution" that has brought prosperity to the region, but defense remains an indispensable way of life along with it. According to the economic minister of Efrîn:

> With the beginning of the revolution, over the first year, we found[ed] a newspaper and TV channel. We formed a people's assembly. We threw out the regime elements among us. We threw out organizations and people connected to the regime but we did not do harm to any place. It was even forbidden to break open a cash box. Before the revolution 450 thousand people were living in Efrîn. After the revolution the population exceeded 1 million. Close to 200 thousand Arabs came and settled here.[24]

In order to maintain economic productivity, the Kurdish administration founded an Economic Development Center in Derik and opened branches concerned with commerce, agriculture, and crafts in Qamişlo, Kobanê, and Efrîn. When craft and commerce associations and trade unions emerged, artisans and merchants could connect easily, all facilitated by a new regime based on municipal elections. There is also the claim to full employment and a taxation system being set into place—none of this would be possible had the self-defense squads not taken up arms after the Syrian military withdrew from Rojava in 2013.[25]

While the PKK shifted from a guerrilla group to localized political practice; the Peshmerga fighters in Iraq are a more well-trained, well-funded military, and the YPG/YPJ in Rojava are more like self-defense units emerging from communities and tribes around Kurdistan that do not have training in offensive military operations.

Conclusion

The geography of Rojava is crucial to the needs of maintaining critical infrastructure to ensure and defend democratic positions. As Cizîrê, with its support from the KRG, provides a base of operations and economic sustainability, Kobanê fortifies the position against IS with strong YPG/YPJ presence and establishes both greater political space for egalitarian systems and tangible protection of civilians from sex slavery, deportation, and execution by IS.[26] Efrîn remains perhaps a key location that maintains coordinated integration throughout Rojava and provides a revolutionary model of economic and political success. With these footholds defended, a broader aggressive formation has been possible, allowing for critical recapturing of key IS positions such as Mount Şingal.[27]

When the Kurds liberated Şingal in what is known as modern-day Iraq, thousands of Êzîdîs held hostage there by IS were released. With the success of Kurdish operations against IS in the region between Rojava and Iraq, the Êzîdîs have risen up to declare autonomy as well.[28] The increased sentiment of self-sufficiency, autonomy, and self-defense continues to spread throughout the region. The struggle against IS has challenged the capacity of the KRG's political hierarchy to respond militarily, and it remains possible that the same transformation happening in Western Kurdistan will begin to take place within the formalized government of the KRG as well. That transition, however, manifests the challenges of confederating the political and social character of Kurdish movements spanning territories of some five nation-states. At the same time, the movement against IS has also empowered the portentous presence of Sunni and Shi'ite militias in Iraq, which likely will pose significant political and military problems in the future.[29]

As the demand for autonomy spreads, the fight against IS also expands. In the city of Cizre in Northern Kurdistan, IS have mounted an insurgency against the Kurdish population. At nightfall, "Tiger Teams" of Kurdish patrols conduct searches of cars and people in order to try and halt the incessant fire of rockets, bullets, and grenades throughout the city. The population has barricaded or dug ditches in every street in the town in order to keep out not only IS but the Turkish police, whom they insist would have made mass arrests long ago were it not for the preventative measures. Locals insist that "Cizre has become Kobanê," but in the midst of the turmoil are developing the councils and institutions of Democratic Confederalism.[30]

Notes

1   David Graeber, "Why Is the World Ignoring the Revolutionary Kurds in Syria?" *Guardian*, October 8, 2014, http://www.theguardian.com/commentisfree/2014/oct/08/why-world-ignoring-revolutionary-kurds-syria-isis, accessed June 30, 2017.

2   TATORT Kurdistan, *Democratic Autonomy in North Kurdistan: The Council Movement, Gender Liberation, and Ecology—In Practice: A Reconnaissance into Southeastern Turkey*, trans. Janet Biehl (Porsgrunn: New Compass Press, 2013), 26.

3   Aylin Ünver Noi, "The Arab Spring, Its Effects on the Kurds, and the Approaches of Turkey, Iran, Syria, and Iraq on the Kurdish Issue," *Global Research in International Affairs*, July 1, 2012.

4   Joshua Virasami, "Rojava's Revolution Is Roaring, Are We Listening?," *Contributoria*, January 1, 2015.

5   Abdulla Öcalan, *Democratic Confederalism*, trans. International Initiative (London: Transmedia, 2011), 28; TATORT Kurdistan, *Democratic Autonomy in North Kurdistan*, 22.

6   TATORT Kurdistan, *Democratic Autonomy in North Kurdistan*, 21.

7   Agence France Presse, "Kurdish woman leads fight against ISIS in Kobane," *Al Arabiya News*, October 14, 2014.

8   TATORT Kurdistan, *Democratic Autonomy in North Kurdistan*, 32–61.

9   Ibid., 147–51.

10 David Graeber and Pinar Öğünç, "No. This Is a Genuine Revolution," *ZNet*, December 26, 2014, https://zcomm.org/znetarticle/no-this-is-a-genuine-revolution/, accessed July 1, 2017.

11 TATORT Kurdistan, *Democratic Autonomy in North Kurdistan*, 31; Janet Biehl, "Impressions of Rojava: A Report from the Revolution," *Roarmag*, December 16, 2014.

12 Biehl, "Impressions of Rojava."

13 There are also contested claims that the KRG trades oil with Israel. See "Kurdistan Denies Selling Oil to Israel," *Rudaw*, June 21, 2014, http://www.rudaw.net/english/kurdistan/210620143, accessed July 9, 2017.

14 "Germany Sends Arms to Kurd Fighters Battling ISIL in Iraq," *Euronews*, September 25, 2014, http://www.euronews.com/2014/09/25/germany-sends-arms-to-kurd-fighters-battling-isil-in-iraq, accessed July 1, 2017.

15 Josh Rogin, "America's Allies Are Funding ISIS," *Daily Beast*, June 14, 2014, http://www.thedailybeast.com/americas-allies-are-funding-isis, accessed July 1, 2017.

16 Hadley Gamble, Matt Clinch, "US Should Stop Syria Not ISIS: Saudi Prince," CNBC, January 21, 2015, http://www.cnbc.com/2015/01/20/us-should-stop-syria-not-isis-saudi-prince.html, accessed July 1, 2017.

17 "Kurds Outraged as Turkey Closes Border to Volunteers for Kobane Fight," *RÛDAW* September 30, 2014, accessed July 1, 2017.

18 Dilar Dirik, "The Western Fascination with 'Badass' Kurdish Women," *Al Jazeera*, October 29, 2014, http://www.aljazeera.com/indepth/opinion/2014/10/western-fascination-with-badas-2014102112410527736.html, accessed July 1, 2017.

19 Stephanie Linning, "Islamic State Group Attacking Kobani from Turkey for the First Time—Indicating Besieged Syrian Town Is Totally Surrounded," *Daily Mail*, November 29, 2014, http://www.dailymail.co.uk/news/article-2853893/Islamic-State-group-attacking-Kobani-Turkey.html, accessed July 1, 2017.

20 ANF, "Muslim: Whoever Is Going to Do Something for Kobanê Must Do It Now," *Firat News*, September 9, 2014, https://anfenglish.com/news/muslim-whoever-is-going-to-do-something-for-kobane-must-do-it-now-9243, accessed July 1, 2017.

21 "YPG Meets Representatives of Arab Tribes from 50 Villages," *Diha News*, January 2, 2015, http://diclenews.com/en/news/content/view/437949, accessed July 1, 2017.

22 Zanyar Omrani, "Inside Kobane: Keeping Islamic State at Bay," *BBC News*, dir. Zanyar Omrani, ed. Kasra Karimi, Assefeh Barrat, ex. prod. Jenny Norton, January 5, 2015

23 Ed Amczyk, "Key Parts of Kobane, Syria, Seized by Kurdish Troops," *UPI*, January 6, 2015.

24 "Efrîn Economy Minister: Rojava Challenging Norms of Class, Gender, and Power," *Rojava Report*, December 22, 2014, https://rojavareport.wordpress.com/2014/12/22/efrin-economy-minister-rojava-challenging-norms-of-class-gender-and-power/, accessed July 1, 2017.

25 "Efrîn Economy Minister."

26 Pierre Rousset, "The Battles of Kobane, Aleppo and the Relearning of Solidarity," *International Viewpoint*, December 19, 2014, http://www.internationalviewpoint.org/spip.php?article3775, accessed July 1, 2017.

27   Michael Cruikshank, "Mt Shingal—The Islamic State's First Major Defeat," *Conflict News*, December 20, 2014, http://www.conflict-news.com/articles/mt-shingal-islamic-states-first-major-defeat, accessed July 1, 2017.

28   ANF, "Êzîdîs Establish Self-administration," *Firatnews.com*, January 18, 2015, http://en.firatajans.com/news/news/ezidis-establish-self-administration.htm, inactive July 1, 2017.

29   Anna Mulrine, "Worse than Islamic State? Concerns Rise about Iraq's Shiite Militias" *Christian Science Monitor*, December 23, 2014, https://m.csmonitor.com/USA/Military/2014/1223/Worse-than-Islamic-State-Concerns-rise-about-Iraq-s-Shiite-militias, accessed July 1, 2017.

30   Gülden Aydın, "Fear and Death Stalking Cizre," *Hürriyet Daily News*, January 22, 2015, http://www.hurriyetdailynews.com/fear-and-death-stalking-cizre.aspx?pageID=238&nid=77179, accessed July 1, 2017; "Democratic Autonomy to Be Established in Þýrnak and Mardin," *ANF*, June 2, 2011, https://anfenglish.com/features/democratic-autonomy-to-be-established-in-thyrnak-and-mardin-3303, accessed July 1, 2017.

Bibliography

Ackelsberg, Martha. *Free Women of Spain: Anarchism and the Struggle for Women's Emancipation*. Oakland: AK Press, 2005.

Arend, Orissa. *Showdown in Desire: The Black Panthers Take a Stand in New Orleans*. Fayetteville: University of Arkansas Press, 2009.

Barrow, Kai Lumumba. "Harm-Free Zones." *Critical Resistance*, 2014, http://criticalresistance.org/wpcontent/uploads/2014/05/HFZ-NY.pdf, inactive July 1, 2017.

Bloom, Joshua, and Waldo E. Martin Jr. *Black against Empire: The History and Politics of the Black Panther Party*. Berkeley: University of California Press, 2013.

Bookchin, Murray. *The Spanish Anarchists: The Heroic Years 1868–1936*. New York: Harper & Row, 1978.

Butler, Judith. *Gender Trouble: Feminism and the Subversion of Identity*. New York: Routledge, 1990.

Cahill, Ann J. *Rethinking Rape*. Ithaca, NY: Cornell University Press, 2001.

Carr, Robert. *The Angry Brigade: A History of Britain's First Urban Guerilla Group*. Oakland: PM Press, 2010.

Churchill, Ward, and Michael Ryan. *Pacifism as Pathology: Reflections on the Role of Armed Struggle in North America*. Oakland: PM Press, 2016 [3rd edition].

Churchill, Ward, and Jim Vander Wall. *Agents of Repression: The FBI's Secret Wars Against the Black Panther Party and the American Indian Movement*. Cambridge: South End Press, 2002 [2nd edition].

Clark, John. *The Impossible Community: Realizing Communitarian Anarchism*. New York: Bloomsbury, 2013.

Cobb, Charles E., Jr. *This Nonviolent Stuff'll Get You Killed: How Guns Made the Civil Rights Movement Possible*. Durham, NC: Duke University Press, 2015.

Crosby, Emilye, ed. *Civil Rights History from the Ground Up: Local Struggles, a National Movement*. Atlanta: University of Georgia Press. 2011.

crow, scott. *Black Flags and Windmills: Hope, Anarchy, and the Common Ground Collective*. Oakland: PM Press, 2014 [2nd edition].

crow, scott, and Malik Rahim. "The Unheard Story of Hurricane Katrina, Blackwater, White Militias & Community Empowerment: An Interview with scott crow and

Malik Rahim." In *Emergency Hearts, Molotov Dreams: A scott crow Reader*. North York, ON: GTK Press, 2015.

Devi, Phoolan. *I, Phoolan Devi: The Autobiography of India's Bandit Queen*. New York: Little, Brown and Company, 1996.

Dolgoff, Sam. *The Anarchist Collectives: Workers' Self-Management in the Spanish Revolution, 1936–39*. New York: Free Life Editions, 1974.

Ervin, Lorenzo Komboa. *Anarchism and the Black Revolution*. Philadelphia: Monkeywrench Press, 1994.

Fanon, Frantz. *Black Skin, White Masks*. Translated by Richard Philcox. New York: Grove Press, 2008.

Fanon, Frantz. *The Wretched of the Earth*. Translated by Richard Philcox. New York: Grove Press, 2004.

Douglass, Frederick. *The Life and Times of Frederick Douglass*. In Frederick Douglass, *Autobiographies*, 453–1045. New York: Library of America, 1994.

Du Bois, W.E.B. *The Souls of Black Folk*. In Du Bois, *Writings*, 357–547. New York: Literary Classics of the United States, 1986.

Dunbar-Ortiz, Roxanne. *Loaded: A Disarming History of the Second Amendment*. San Francisco: City Lights, 2018.

Foner, Philip S., ed. *The Black Panthers Speak*. Chicago: Haymarket Books, 2014.

Garnet, Henry Highland. "Let Your Motto Be Resistance!" In *Let Nobody Turn Us Around: An African American Anthology*, edited by Manning Marable and Leith Mullings, 56–62. Lanham, MD: Rowman & Littlefield, 2009 [2nd edition].

Gelderloos, Peter. *How Nonviolence Protects the State*. Boston: South End Press, 2007.

Gilmore, Ruth Wilson. *The Golden Gulag: Prisons, Surplus, Crisis, and Opposition in Globalizing California*. Berkeley: University of California Press, 2007.

Goodleaf, Donna K. *Entering the Warzone: A Mohawk Perspective on Resisting Invasion*. Penticton: Theytus Books, 1995.

Gossett, Che, Reina Gossett, and AJ Lewis. "Reclaiming Our Lineage: Organized Queer, Gender-Nonconforming, and Transgender Resistance to Police Violence." *The Scholar & Feminist Online* 10, nos. 1–2 (Fall 2011/Spring 2012).

Graeber, David. *Possibilities: Essays on Hierarchy, Rebellion, and Desire*. Oakland: AK Press, 2007.

Hayes, Worth K. "No Service Too Small: The Political Significance of the Survival Programs of the New Orleans Black Panther Party." *Xulanexus* 3 (2004). http://www.xula.edu/communications/xulanexus/issue3/BBP.html, archived at https://web.archive.org/web/20070928005919/http://www.xula.edu/xulanexus/issue3/BBP.html.

Hill, Lance. *The Deacons for Defense: Armed Resistance and the Civil Rights Movement*. Chapel Hill: University of North Carolina Press, 2004.

Holm, Rasmus. *Welcome to New Orleans*. Originally produced for Danish Television 2006. https://www.youtube.com/watch?v=V__lSdR1KZg, accessed July 2, 2017.

Hornung, Rick. *One Nation Under the Gun; Inside the Mohawk Civil War*. Toronto: Stoddart Pub. Co. Ltd., 1991.

INCITE! Women of Color Against Violence. *Color of Violence: The INCITE! Anthology*. Cambridge: South End Press, 2006.

Jackson, George L. *Blood in My Eye*. New York: Random House, 1972.

Jones, Charles E., ed. *The Black Panther Party [Reconsidered]*. Baltimore: Black Classic Press, 1998.

Lew-Lee, Lee, dir. *All Power to the People: The Black Panther Party and Beyond*. Electronic News Group/ZDF, 1996, https://www.youtube.com/watch?v=rn0LuTH2W50, accessed July 2, 2017.

Lugones, María. "Toward a Decolonial Feminism." *Hypatia* 25, no. 4 (Fall 2010): 742–59.

MacLaine, Craig, Michael S. Baxendale, and Robert Galbraith, *This Land Is Our Land: Mohawk Revolt at Oka*. Montreal: Optimum, 1990.

Malatesta, Errico. *The Anarchist Revolution: Polemical Articles 1924–31*. London: Freedom Press, 1995.

Malcolm X. "The Ballot or the Bullet." In *Let Nobody Turn Us Around: An African American Anthology*, edited by Manning Marable and Leith Mullings, 404–13. Lanham, MD: Rowman & Littlefield, 2009 [2nd edition].

Malcolm X. "Communication and Reality." Speech to Domestic Peace Corps, December 12, 1964. In *Malcolm X: The Man and His Times*, by John H. Clarke, 307–20. New York: Macmillan, 1970.

Malcolm X. "Organization of Afro-American Unity (OAAU) Founding Rally in Harlem," June 28, 1964.

Marcos (Subcomandante), and Juana Ponce de Leon, eds. *Our Word Is Our Weapon: Selected Writings*. New York: Seven Stories Press, 2001.

McCaughey, Martha. *Real Knockouts: The Physical Feminism of Women's Self-Defense*. New York: New York University Press, 1997.

Meltzer, Jamie. *Informant*. Music Box Films, 2013.

Omi, Michael, and Howard Winant. *Racial Formation in the United States*. New York: Routledge, 2014.

Pankhurst, Sylvia. "Jiu-Jitsu for Militants: Sylvia Pankhurst Also Wants Them Drilled and to Carry Sticks." *New York Times*, August 20, 1913, 4, http://query.nytimes.com/mem/archive-free/pdf?res=9904E6DB163DE633A25753C2A96E9C946296D6CF&mcubz=2, accessed July 9, 2017.

Pellow, David Naguib. *Total Liberation: The Power and Promise of Animal Rights and the Radical Earth Movement*. Minneapolis: University of Minnesota Press, 2014.

Richards, Vernon. *Lessons of the Spanish Revolution*. London: Freedom Press, 1983 [3rd edition].

Richards, Vernon, ed. *Life and Ideas: The Anarchist Writings of Errico Malatesta*. Oakland: PM Press, 2015.

Rose City Copwatch. "Alternatives to Police." Portland, Oregon, 2008, http://cobp.resist.ca/sites/cobp.resist.ca/files/alternatives-to-police-web.pdf, accessed July 2, 2017.

Ross, Alexander Reid. *Against the Fascist Creep*. Chico, CA: AK Press, 2017.

Seale, Bobby. *Seize the Time: The Story of the Black Panther Party and Huey P. Newton*. New York: Random House, 1970.

Shakur, Assata. *Assata: An Autobiography*. Chicago: Lawrence Hill & Co., 2001.

Skirda, Alexandre. *Nestor Makhno—Anarchy's Cossack: The Struggle for Free Soviets in the Ukraine 1917–1921*. Oakland: AK Press, 2004.

Smith, J., and André Moncourt. *The Red Army Faction: A Documentary History— Volume 1: Projectiles for the People*. Oakland: PM Press, 2010.

Strain, Christopher B. *Pure Fire: Self-Defense as Activism in the Civil Rights Era.* Athens: University of Georgia Press, 2005.

Thoreau, Henry David. "A Plea for Captain John Brown." In *Essays: A Fully Annotated Edition,* edited by Jeffrey S. Cramer, 190–216. New Haven: Yale University Press, 2013.

Umoja, Akinyele Omowale. *We Will Shoot Back: Armed Resistance in the Mississippi Freedom Movement.* New York: New York University Press, 2013.

Western Unit Tactical Defense Caucus. *Desire Armed: An Introduction to Armed Resistance and Revolution.* Pamphlet, 2006 [1st edition].

Williams, Kristian, Lara Messersmith-Glavin, William Munger, eds. *Life During Wartime: Resisting Counterinsurgency.* Oakland: AK Press, 2013.

Williams, Robert, and Mabel Williams. *Negroes with Guns.* New York: Marzani & Munsell, 1962.

Yancy, George. *Black Bodies, White Gazes: The Continuing Significance of Race.* Lanham, MD: Rowman & Littlefield, 2008.

York, Geoffrey, and Loreen Pindera. *People of the Pines: The Warriors and the Legacy of Oka.* Toronto: Little, Brown and Co. Ltd., 1992 [paperback edition].

Young, Iris Marion. "Throwing like a Girl." In *On Female Body Experience,* edited by Iris Marion Young, 27–45. New York: Oxford University Press, 2005.

Zinn, Howard. *A People's History of the United States.* New York: Harper Perennial, 2003 [reprint edition].

Glossary

Civil society
A term I adopted from Zapatismo. I use it here to refer to individuals, organizations, and even institutions, as opposed to the state apparatus or even the multinational corporations that use force to reinforce their power. Civil society is you and I and everyone else who associates without coercion.

Marginalized or neglected communities
I use these terms instead of, or sometimes interchangeably with, typical sociopolitical language (like working-class, queer, poor, etc.) that have been used to qualify people or communities pushed to the margins in civil society. Traditional political language takes many of the complex relationships within civil society that make up people and communities, making them one-dimensional. This leaves out the complex humanity of those involved. People and communities are often marginalized for more than one reason. These phrases address the fact that there are multiple issues at stake, instead of running a laundry list to illustrate the marginalization or neglect.

Power
I use this term in three ways:
1. **power (with a little "p")**: power that is exercised directly by individuals and communities as part of civil society, working to make changes in the world. It is what grassroots democracy is based on. This kind of power is derived from recognizing that we do have the abilities, creativity, and strength to make the world better. It

is the collective power of everyone, from the middle class to the marginalized.

2. **Power (with a capital "P")**: concentrations of authority and privilege in economic, political, or cultural institutions that exercise undue influence on the world. In this sense, Power is identical with the state, multinational corporations, or the rich, who are unaccountable to and derisive of civil society. It operates through bureaucracies, executive boards, the military, and transnational corporations and corporate media of all forms. It is exercised through brute force, neglect, and manipulation or corruption of economies, for example. It results in control over resources as well as social and cultural norms.

3. I sometimes use the phrase **those who assume to have Power**. It is my way of recognizing that such forms of Power do not have legitimate claims of authority over civil society. It is also a reminder not to automatically give legitimacy to those institutions or people who don't deserve it. My underlying philosophy is that once we see past this illegitimacy, we begin to recognize that we have the collective capacities to directly make changes and influence the world ourselves, rather than appealing to these coercive hierarchies and bureaucracies that claim this Power over us.

Acknowledgments

It cannot be said enough that it takes an ecosystem to bring books to life. I wish to thank deeply and sincerely those who have supported and contributed to bring this book to publication over these long years. *Kristian Williams*, an excellent editor, writer, and friend. Your keen insight, writer's eye, and deep analysis of our complex world and your contributions to this book and my writing have been invaluable.

Alexander Reid Ross for stepping in during some dark times to keep this book going with your editing and support when I was going to give it up.

Leon Alesi for your friendship, collaborations, and wonderful photographic eye. The front cover conveys a lot.

Elaine Cohen and *Kevin Van Meter*, who took the time to read the developing thoughts and give feedback.

Ward Churchill for the legacy of controversial writing around these issues.

Shelley Fleming at Word Ranch for continually keeping the transcriptions and copyediting going through the years.

Ann Harkness, my love, for the fun and support all these years and especially on this book.

J. Clark for keeping me going, bouncing off ideas, and help with research over the years. Your counsel is always appreciated and your heart is big.

PM Press: Ramsey for support of this project and a little hand-holding.

John Yates/Stealworks for another excellent cover design.

To all of the contributors, both past and present, whose engagements and writing has helped shape this developing theory and book: Ashanti Alston, Anti-Fascist Action UK, Paul Avrich, Dennis Banks, Kalika Baruti, Lamont Carter, David Cecelski, Ward Churchill, Kathleen Cleaver, Nikki Craft, J. Clark, Helge Döhring, Laura Gallery, Gord Hill, Mo Karnage, Chad Kautzer, Erick Khafre, Gabriel Kuhn, Ian LaVallee, Peter Little, George Ciccariello-Maher, North Carolina Piece Corps, Leslie James Pickering, Gustavo Rodríguez, Alexander Reid Ross, Simón Sedillo, Suncere Shakur, Neal Shirley, Shawn Stevenson, Dave Strano, Subcomandante Marcos, Dr. Akinyele Omowale Umoja, Michele Rene Weston, Western Unit Tactical Defense Caucus, Kristian Williams, Mabel Williams.

Shout-Outs and Inspirations:
Stella Alesi, Anarchist Black Cross Tactical Defense Caucus, theAnarchistLibrary.org, Aragorn Bang, Gerry Bello, Jake Bird, Black Guns Matter, Belinda Bonnen, Bob Buzzanco, Civil Liberties Defense Center, Kathleen Cleaver, Charles E. Cobb Jr., Common Ground Collective, Jamie Connatser, Emilye Crosby, *Fifth Estate* magazine, Lisa Fithian, Girl Army, Godspeed You! Black Emperor, Andrej Grubačić, Arielle Hansen, Sue Hilderbrand, Tim Holland, Huey Newton Gun Club (Dallas), It's Going Down! Collective, libcom.org, Dot Matrix, Heather McCurry, Daniel McGowan, Abby Martin, Paul Messersmith-Glavin, Lara Messersmith-Glavin, Cindy Milstein, Beverly Baker Moore, Mutual of Emma, North Carolina Piece Corps, DJ Pangburn, Scott Parkin Beth Payne, P&L Printing Coop (defunct), Lauren Regan, Redneck Revolt, Patrick Ross, Josie Shapiro, sole and DJ Pain1, Sarah Somera, Chris "Time" Steele, SURVIVE, Treasure City Thrift, Total Unicorn, Peter Werbe, Albert Woodfox.

Contributors

Editor

scott crow is a speaker, author, musician, storyteller, and anarchist. Over the last thirty years he has been involved with many political and cooperative projects and businesses, including cofounding Common Ground Collective, Treasure City Thrift, Century Modern, Red Square Gallery, and others. He is also the author of *Black Flags and Windmills: Hope, Anarchy, and the Common Ground Collective*, which has been translated into Spanish and Russian, and *Emergency Hearts, Molotov Dreams: A scott crow Reader*. He contributed to the books *Grabbing Back: Essays against the Global Land Grab, Witness to Betrayal, Black Bloc Papers*, and *What Lies Beneath: Katrina, Race, and the State of the Nation*, as well as being a featured subject in the books *The Power and Promise of Animal Rights and the Radical Earth Movement* and *Surveillance in America: Critical Analysis of the FBI, 1920 to the Present*. He has appeared regularly in international media both as a commentator and a subject, as well as in the documentary films *Informant, Better This World, American Totem*, and *Welcome to New Orleans*. In 2004, he coproduced, with his partner Ann Harkness, the documentary film *The Angola 3: Black Panthers and the Last Slave Plantation*. Beginning in the late 1990s and for over a decade, crow was targeted by the FBI for political activities as an alleged domestic terrorist without charges ever being brought. Find him virtually at www.scottcrow.org.

Contributors

Ashanti Alston is an anarchist activist, speaker, writer, and former member of the Black Panther Party and the Black Liberation Army (BLA).

For his role in the BLA he spent more than a decade in prison as a U.S. political prisoner. Alston is cochair of the National Jericho Movement, *Estación Libre*, and a longtime board member of the Institute for Anarchist Studies. He is a former coordinator for Critical Resistance. Since 1999, he has produced four issues of the zine *@narchist Panther* (the name being a reference to his current affiliation as an anarchist and his past membership in the Black Panther Party). Alston has identified himself as a black anarchist as well as a postmodern anarchist.

Anti-Fascist Action UK was a militant anti-fascist organization founded in 1985 by a wide-ranging network of anti-racist and anti-fascist groups. It was active in fighting far-right organizations, particularly the National Front and the British National Party. AFA had what they called a "twin-track" strategy: physical confrontation of fascists on the streets and ideological struggle against fascism in working-class communities.

Paul Avrich (1931–2006) was a professor and historian at Queens College, City University of New York. He was a pioneer in reviving the history of the anarchist movement in Russia and the United States. He wrote numerous books on the subject that have been reprinted in many languages, including: *The Russian Anarchists*; *Kronstadt, 1921*; *The Anarchists in the Russian Revolution*; *An American Anarchist: The Life of Voltairine de Cleyre*; and *Anarchist Voices: An Oral History of Anarchism in America*.

Dennis Banks is a Native American leader, teacher, lecturer, activist, and author. He has been a longtime leader of the American Indian Movement, which he cofounded in 1968 in Minneapolis. Dennis is the coauthor of two books, *Ojibwa Warrior: Dennis Banks and the Rise of the American Indian Movement* (University of Oklahoma Press), with Richard Erdoes, and *Seinaru Tamashii: Gendai American Indian Shidousha no Hansei*, with Yuri Morita. He has also appeared in a number of films as subject or actor including *War Party* (1988), *The Last of the Mohicans* (1992), *Thunderheart* (1992), *Older Than America* (2008), and the documentary on his life, *A Good Day to Die* (2010).

Kilaika Anayejali Kwa Baruti, also known as Angel, resides in Dallas and is a cadre member of the United States of Africa Revolutionary Party.

She has served as the secretary for the Department of International Affairs in Sierra Leone with the African Socialist Movement, founded and publishes the *Medase Initiative,* and coordinates with the Guerilla Mainframe project. Kilaika currently serves as the executive director of George Jackson University, is a contributing writer to the *African World Report Online* and *The New Black Panther Party Political Prisoners Magazine,* and is editing an anthology on the writings of New Afrikan political prisoners currently held in solitary confinement in Pelican Bay State Prison, California.

Lamont Carter is a writer/organizer currently living in the Pacific Northwest. His most recent projects have included organizing around the Black Lives Matter movement and organizing with tenants.

David Cecelski is a historian and professor who is a graduate of Duke University and the Harvard Graduate School of Education. He has written extensively on U.S. southern politics and history. His books include *The Waterman's Song: Slavery and Freedom in Maritime North Carolina* and *Along Freedom Road: Hyde County, North Carolina, and the Fate of Black Schools in the South.* He coedited *Recollections of My Slavery Days* and *Democracy Betrayed: The Wilmington Race Riot of 1898 and Its Legacy.*

Ward Churchill was, until moving to Atlanta in 2012, a member of the leadership council of Colorado AIM. A past national spokesperson for the Leonard Peltier Defense Committee and UN delegate for the International Indian Treaty Council, he is a life member of Vietnam Veterans Against the War and currently a member of the Council of Elders of the original Rainbow Coalition, founded by Chicago Black Panther leader Fred Hampton in 1969. Now retired, Churchill was professor of American Indian Studies and chair of the Department of Ethnic Studies until 2005, when he became the focus of a major academic freedom case. Among his two dozen books are *Wielding Words like Weapons* (2016), *Fantasies of the Master Race* (1992, 1998), *Struggle for the Land* (1993, 2002), *On the Justice of Roosting Chickens* (2003), *A Little Matter of Genocide* (1997), *Acts of Rebellion* (2003), and *Kill the Indian, Save the Man* (2004); as well as, with Jim Vander Wall, *Agents of Repression* (1988, 2002) and *The COINTELPRO Papers* (1990, 2002).

George Ciccariello-Maher teaches political theory at Drexel University in Philadelphia, where he also organizes against the police. He is the author of *We Created Chávez: A People's History of the Venezuelan Revolution* (2013), *Building the Commune: Venezuela's Radical Democracy* (2016), and *Decolonizing Dialectics* (2016).

J. Clark is an organizer and writer from Texas who focuses on fascism, repression, and radical legal support. He is a former member of the Anti-Racist Action network.

Kathleen Neal Cleaver has been involved in the human rights movement most of her life. In 1967, while a staff member of the Student Nonviolent Coordinating Committee (SNCC) she moved to California and joined the Black Panther Party for Self-Defense. She and her husband Eldridge Cleaver founded the International Section of the Black Panther Party in Algiers, Algeria, and worked there until 1973. Cleaver graduated from Yale Law School in 1988 and practiced law in New York before joining the faculty at Emory Law School. She has worked to free imprisoned political activists, including Geronimo ji-Jaga, Mumia Abu-Jamal, and Marilyn Buck. She coedited (with George Katsiaficas) the collection *Liberation, Imagination, and the Black Panther Party* and edited the posthumously published *Target Zero: A Life in Writing* by Eldridge Cleaver. She is the author of the memoir *Memories of Love and War*.

Nikki Craft is an American political activist, radical feminist, artist, and writer involved in anti-rape and feminist organizing since the early 1970s. Among her many projects, she cofounded Women Armed for Self-Protection, the Kitty Genovese Women's Project, and the Myth California Anti-Pageant. She can be found at nikkicraft.com.

Angela Y. Davis is an activist, scholar, writer, distinguished professor emerita at the University of California, Santa Cruz, and a cofounder of Critical Resistance. Some of her many books include: *Angela Davis: An Autobiography*; *Freedom Is a Constant Struggle: Ferguson, Palestine, and the Foundations of a Movement*; and *Abolition Democracy: Beyond Prisons, Torture, and Empire*.

Helge Döhring is a cofounder of the *Institut für Syndikalismusforschung* (SyFo) in Bremen and has authored numerous works on the history of anarcho-syndicalism in Germany. His 2011 release *Schwarze Scharen. Anarcho-Syndikalistische Arbeiterwehr (1929–1933)* is the first German book-length study of the *Schwarze Scharen*.

Laura Gallery is a graduate from University at Albany. She got her undergraduate in women's studies, with minors in both sociology and Latin American studies, and her master's in Latin American and Caribbean studies.

Gord Hill is a member of the Kwakwaka'wakw nation and has been involved in Indigenous and anarchist social movements since the late 1980s. A prolific writer and artist, he is the author of *The 500 Years of Resistance Comic Book* and *The Anti-Capitalist Resistance Comic Book*, as well as *500 Years of Indigenous Resistance*.

Mo Karnage is an anarchist living in Hanover County, Virginia. She is a cofounder and member of the Wingnut Anarchist Collective and the author of the book *The South Is Still Rising*. Mo is self-employed as a carpenter and writer and spends time organizing with Food Not Bombs and Copwatch and writing. Mo can be found online at www.mokarnage.com.

Chad Kautzer is an associate professor of philosophy at Lehigh University in Bethlehem, Pennsylvania. He is the author of *Radical Philosophy: An Introduction* and coeditor of *Pragmatism, Nation, and Race: Community in the Age of Empire*.

Chairman Erick Khafre has been actively organizing locally and nationally for all of his adult life. He founded an organization called Freedom Now in his youth and is a cofounder and current leader of Guerrilla Mainframe (GMF-RM) and a cofounder and leader within the Huey P. Newton Gun Club. He also serves as a coordinator in the George Jackson University.

Gabriel Kuhn is an Austrian-born author and translator living in Sweden. Among his publications with PM Press are *Erich Mühsam:*

Liberating Society from the State and Other Writings; *All Power to the Councils! A Documentary History of the German Revolution of 1918–1919*; *Antifascism, Sports, Sobriety: Forging a Militant Working-Class Culture*; and *Turning Money into Rebellion: The Unlikely Story of Denmark's Revolutionary Bank Robbers*.

Ian LaVallee organizes with Iraq Veterans Against the War and Rising Tide in Portland, Oregon.

Peter Little has participated in anti-fascist and workplace organizing in the Pacific Northwest since the 1990s.

North Carolina Piece Corps is a small anarchist publishing project, primarily interested in topics related to the legitimacy and utility of violence in political resistance, radical perspectives on southern history, self-defense training, race treason, and critical insurrectionary perspectives.

Leslie James Pickering served as spokesperson for the Earth Liberation Front Press Office during the late 1990s and early 2000s. He currently co-owns Burning Books, a radical bookstore in Buffalo that was the target of an attempted ecoterrorism conspiracy frame-up by the FBI from 2012 to 2014. He is the author of *The Earth Liberation Front: 1997–2002* and *Mad Bomber Melville* and editor of *Conspiracy to Riot in Furtherance of Terrorism: The Collective Autobiography of the RNC 8*.

Gustavo Rodríguez is an anarchist writer, activist, and speaker in Mexico. In the 1980s, he was part of the anarcho-syndicalist initiative Workers Solidarity Alliance (WSA), the political prisoner support network Latin American Anarchist Black Cross, and the Revolutionary Anarchist Network. Today he works informally with many groups across the U.S. and Mexico.

Alexander Reid Ross teaches geography at Portland State University. He is the author of *Against the Fascist Creep* and the editor of *Grabbing Back: Essays Against the Global Land Grab*.

Simón Sedillo is a bilingual documentarian, journalist, and filmmaker who splits his time between the U.S. and Mexico. On his own and with El Enemigo Común Collective he has contributed to the production of a wide variety of documentary films including *El Factor Demarest* (The Demarest Factor) and *Guarda Bosques* (Forest Keepers). He has contributed articles to many Spanish- and English-language periodicals. Sedillo tours universities and community centers throughout the U.S., screening films and facilitating discussions and workshops on political economy and geopolitics in Mexico and the USA. See https://elenemigocomun.net/author/simon/.

Suncere Shakur, born Luther Lee Jones Jr., was raised in Washington, DC. From the '90s, Suncere was active in many DC organizations he either cofounded or joined, including the Black Basement Brigade and T.R.I.B.E., as well as co-owning Café Maowangi. He left DC in the days after Hurricane Katrina to cofound the Common Ground Collective, Common Ground Legal, and the HOPE Project in Louisiana. Since Katrina, Suncere was part of disaster efforts in Haiti and Hurricane Sandy and founded and runs the Hali Stone Free Breakfast Program in Cleveland, Ohio.

Neal Shirley is a coauthor of the book *Dixie Be Damned: 300 Years of Insurrection in the American South*. As a teenager he started skipping off to anti-globalization demos, got involved with prisoner solidarity work, and has been exploring different ways to get in trouble ever since.

Shawn Stevenson is an educator living in Washington State. He writes on anarchist history, theory, and praxis. When not writing he organizes with the Industrial Workers of the World and with the IWW's General Defense Committee.

Dave Strano is a working-class anarchist organizer and occasional writer currently based in Phoenix. He is a cofounder of Kansas Mutual Aid, the short-lived John Brown Gun Club in Lawrence, Kansas, and the national network Redneck Revolt.

Subcomandante Marcos was the nom de guerre of former University of Mexico philosophy professor Rafael Sebastián Guillén Vicente. Since

1982, he has been a leader and spokesperson within the Zapatista Army of National Liberation (EZLN) in Chiapas, Mexico. Marcos is a prolific writer and has published hundreds of essays and multiple books. Most of his writings focus on his anti-capitalist ideology and the advocacy indigenous people's rights, but he has also written poetry and novels. A selection includes: *Our Word Is Our Weapon: Selected Writings of Subcomandante Insurgente Marcos*; *The Story of Colors*; *Questions and Swords: Folktales of the Zapatista Revolution*; and *Postmodern and Mexican Stories: An Anthology of Ultrashort, Hybrid, and Lucid Prose.*

Akinyele Omowale Umoja is a professor and chair of the Department of African-American Studies at Georgia State University. For over forty years he has been engaged in the liberation struggle of Afrikan people and political prisoners. Umoja is a founding member of the New Afrikan Peoples Organization and the Malcolm X Grassroots Movement and a longtime coordinator with the New Afrikan Independence Movement. He is author of the book *We Will Shoot Back: Armed Resistance in the Mississippi Freedom Movement*. He has appeared in the documentary films *COINTELPRO 101* and *Bastards of the Party*.

Western Unit Tactical Defense Caucus was a pseudonymous pen name used by a collective of people within Kansas and Texas to publish a zine on community armed self-defense called *Desire Armed: An Introduction to Armed Resistance and Revolution*, in 2006.

Michele Rene Weston is a Turtle Island anarchist who grew up on the plains of Nebraska, Kansas, Iowa, and South Dakota. She remains a student and writer of American history, feminist prose, and environmental journalism. She is "iyeshka," or mixed-breed of hillbilly and Cherokee/Choctaw descent. Most of her family still reside in Oklahoma and many of them still support AIM.

Kristian Williams is the author of *Our Enemies in Blue: Police and Power in America* and *American Methods: Torture and the Logic of Domination*, along with the collections: *Fire the Cops!*; *Witness To Betrayal/Profiles of Provocateurs*; *Hurt: Notes of Torture in a Modern Democracy*; and *Between the Bullet and the Lie: Essays on Orwell*. He lives in Portland, Oregon.

Mabel Williams (1931–2014) was a U.S. civil rights activist and organizer with the National Association for the Advancement of Colored People (NAACP), who, with her husband Robert F. Williams, called for and organized community armed self-defense against racist violence in the South during the 1950s and '60s. Due to threats on their lives from local law enforcement and the Klan, they fled and lived in exile in Cuba and China for a time, where they produced a revolutionary radio program called *Radio Free Dixie*. She also coauthored, uncredited until later, the seminal book *Negroes with Guns*.

Index

Page numbers in *italic* refer to illustrations. "Passim" (literally "scattered") indicates intermittent discussion of a topic over a cluster of pages.

ABOUT PM PRESS

PM Press was founded at the end of 2007 by a small collection of folks with decades of publishing, media, and organizing experience. PM Press co-conspirators have published and distributed hundreds of books, pamphlets, CDs, and DVDs. Members of PM have founded enduring book fairs, spearheaded victorious tenant organizing campaigns, and worked closely with bookstores, academic conferences, and even rock bands to deliver political and challenging ideas to all walks of life. We're old enough to know what we're doing and young enough to know what's at stake.

We seek to create radical and stimulating fiction and non-fiction books, pamphlets, T-shirts, visual and audio materials to entertain, educate, and inspire you. We aim to distribute these through every available channel with every available technology—whether that means you are seeing anarchist classics at our bookfair stalls, reading our latest vegan cookbook at the café, downloading geeky fiction e-books, or digging new music and timely videos from our website.

PM Press is always on the lookout for talented and skilled volunteers, artists, activists, and writers to work with. If you have a great idea for a project or can contribute in some way, please get in touch.

PM Press
PO Box 23912
Oakland, CA 94623
www.pmpress.org

FRIENDS OF PM PRESS

These are indisputably momentous times—the financial system is melting down globally and the Empire is stumbling. Now more than ever there is a vital need for radical ideas.

In the years since its founding—and on a mere shoestring—PM Press has risen to the formidable challenge of publishing and distributing knowledge and entertainment for the struggles ahead. With over 300 releases to date, we have published an impressive and stimulating array of literature, art, music, politics, and culture. Using every available medium, we've succeeded in connecting those hungry for ideas and information to those putting them into practice.

Friends of PM allows you to directly help impact, amplify, and revitalize the discourse and actions of radical writers, filmmakers, and artists. It provides us with a stable foundation from which we can build upon our early successes and provides a much-needed subsidy for the materials that can't necessarily pay their own way. You can help make that happen—and receive every new title automatically delivered to your door once a month—by joining as a Friend of PM Press. And, we'll throw in a free T-shirt when you sign up.

Here are your options:

- **$30 a month** Get all books and pamphlets plus 50% discount on all webstore purchases

- **$40 a month** Get all PM Press releases (including CDs and DVDs) plus 50% discount on all webstore purchases

- **$100 a month** Superstar—Everything plus PM merchandise, free downloads, and 50% discount on all webstore purchases

For those who can't afford $30 or more a month, we have **Sustainer Rates** at $15, $10 and $5. Sustainers get a free PM Press T-shirt and a 50% discount on all purchases from our website.

Your Visa or Mastercard will be billed once a month, until you tell us to stop. Or until our efforts succeed in bringing the revolution around. Or the financial meltdown of Capital makes plastic redundant. Whichever comes first.

Black Flags and Windmills: Hope, Anarchy, and the Common Ground Collective

scott crow with forewords
by Kathleen Cleaver and John P. Clark

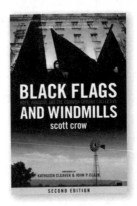

ISBN: 978-1-60486-453-3
$20.00   288 pages

When both levees and governments failed in New
Orleans after Hurricane Katrina, the anarchist-
inspired Common Ground Collective was created to fill the void. With the motto
of "Solidarity Not Charity," they worked to create power from below—building
autonomous projects, programs, and spaces of self-sufficiency like health clinics
and neighborhood assemblies, while also supporting communities defending
themselves from white militias and police brutality, illegal home demolitions, and
evictions.

Black Flags and Windmills—equal parts memoir, history, and organizing philosophy—
vividly intertwines Common Ground cofounder scott crow's experiences and ideas
with Katrina's reality, illustrating how people can build local grassroots power for
collective liberation. It is a story of resisting indifference, rebuilding hope amid
collapse, and struggling against the grain to create better worlds.

The expanded second edition includes up-to-date interviews and discussions
between crow and some of today's most articulate and influential activists and
organizers on topics ranging from grassroots disaster relief efforts (both economic
and environmental); dealing with infiltration, interrogation, and surveillance from
the State; and a new photo section that vividly portrays scott's experiences as an
anarchist, activist, and movement organizer in today's world.

*"scott crow's trenchant memoir of grassroots organizing is an important contribution to
a history of movements that far too often goes untold."*
—Amy Goodman, host and executive producer of *Democracy Now!*

*"This revised and expanded edition weaves scott crow's frontline experiences with a
resilient, honest discussion of grassroots political movement-building."*
—Will Potter, author of *Green Is the New Red: An Insider's Account of a Social
Movement Under Siege*

*"It is a brilliant, detailed, and humble book written with total frankness and at the same
time a revolutionary poet's passion. It makes the reader feel that we too, with our
emergency heart as our guide, can do anything; we only need to begin."*
—Marina Sitrin, author of *Horizontalism: Voices of Popular Power in Argentina*

Pacifism as Pathology: Reflections on the Role of Armed Struggle in North America Third Edition

Ward Churchill and Michael Ryan with a Preface by Ed Mead and Foreword by Dylan Rodríguez

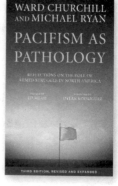

ISBN: 978-1-62963-224-7
$15.95   192 pages

Pacifism as Pathology has long since emerged as a dissident classic. Originally written during the mid-1980s, the seminal essay "Pacifism as Pathology" was prompted by veteran activist Ward Churchill's frustration with what he diagnosed as a growing—and deliberately self-neutralizing—"hegemony of nonviolence" on the North American left. The essay's publication unleashed a raging debate among activists in both the U.S. and Canada, a significant result of which was Michael Ryan's penning of a follow-up essay reinforcing Churchill's premise that nonviolence, at least as the term is popularly employed by white "progressives," is inherently counterrevolutionary, adding up to little more than a manifestation of its proponents' desire to maintain their relatively high degrees of socioeconomic privilege and thereby serving to stabilize rather than transform the prevailing relations of power.

This short book challenges the pacifist movement's heralded victories—Gandhi in India, 1960s antiwar activists, even Martin Luther King Jr.'s civil rights movement—suggesting that their success was in spite of, rather than because of, their nonviolent tactics. Churchill also examines the Jewish Holocaust, pointing out that the overwhelming response of Jews was nonviolent, but that when they did use violence they succeeded in inflicting significant damage to the nazi war machine and saving countless lives.

As relevant today as when they first appeared, Churchill's and Ryan's trailblazing efforts were first published together in book form in 1998. Now, along with the preface to that volume by former participant in armed struggle/political prisoner Ed Mead, new essays by both Churchill and Ryan, and a powerful new foreword by leading oppositionist intellectual Dylan Rodríguez, these vitally important essays are being released in a fresh edition.

"This extraordinarily important book cuts to the heart of the central reasons movements to bring about social and environmental justice always fail. The fundamental question here is: is violence ever an acceptable tool to bring about social change? This is probably the most important question of our time, yet so often discussions around it fall into clichés and magical thinking: that somehow if we are merely good and nice enough people, the state will stop using its violence to exploit us all. Would that this were true."
—Derrick Jensen, author of *Endgame*

Wielding Words like Weapons: Selected Essays in Indigenism, 1995-2005

Ward Churchill
with a Foreword by Barbara Alice Mann

ISBN: 978-1-62963-101-1
$27.95   616 pages

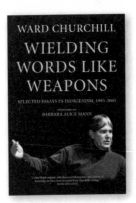

Wielding Words like Weapons is a collection of acclaimed American Indian Movement activist-intellectual Ward Churchill's essays in indigenism, selected from material written during the decade 1995-2005. It includes a range of formats, from sharply framed book reviews and equally pointed polemics and op-eds to more formal essays designed to reach both scholarly and popular audiences. The selection also represents the broad range of topics addressed in Churchill's scholarship, including the fallacies of archeological and anthropological orthodoxy such as the insistence of "cannibalogists" that American Indians were traditionally maneaters, Hollywood's cinematic degradations of native people, questions of American Indian identity, the historical and ongoing genocide of North America's native peoples and the systematic distortion of the political and legal history of U.S.-Indian relations.

Less typical of Churchill's oeuvre are the essays commemorating Cherokee anthropologist Robert K. Thomas and Yankton Sioux legal scholar and theologian Vine Deloria Jr. More unusual still is his profoundly personal effort to come to grips with the life and death of his late wife, Leah Renae Kelly, thereby illuminating in very human terms the grim and lasting effects of Canada's residential schools upon the country's indigenous peoples.

A foreword by Seneca historian Barbara Alice Mann describes the sustained efforts by police and intelligence agencies as well as university administrators and other academic adversaries to discredit or otherwise "neutralize" both the man and his work. Also included are both the initial "stream-of-consciousness" version of Churchill's famous—or notorious—"little Eichmanns" opinion piece analyzing the causes of the attacks on 9/11, as well as the counterpart essay in which his argument was fully developed.

"Compellingly original, with the powerful eloquence and breadth of knowledge we have come to expect from Churchill's writing."
—Howard Zinn

"This is insurgent intellectual work—breaking new ground, forging new paths, engaging us in critical resistance."
—bell hooks

500 Years of Indigenous Resistance

Gord Hill

ISBN: 978-1-60486-106-8
$12.00   96 pages

The history of the colonization of the Americas by Europeans is often portrayed as a mutually beneficial process, in which "civilization" was brought to the Natives, who in return shared their land and cultures. A more critical history might present it as a genocide in which Indigenous peoples were helpless victims, overwhelmed and awed by European military power. In reality, neither of these views is correct.

500 Years of Indigenous Resistance is more than a history of European colonization of the Americas. In this slim volume, Gord Hill chronicles the resistance by Indigenous peoples, which limited and shaped the forms and extent of colonialism. This history encompasses North and South America, the development of nation-states, and the resurgence of Indigenous resistance in the post-WW2 era.

Gord Hill is a member of the Kwakwaka'wakw nation on the Northwest Coast. Writer, artist, and militant, he has been involved in Indigenous resistance, anti-colonial and anti-capitalist movements for many years, often using the pseudonym Zig Zag.

Antifascism, Sports, Sobriety: Forging a Militant Working-Class Culture

Julius Deutsch
Edited and translated by Gabriel Kuhn

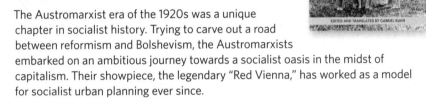

ISBN: 978-1-62963-154-7
$14.95   128 pages

The Austromarxist era of the 1920s was a unique chapter in socialist history. Trying to carve out a road between reformism and Bolshevism, the Austromarxists embarked on an ambitious journey towards a socialist oasis in the midst of capitalism. Their showpiece, the legendary "Red Vienna," has worked as a model for socialist urban planning ever since.

At the heart of the Austromarxist experiment was the conviction that a socialist revolution had to entail a cultural one. Numerous workers' institutions and organizations were founded, from education centers to theaters to hiking associations. With the Fascist threat increasing, the physical aspects of the cultural revolution became ever more central as they were considered mandatory for effective defense. At no other time in socialist history did armed struggle, sports, and sobriety become as intertwined in a proletarian attempt to protect socialist achievements as they did in Austria in the early 1930s. Despite the final defeat of the workers' militias in the Austrian Civil War of 1934 and subsequent Fascist rule, the Austromarxist struggle holds important lessons for socialist theory and practice.

Antifascism, Sports, Sobriety contains an introductory essay by Gabriel Kuhn and selected writings by Julius Deutsch, leader of the workers' militias, president of the Socialist Workers' Sport International, and a prominent spokesperson for the Austrian workers' temperance movement. Deutsch represented the physical defense of the working class against its enemies like few others. His texts in this book are being made available in English for the first time.

"An almost completely forgotten episode in labor history."
—Murray Bookchin, author of *Anarchism, Marxism and the Future of the Left*

"A foretaste of the socialist utopia of the future in the present."
—Helmut Gruber, author of *Red Vienna: Experiment in Working-Class Culture, 1919-1934*

Look for Me in the Whirlwind: From the Panther 21 to 21st-Century Revolutions

Sekou Odinga, Dhoruba Bin Wahad, Jamal Joseph
Edited by Matt Meyer & déqui kioni-sadiki
with a Foreword by Imam Jamil Al-Amin,
and an Afterword by Mumia Abu-Jamal

ISBN: 978-1-62963-389-3
$26.95   648 pages

Amid music festivals and moon landings, the tumultuous year of 1969 included an infamous case in the annals of criminal justice and Black liberation: the New York City Black Panther 21. Though some among the group had hardly even met one another, the 21 were rounded up by the FBI and New York Police Department in an attempt to disrupt and destroy the organization that was attracting young people around the world. Involving charges of conspiracy to commit violent acts, the Panther 21 trial—the longest and most expensive in New York history—revealed the illegal government activities which led to exile, imprisonment on false charges, and assassination of Black liberation leaders. Solidarity for the 21 also extended well beyond "movement" circles and included mainstream publication of their collective autobiography, *Look for Me in the Whirlwind*, which is reprinted here for the first time.

Look for Me in the Whirlwind: From the Panther 21 to 21st-Century Revolutions contains the entire original manuscript, and includes new commentary from surviving members of the 21: Sekou Odinga, Dhoruba Bin Wahad, Jamal Joseph, and Shaba Om. Still-imprisoned Sundiata Acoli, Imam Jamil Al-Amin, and Mumia Abu-Jamal contribute new essays. Never or rarely seen poetry and prose from Afeni Shakur, Kuwasi Balagoon, Ali Bey Hassan, and Michael "Cetewayo" Tabor is included. Early Panther leader and jazz master Bilal Sunni-Ali adds a historical essay and lyrics from his composition "Look for Me in the Whirlwind," and coeditors kioni-sadiki, Meyer, and Panther rank-and-file member Cyril "Bullwhip" Innis Jr. help bring the story up to date.

At a moment when the Movement for Black Lives recites the affirmation that "it is our duty to win," penned by Black Liberation Army (BLA) militant Assata Shakur, those who made up the BLA and worked alongside of Assata are largely unknown. This book—with archival photos from David Fenton, Stephen Shames, and the private collections of the authors— provides essential parts of a hidden and missing-in-action history. Going well beyond the familiar and mythologized nostalgic Panther narrative, *From the Panther 21 to 21st-Century Revolutions* explains how and why the Panther legacy is still relevant and vital today.